W. G. HOSKINS

The Making of
THE ENGLISH
LANDSCAPE

The Making of THE ENGLISH LANDSCAPE

W. G. HOSKINS

Emeritus Professor of English Local History

with an Introduction and Commentary by
CHRISTOPHER TAYLOR

Colour photographs by ANDREW BUTLER

HODDER AND STOUGHTON
London   Sydney   Auckland   Toronto

FRONTISPIECE: *Fingest church. Stylistically Fingest church is likely to be at least fifty years earlier than 1163 when the settlement is first recorded. In any case the tower is so large when compared with the nave that Sir Alfred Clapham and others have suggested that it may have in origin been a nave itself, as were other late Saxon towers. This would imply that the church, and thus perhaps the hamlet, is considerably older than the twelfth century.*

British Library Cataloguing in Publication Data

Hoskins, W. G. (William George)
  The making of the English landscape.
  1. England. Historical geography
  I. Title
  911′.42

  ISBN 0-340-39971-6

Published by Hodder & Stoughton
a division of Hodder & Stoughton Limited,
Mill Road, Dunton Green, Sevenoaks, Kent TN13 2YA
Hodder & Stoughton Editorial Office:
47 Bedford Square, London WC1B 3DP.

Typeset by SX Composing Limited.
Printed in Italy by L.E.G.O., Vicenza

CONTENTS

GENERAL INTRODUCTION
by Christopher Taylor

To be asked to revise and up-date Professor Hoskins' *The Making of the English Landscape* is a great honour but the task carries with it a grave responsibility. *The Making of the English Landscape* is one of the greatest history books ever written. It is great because it established landscape history as a new and proper branch of historical study. It is great because it is written in a language which is easy to understand and a pleasure to read. It is great because it has inspired two, and perhaps now more, generations of historians, archaeologists, geographers and botanists to follow the master's footsteps and to explore the mysteries of our country's landscape. But its greatest achievement, only matched perhaps by the works of Macaulay and Trevelyan, is that it reached out to, and profoundly affected, hundreds of thousands of ordinary people who would otherwise have never thought about the past.

The book, first published in 1955, cannot therefore be, nor should it be, rewritten and it is a pleasure to record that, from the very beginning, the publishers and I were in complete agreement that Professor Hoskins' original text should remain as he left it in 1976. Whatever details are out of date, it remains a milestone in the study of history, a brilliant exercise in methodology and an exquisitely written account of the development of the English landscape.

Yet the very fact that the book was the beginning of an entirely new form of history and that it drew to that study so many disciples and disciplines means that it is in many places out of date. For over thirty years now hosts of scholars, both professional and amateur, have continued where Professor Hoskins left off and pushed back the frontiers of knowledge, almost always along the lines that he would have followed him-self if circumstance had allowed. It thus seemed timely to attempt, however inadequately, to point out some of these advances and to confirm the correctness of so much that Professor Hoskins conjectured. In the following pages all I have tried to do is to indicate the places where this new scholarship has advanced our thinking. This has been done in the hope that a new generation of readers will draw the same pleasure and inspiration from Professor Hoskins' work as I and my generation have done and that they too will come to admire him and recognise him as one of the greatest historians of our time and continue to explore the landscape of our country.

The notes which accompany the original text are, inevitably, a very personal view of the origins and development of the English landscape. Scholars and laymen alike will no doubt disagree over details, just as they did with Professor Hoskins in the 1950s. But I believe that, details apart, the outlines of the new assessment generally reflect modern thought and research. In addition there are a few specific points which must be made in this General Introduction. The first is that, overall, the present picture of the making of the landscape is a much more clouded one than Professor Hoskins' clear view. This partly reflects a lack of confidence by landscape historians of the 1980s in their ability to understand that landscape. The more detail we have gone into and the more carefully we have looked at the evidence, both on the ground and in documents, the more uncertain we have become of our conclusions. Much that we previously felt we could explain now seems doubtful. Many things that have always been accepted as obvious now seem less so. All that we can be sure about is that the making of the English landscape was much more complicated, took place over a

The withy levels near Lyng, Somerset.

much longer period and is therefore much more fascinating and rewarding to study, than anyone could have thought possible in 1955.

Certainly the story as it continues to emerge grows in complexity. This is particularly true of the age between the fifth and ninth centuries AD which, despite an enormous amount of new work, seems to be more dark than ever. It is still not clear what Saxon England actually looked like. We can be sure that Hoskins' view and the view of his contemporaries is not correct but it remains very difficult to see what the true picture was. We have removed nucleated villages from the early Saxon landscape but have little with which to replace them. We can now perhaps put these nucleated villages, as they survive on the ground, in the years between the ninth and thirteenth centuries, but the mechanism behind their formation still eludes us.

It is also becoming increasingly difficult to disentangle the palimpsest of fields that lie scattered over England. Some of the fields in, say, south Wiltshire, which twenty years ago I could date firmly to the thirteenth century, now seem possibly to be of the Iron Age. Ditches in the Somerset Levels, always said to be the work of medieval reclaimers, might now well be, in part, Roman. Hedge lines in Norfolk, previously clearly assigned to the sixteenth and seventeenth century, could now be of Saxon date.

This brings us to the problem of the age of the English landscape. Professor Hoskins always emphasised that 'everything is older than we think' but even he did not realise just how far back in time much of the basic man-made framework of this country actually goes. We need to understand events which took place six to seven thousand years ago. In particular, the idea of great areas of primeval woodland, whose clearance in Saxon, medieval and even later times is such a feature of Professor Hoskins' work and is still repeated endlessly today, continues to mislead us. As Dr Rackham has pointed out, the clearance of primeval forest began in Mesolithic times around 8000 BC and by the time of Domesday Book little or no natural woodland was left. What existed then was the result of successive phases of clearance, regeneration and renewed clearance, and such fragments of forest that remained were carefully managed and protected. We shall never understand the history of the English landscape until we remove from our minds the concept of the primeval woodland that our prehistoric ancestors had largely removed from the landscape by 1000 BC.

Another aspect of the English landscape is that its story, even if unclear, has one over-riding feature about which we can be absolutely sure, namely that it has always been changing. This point was, of course, well appreciated by Professor Hoskins and, indeed, perhaps the major theme of his work here, and in many other of his publications, was the emphasis on change. It is perhaps curious therefore that he, like so many other people, feared and disliked the changes of the twentieth century. Granted many of the changes today are more destructive, more extensive and the results arguably less aesthetically pleasing than those that have gone before, but the fact that change has always taken place should make us less fearful of change today. People have always been afraid of change in certain aspects of their lives and their environment, yet it has always gone on. It is likely that small Bronze Age farmers in Wessex decried the total replanning of the downland which must have been on a scale far greater than that of the parliamentary enclosure in that area during the eighteenth and nineteenth centuries. Similarly the disruption caused by the arrival of the Romans in AD 43 with all their new-fangled ideas on architecture, building materials, agricultural methods and commercial exploitation, as well as their suppression of a long tradition of incessant warfare, must have seemed to late Iron Age people far more serious than the impact of the Norman invaders of 1066. Likewise the introduction of artillery, which revolutionised warfare, spoilt the gentlemanly sport of polite conflict, made every existing fortress redundant and arguably helped hasten the end of the feudal system, must have been regarded by some people then as an event as momentous as the invention of the atomic bomb was in our century.

There is, however, an important feature about change in the English landscape which has not hitherto been stressed. While change at a relatively minor level has always gone on, from the fluctuating clearance and regeneration of woodland between 5000 and 3000 BC, through the gradual replacement of circular wooden huts by stone-built houses in the early Roman period, to the destruction of the monasteries and the break-up of their great land-holdings in the sixteenth century, it now seems clear that there have also been three major periods of change in the history of the English landscape.

These periods of change were so profound and so extensive that it is perhaps not going beyond the bounds of truth to call them revolutions. Each of the revolutions took place over perhaps two to three hundred years, and possibly longer. Not every part of England was equally affected by them, as we shall see. Further, none of these revolutions burst upon the world suddenly and without warning. Each perhaps had a period of preparation, innovation and population change beforehand. Yet in the end each revolution led to the total transformation of both the appearance and organisation of large parts of the landscape.

The first of these revolutions took place in the later Bronze Age, perhaps around 1800-1400 BC. Up to then there had been a slow expansion of population, a gradual but fluctuating and piecemeal clearance of woodland and a slow growth in settlement size and numbers. Then, apparently relatively quickly, the population rose, settlements multiplied both numerically and in type and, most important of all, vast areas of land were not only reclaimed but both new and older reclaimed areas were replanned on a massive scale. Large parts of England, for example in Wessex, in the north-east Midlands and on Dartmoor, to name only the best documented, were completely transformed. The following centuries, during the immediate pre-Roman Iron Age and the Roman period itself, saw the consolidation of this revolution and its further expansion in many ways.

The coming of the Saxons had little effect on the landscape except perhaps in a negative sense with a reduction of population and a collapse of the existing political, administrative and economic organisations, which probably produced an abandonment of land and settlements. It is not until the end of Saxon times that the second revolution began. This again may have been connected with a rise in population, but its effect over certain parts of England was immense. The nucleated English village appeared, often as a result of conscious planning, perhaps accompanied by a total reorganisation of agriculture and the growth of the fully developed open or common field system. Towns began, were planned and expanded. Again, this revolution occurred over a relatively short period, perhaps between the ninth and the twelfth centuries. It was followed by further consolidation and local expansion but this ended with the economic decline of the fourteenth century and the social and political upheavals of the later fourteenth and fifteenth centuries.

The third revolution, based on technical innovations and social change, began as early as the sixteenth and seventeenth centuries and continued in the eighteenth century with the enclosure movement and the development of industry. This revolution is still with us and its end is not, at the moment, in sight.

If this concept of landscape revolution rather than continuous change is accepted, then it is possible to understand the English landscape rather more clearly than hitherto. Yet such a concept needs to be set alongside another in order to appreciate the true complexities of the landscape. For if the making of the English landscape was merely the result of these three massive revolutions, it would all look very much the same. It certainly does not, a fact that makes it so interesting. The landscape of Kent is quite different from that of Essex, despite being geographically very close to it, while Dorset is not the same as Devon.

Of course many of these contrasts are due to the basic differences in geology and geomorphological history. Yet this is not the only reason, for the differences in detail far outweigh the constraints laid on man by nature in these areas. Why, for example, do we seem to have prehistoric fields still in use in Cornwall and Norfolk, but not in Worcestershire? Why are nucleated villages largely confined to a broad strip across England from north to south, yet rare in the south-west, East Anglia and along the Welsh border? Why do we have numerous small medieval towns in, say, Cornwall and Wiltshire, but relatively few in Dorset and Hampshire?

Neither the concept of revolution nor mere geography can fully answer these types of questions. The solution perhaps lies in the concept of continuity and change. That is, throughout England as a whole, there are areas whose landscape sometimes reflects periods of continuity and sometimes periods of change, the latter often the direct result of the revolutions. For example, as Professor Everitt has shown, the landscape of north Kent is one of continuity, certainly from Roman times and probably even from an earlier period, while the southern part of that county is the result of great changes which took place in later Saxon times and the early medieval period. In a wider context it is possible to see how each of the great landscape revolutions affected the English countryside in different ways or sometimes not at all. Thus it is the combination of continuity through the revolutions and changes caused by them that has produced the complexities of landscape which we are now struggling to unravel.

In Devon, therefore, we have a landscape which was greatly affected by the first revolution in prehistoric times. It produced a new landscape, a landscape of change. But this subsequently became a landscape of continuity. There are, for example, few large nucleated villages in the area and only rarely evidence of open fields. The basic settlement and field pattern visible today is the result of the first revolution. That is because not only did the second revolution largely pass it by, though not of course completely, but the third revolution also did so to a large extent. On the other hand on the Wessex downlands all three revolutions had an impact. There we not only have traces of planned landscapes of the prehistoric period, and evidence of the villages and fields of late Saxon times, but also the great enclosures of the eighteenth and nineteenth centuries.

In essence therefore our view of the English landscape and our interpretation of it must be the result of a balance between both these concepts of revolution and of continuity and change. Neither must it be at only a broad regional or county level. Individual parishes and settlements need to be studied in terms of these concepts.

One final point must be made. Because the evolution of the English landscape can now be seen to be so complicated and spread over so long a period of time, the study of it is also complicated and perhaps requires a range of expertise that no one person can fully have. It is asking too much for an historian to understand fully the complexities and methodology of interpretation needed on a large-scale excavation, just as it is to expect an archaeologist to appreciate the subtleties of medieval legal documents. Professor Hoskins was, perhaps, the last of the polymaths. Those of us who attempt to follow him may have to lower our sights and work together more closely if we are to continue in his footsteps.

Christopher Taylor
1988

INTRODUCTION
to the 1977 edition by W. G. Hoskins

Back in 1955, when I first published this book it was a pioneer work. There I began by saying that 'despite the multitude of books about English landscape and scenery, and the flood of topographical books in general, there is not one book which deals with the historical evolution of the landscape as we know it. At the most we may be told that the English landscape is the man-made creation of the seventeenth and eighteenth centuries, which is not even a quarter-truth, for it applies only to country houses and their parks, and to the parliamentary enclosures that gave us a good deal of our modern patterns of fields, hedges, and by-roads. It ignores the fact that more than a half of England never underwent this kind of enclosure, but evolved in an entirely different way, and that in some regions the landscape had been virtually completed by the eve of the Black Death.'

This book opened up a huge field of history which has been, and is still being, exploited by other writers. The literature of landscape history is growing quickly, both in books dealing with special aspects (such as *Anglo-Saxon Settlement and Landscape*, edited by Trevor Rowley in 1974) or with microscopic local studies like Thorpe's *The Lord and the Landscape* (Wormleighton in Warwickshire, published in 1965) and Jack Ravensdale's *Liable to Floods* (three Fen-edge villages in Cambridgeshire, published in 1974). These represent in their different ways two of the most fruitful approaches to landscape history, from which we are likely to learn a great deal that is new and often unexpected.

Archaeologists, too, have added enormously to our knowledge of the antiquity of the present landscape, above all perhaps their widespread investigations of river gravels enforced by the urgent need to do 'rescue digs' before the gravel is poured ultimately into the new motorways. 'Rescue digs' have many disadvantages, as has anything done at speed; but at least they uncover a vast amount of evidence that might have remained buried for ever or discovered only at long intervals and by accident. Even the claylands of the Midlands, once thought so inhospitable to early settlement, have produced an average of four Romano-British settlements per mile along the M5 route through the keuper marls of south Gloucestershire, including arable fields of the same period. So another myth about the English landscape has been exploded.

All our previous estimates of population in Romano-British times, and possibly even in the prehistoric period, have been far too low. And this means too that our knowledge of how much of our land had been cleared and brought into cultivation by, say, Roman times if no earlier, needs complete revision, for people imply farming systems for their material needs. One can hardly over-estimate the contribution of archaeologists in this field, with the proviso that landscapes may have been cleared at much earlier dates than we had previously thought, but that they may have been lost again by natural changes such as submergence of land-levels in the Fens and elsewhere or by human changes in farming practice. Thus a great deal of our evidence for farming and for field-systems at various periods comes from aerial photography and nothing is usually visible on the ground itself. The most remarkable area of England in which to see Roman fields is the fenlands of Lincolnshire, north Cambridgeshire, and north-west Norfolk. Most have been obliterated because of the intensity of modern farming on valuable land, but they can be seen and mapped

Hackpen Hill, Broad Hinton, Wiltshire.

from the air (Christopher Taylor, *Fields in the English Landscape*, 1975).

When one thinks, too, of the neolithic 'axe-factories' recently discovered high on the mountains of the Inner Lake District and the clearance of woodland this involved up to two thousand feet above sea-level, or at the other end of the scale the discovery of Neolithic wooden trackways through parts of the Somerset marshlands, an area that had to be reclaimed again by the rich abbeys of that region from the tenth century onwards, one can sum it up safely in the phrase *Everything is older than we think*. There is even some evidence that woodland clearance began in Mesolithic times, say seven or eight thousand years ago, though their farming could only have produced very limited clearances in the woods and all the signs have been lost in the re-invasion by trees and heaths (as on the Dorset Heaths, above all at Winfrith Newburgh).

Not only have archaeologists greatly enlarged our time-scale in the making of the English landscape, but they have also shown how complicated a pattern of past landscapes we may have to take into account. Thus in *The Upper Thames Valley: an archaeological survey of the river gravels* (Benson and Miles, 1974) David Miles has this to say: 'The maps showed that in the Upper Thames Valley we were not just dealing with a series of isolated sites, but rather with overlapping and often interrelated prehistoric, Roman and Saxon landscapes underlying the present surface and, sometimes moulding it and in some places even breaking through. . .' The student of the English landscape therefore faces at times the possibility of underground evidence; though in this book I have striven to analyse what can be seen on the surface today as an end in itself. The visible landscape offers us enough stimulus and pleasure without the uncertainty about what may lie underneath. In other words, the borderline between landscape history as I conceive it and archaeology is a fine one, and I am not prepared to define it at this early stage even if I were competent to do so.

I have said above that everything in the landscape is older than we think. Nor is the evidence for this statement buried, and the province of professional archaeologists only. In many parts of England more or less massive boundary banks survive, some of them still awaiting explanation. In Oxfordshire, the boundaries of the Roman villa estate of Ditchley have been traced with considerable certainty, enclosing an area of about 875 acres. A good deal of these boundaries consist of earthen banks thrown up about the middle of the first century AD, known in parts as Grim's Dike. There are gaps where dense woodland afforded sufficient protection. Even to this day a nearly complete periphery of ancient woodland can be traced around the villa estate. The other remarkable thing is that most of this extensive boundary dating from the first century is followed by parish boundaries of Saxon origin: in other words there was still a farming unit here which was recognisable in Saxon times. Landlords come and go, but farming goes on. Every harvest was

a gamble whatever work went into the preparation: villas may have been destroyed or even decayed like many a modern house, but the tenant farmers go on from year to year and generation to generation.

Across in Suffolk a massive embankment, deeply ditched on both sides, divides the hundreds of Bosmere and Hartismere and it has its own name – Hundred Lane – followed by parish boundaries for miles. As a hundred boundary it must date from the early tenth century. It is slowly being destroyed by modern farming machinery, but the surviving parts should be scheduled as an ancient monument. What is more, I am certain that it was already in existence in the tenth century and was probably the boundary of a Romano-British villa estate centred perhaps on Stonham Aspal. On the southern side of this great embankment with its two ditches is a parish named Mickfield which means literally 'the great field'. What did the Old English colonists see when they moved in here? I think they saw a large area already cleared for farming, part of the old villa estate, and that they took over the boundary ready-made. Why bother to erase it? It takes modern machinery to do that. So I believe in general that *boundaries* are one of the most ancient features in the English landscape – parish, county, hundred, estate – allowing for the fact that in modern times some lesser boundaries have been erased or changed.

This speculation, for such it is so far about the Hundred Lane and its possible link with a Roman villa estate, leads us on to the conjunction of place-names ending in -*field* and their relationship to known (and unknown) Romano-British sites. I think it probable that the word 'field' carries this ancient meaning and should be explored accordingly. Norman Scarfe, in his book *The Suffolk Landscape*, discusses the name Bradfield at length in this context, and its relation to known Roman roads and sites in the neighbourhood.

In mid-Essex there is a remarkable group of 'field' place-names in the Braintree-Finchingfield district. There are three Bardfields, Finchingfield, Wethersfield, Gosfield, Panfield; while Felsted, not far away, contains the same element of 'field'. And this is an area where important Roman roads cross, with villa-sites and other Romano-British evidence known and more undoubtedly awaiting discovery. This small tract of England would make a marvellous study under the microscope of the local historian.

All this raises the important question of How old is the English village? We must not allow ourselves to be deceived by some clearly Old English place-name or in eastern England a Scandinavian place-name. This is admittedly dangerous ground, not to be lightly ignored, but we know certain places that have changed their names from British to Old English, and from Old English to Scandinavian. One small example must suffice here, though we do not know the answer yet. The Roman city of Exeter had a port four miles down the river Exe, a place now called Topsham – 'Toppa's *ham*', pure English. But it must have had quite another name during the four centuries or so it existed as a Roman riverside settlement. David Miles has investigated closely a small area near Oxford (Barton Court/Barrow Hills, near Radley) and concludes that the whole area has been extensively exploited for over five thousand years.

In west Norfolk, in the valley of the river Nar, Mr. J. P. Smallwood writes of the parish of Shouldham (again an Old English place-name, though of uncertain meaning) that it has produced evidence of occupation stretching back over five thousand years. In the Norfolk Research Committee's Newsletter for March 1976 he says: 'Neolithic and Early Bronze Age flint implements are found on its fields. The Abbey Farm is built on the site of the Gilbertine Priory, the only example in Norfolk of this unique English order. Beneath the destruction layer of the Priory lies a Late Bronze Age cemetery . . . In the fields at the back of the Abbey Farm lay an Iron Age farm and a Roman industrial settlement where iron was smelted and pottery and tiles made from the clay which outcrops in the parish.' From the ruined church of St Margaret has come evidence of more Roman occupation and an Iron Age warrior burial. 'The church site is also surrounded by traces of Middle and Late Saxon, and Medieval occupation. The village has shifted farther to the west and in the meadow by the surviving church (the village formerly had two churches, an arrangement not uncommon in East Anglia) are traces of the abandoned street and crofts of the old village. The list is apparently endless. . .' Further discoveries were made in the spring of 1975. Nor is Shouldham unique amongst Norfolk villages in possessing a rich and varied history of settlement. The neighbouring villages of Wormegay, Pentney, and West Dereham 'offer as enticing a prospect for research . . . in fact in north-west Norfolk alone it would not be difficult to draw up a list of twenty or thirty villages which would repay close attention.' We know all this because Norfolk possesses an active Research Committee, yet even so we are scarcely scratching the surface. Nor is Norfolk unique in holding such a rich field of evidence for the antiquity of its villages and their fields. This is not to assert that the evidence points to thousands of years of *continuous* occupation: that is a problem to which we may never know a certain answer. Many villages have changed their sites for different reasons, but most probably have not. They have been built over again and again and their true age lies buried several feet down in the humus and debris of village gardens and the floors of houses. In my own county of Devon, on the fertile lands of the New Red Sandstones, it seems to me highly likely that the burial-mounds of the middle Bronze Age are associated with the 'ancient fields' revealed by air photography in the river gravels of the middle Exe valley. This remains to be proved, but I myself believe that these fertile soils have been farmed continuously for some four thousand years, if not longer.

When I wrote the concluding pages of this book over twenty years ago I described the landscape as seen from the window of a Victorian vicarage in deepest Oxfordshire. Now I live in what many would call a suburban road in my native city and it might be thought it had little or no interest. The road itself began to be built up in 1839 on what were until then empty fields. Yet a few yards from my study runs a lane of Anglo-Saxon origin towards an Old English farm called *Madaworthi* (now called Matford). This lane itself comes off the Roman road that ran from Exeter to its port at Topsham. Matford Lane, still so-called, has a right-angled bend in it, quite inexplicable as there are no physical obstacles to make it bend like this; so I assume that it was contrived to run around some Saxon estate that already existed. Even an early Victorian suburb can produce its own landscape and its own problems.

It might be thought after twenty years or so, and the amount of new work which has been done, that this book should be revised.But there is so much we still do not know, so much work in progress, that a revision is still premature. There is continual change in the English landscape, at an accelerating pace during the past generation or so. The most obvious of these changes are enormous removal of hedges, some thousands of miles torn up every year now in order to accommodate ever-larger farming machinery, and the consequent enlargement of fields, above all in eastern England where the 'barley barons' hold sway. Then there is the widespread digging for gravel for new roads and other constructions, above all in the Welland valley in the east Midlands and in the upper Thames valley, and the construction of the motorways themselves. It is sometimes said that this is the greatest revolution in road-building since the Romans, but this is to forget the great mileage of turnpike roads in the seventeenth and eighteenth centuries. Conversely thousands of miles of railways have been obliterated, leaving behind only their earthworks in the form of cuttings and embankments and forlorn and wrecked stations. In the world of nature Dutch elm disease has decimated whole landscapes, more so in some parts of England than others. And finally, so many 'old' villages have spawned outwards with little bungalows on all sides that they have lost their historic shape (though here again we must not forget that villages in past centuries were continually growing or retreating). These are some of the major changes and it would be premature to assess how permanent some of them will prove to be. Such changes are, as has been said, often localised: many parts of the English landscape remain just as our forefathers left them a long time ago. It is to these quiet solitudes, above all perhaps our old common lands, that we can still gratefully turn for refreshment and sanctuary from noise and meaningless movement.

W. G. Hoskins
Exeter
November 1976

Chapter 1
THE LANDSCAPE BEFORE THE ENGLISH SETTLEMENT

Introduction

Professor Hoskins was somewhat dismissive of the impact and relevance of prehistoric and Roman people in the making of the English landscape. Writing first in 1955 when field archaeology in this country can be said to have been in its infancy, neither he nor anyone else could have had any conception of the part which archaeological studies were to play in the understanding of the development of the landscape. By 1976, as he pointed out in his Introduction to the 1977 edition of this book, a revolution in knowledge was already under way and he was well aware of it. However Hoskins was, rightly perhaps, largely concerned with the history of the visible landscape and he felt that the 'underground' evidence of archaeology was not a vital part of that history.

While perhaps prehistoric and Roman activities have had little direct effect on much of the later development of the English landscape, there is no doubt that when we search for the beginnings of that landscape we cannot ignore the influence of prehistoric and Roman peoples, even if at first sight it is difficult to understand or appreciate. The majority of the habitations of early people are largely invisible, except sometimes from the air. The detailed examination of ploughed fields for fragments of pottery and other debris, and complex and expensive excavations show, however, that much of the basic framework of the English countryside, including fields, boundaries, roads and tracks was fixed in Roman and even in prehistoric times. Thus we cannot, indeed must not, ignore the work of our remote ancestors. To do so would be to belittle their considerable achievements and totally to misunderstand the great complexity and age of the landscape in which we have our homes.

Perhaps the most notable feature of pre-Saxon times which recent archaeological research has revealed is the very high population levels which existed then. Inevitably no exact figures are available, nor will they ever be, but it is now clear that there were far more people living in England in Roman and prehistoric times than has hitherto been realised. England, far from being a largely empty country with vast unpopulated areas until Saxon times, at least in the later prehistoric and Roman periods had far more people within it than at the time of the Norman Conquest. This single fact implies a much greater degree of landscape exploitation and development than earlier writers, including Professor Hoskins, appreciated. The evidence for thousands of prehistoric and Roman settlements, tens of thousands of acres of fields and countless miles of trackways shows the influence of early people in the making of the English landscape.

In early prehistoric times, between 10000 BC at the end of the last Ice Age and 5000 BC, England was indeed an empty land with perhaps no more than a few thousand people eking out a fairly precarious living by hunting wild animals, fishing and gathering the natural fruits of the earth. But these people were by no means confined to 'good' light soils, nor river banks. They lived almost everywhere, as the discovery of their temporary habitations in their thousands has shown. The homes of these people have been found on the high Pennine moors, the Wessex downlands, in the Midland claylands and on the sandy heaths of East Anglia, as well as many other places. And though they were relatively few in number, in a very real sense, as a result of their wanderings, they laid down much of the basic framework of our later pattern of communications.

In following the migrating herds of deer or wild cattle or in seeking out suitable fishing places and woodland grazing areas they, and their animals, produced routeways which were later to become many of our existing roads and tracks. These were much more than merely the traditional so-called prehistoric trackways such as the Icknield Way, or the numerous ridgeways, but many of the minor and major roads of the claylands and mountains of England. Later people merely redefined and extended this basic framework.

The impact of the Neolithic people who occupied this country between about 5000 BC and 2500 BC was even more marked. Most of their visible remains are of their great ritual and burial monuments such as Avebury in Wiltshire and Arbor Low in Derbyshire and the

PLATE 1. *Hambledon Hill, Dorset. This great defensive structure of the Iron Age dominates the landscape. It was probably the centre of a huge estate or tribal unit.*

PLATE 2. *This is a modern recreation of a Neolithic trackway, on Shapwick Heath, Somerset. It gives a vivid impression of one type of prehistoric routeway.*

numerous chambered and unchambered long barrows or burial mounds. While these are of considerable archaeological importance they seem to have little significance in the wider history of the landscape. To some extent this is true, though it should be remembered that these great monuments do show the complex and sophisticated society that had emerged by this time. They should also suggest to us that the builders of such monuments would also have been very capable of modifying the landscape if they so chose. Other less vivid archaeological evidence shows that they did.

The actual number of Neolithic people was relatively small, perhaps no more than thirty to fifty thousand at any one time, but over two and a half thousand years they created many and varied settlements ranging from small farmsteads to large semi-fortified hill-top settlements such as that discovered at Carn Brea in Cornwall. More important, these people were farmers who removed vast areas of the primeval woodland by burning or by using their fine flint axes and subsequently cultivated the fields they had created.

As the centuries passed knowledge of metal-workng was acquired and local and regional specialisations in agriculture developed with pastoral farming in certain areas and primarily arable in others. The population continued to grow slowly and more and more of England was subjected to man's control.

Then, perhaps, quite suddenly, the first revolution in the English landscape occurred, usually termed the later Bronze Age by archaeologists. For reasons which are by no means understood, around 1600 BC the population of England seems to have exploded. It perhaps rose to as many as one million people within a few centuries. Thousands of new settlements appeared, most of which are now only visible from the air or revealed by excavation, though many survive on the fringes of Dartmoor or on the high hills of the Cheviots and the Pennines as

groups of hut-circles or small enclosures, or merely levelled platforms for former huts. These settlements also filled the river valleys, occupied parts of what later became the eastern fenlands and extended over the southern downlands. In addition, perhaps because the countryside was becoming over-full, fortified hill-top villages appeared and these, complemented by the archaeological finds of swords, spears, shields and daggers of this period, show that warfare was becoming endemic. The fort on Mam Tor in Derbyshire is one of these defensive sites, as is perhaps the huge enclosure at Borough Hill near Daventry, Northamptonshire. All these settlements were linked together by trackways, many of which can also be seen on air photographs, and the majority of which we still use today.

Equally important was the development of fields and field systems. In some places archaeologists have found the traces of small areas of cultivated land similar to those of the previous three thousand years. Of greater significance is the evidence for planned agricultural landscapes covering thousands of acres. On Dartmoor, and on the Wiltshire, Dorset and Berkshire downs, the remains of very large field systems have been discovered, often laid out from clearly defined base lines and with tracks and settlements fully integrated within them. On the fen edges of East Anglia, excavations have produced evidence for similar large-scale land allotment at this period, while air photographs have shown that hundreds of square miles in north Nottinghamshire and south Yorkshire, as well as along the edges of the River Trent further south, were divided into a regular pattern of fields and boundaries. All these, as well as similar field systems elsewhere, indicate that a total remodelling of great parts of the English landscape took place over a short period of time, presumably produced not by the sheer numbers of people involved, though this must have lain behind it, but by deliberate decisions by those in power. We do not know, and perhaps will never know, who these people were, or what economic, social or political forces lay behind their work. But we can be sure that the whole landscape was drawn out anew, leading to a further period of expansion after 1200 BC, conventionally called the Iron Age.

In these years the population continued to grow, so by the time of the Roman Conquest in AD 43 there were perhaps two million people in England. By then they had developed and expanded the Bronze Age landscape, sub-dividing fields, creating specialised areas of cattle ranching defined by miles of ditches, and pushing agriculture even further into the upland moors and heavy claylands of the Midlands. Perhaps the most remarkable evidence is that from eastern England. There over large parts of south-east Essex, north Suffolk and south Norfolk it has recently been recognised that much of the basic framework of the modern fields is actually pre-Roman in origin. There is even evidence that in the last few centuries of prehistoric times the exploitation of the countryside was becoming too intensive and that the natural balance of nature was being affected with break-down of soils and large-scale erosion occurring.

Alongside these fields, both old and new, lay thousands of settlements. These ranged from isolated farmsteads comprising a small group of huts, through hamlets to considerable villages. Above them lay hill-top fortresses also with a great variation in size ranging from the great town-like complexes of Maiden Castle and Hambledon Hill in Dorset to minor fortified settlements in the Midland counties.

By the end of the prehistoric period, England was crowded, perhaps over-crowded, with most of its land exploited to a great or lesser extent. The primeval forests had long since gone and what remained, perhaps less than exists today, was the product of two or three phases of clearance and regeneration and was also carefully managed. Whatever the influence of later people on the making of the English landscape, their contribution was merely fitted into a framework which had been established and modified a number of times by prehistoric people.

The four centuries during which England was part of the Roman empire saw the intensification of all that had been taking place in the previous fifteen hundred years or so. Membership of the Empire brought with it various technological, economic and political changes which halted the trend towards over-exploitation of the landscape and enabled it to continue to develop. New and better ploughs were introduced, the potential for export to the continent became available and an imposed peace brought the incessant warfare to an end. All this led to yet another rise in population, perhaps to a level of four million people by the third century AD. This in turn inevitably produced a further expansion of arable land as well as pastoral farming and, of course, led to even more settlements of every size and form. It is the sheer number of rural settlement sites that is perhaps the most difficult fact about the Roman period in England for the non-archaeologist to appreciate. In eastern Northamptonshire, for example, there is a *minimum* of four settlements every square mile. In Bedfordshire Roman settlements are usually no more than five hundred yards apart, almost regardless of soils and situation, and on the Northumberland hills they lie less than two hundred yards from each other in some places. On parts of the silt fens of eastern England, which were drained and exploited from the late first century AD onwards, Roman occupation sites occur less than a hundred yards apart.

Again these settlements varied in extent. Many were just farmsteads or hamlets, but others were of considerable size. Some of the latter were arranged in such a regular way that one can only interpret them as planned villages. The term villa, familiar to anyone interested in the Roman period, also covers a wide spectrum of functions from rather modest farmhouses through small country houses to magnificent palaces. Moreover, many villas which were in the past assumed to be isolated buildings have now been recognised as parts of extensive Roman villas. In addition the Roman administration introduced the first real towns into England as deliberately planned creations. The concept of urban life was apparently much favoured and as well as formal Roman towns, England was eventually dotted by huge semi-urban complexes, often much larger than the towns themselves.

When the Saxons finally arrived in England, they thus came, not to an empty land of forests, marshes and moorland with the insubstantial remains of a few thousand primitive people, but to a crowded, totally exploited country, covered in fields, roads, towns, villages and farmsteads, all organised into a complex system of land-holding and with political, administrative and religious boundaries not only fixed but of great antiquity.

1

THE LANDSCAPE BEFORE THE ENGLISH SETTLEMENT

Wordsworth in his *Guide through the District of the Lakes* – one of the best guide-books ever written, for poets make the best topographers – opens his description of the scenery of the Lakes with a View of the Country as formed by Nature. He then passes, in his second section, to the Aspect of the Country, as affected by its Inhabitants, and this he begins by asking the reader to envisage what the landscape, finished by the great impersonal forces of Nature and awaiting its first human inhabitants, looked like in its primeval freshness.

He will form to himself an image of the tides visiting and revisiting the friths, the main sea dashing against the bolder shore, the rivers pursuing their course to be lost in the mighty mass of waters. He may see or hear in fancy the winds sweeping over the lakes, or piping with a loud voice among the mountain peaks and, lastly, may think of the primæval woods shedding and renewing their leaves with no human eye to notice, or human heart to regret or welcome the change.

How often one has tried to form these images in various parts of England, seated beside a wide, flooding estuary as the light thickens on a winter evening, dissolving all the irrelevant human details of the scene, leaving nothing but the shining water, the sky, and the darkening hills, and the immemorial sound of curlews whistling over the mud and fading river-beaches. This, we feel, is exactly as the first men saw it when they reached the shingled margin of the river a hundred generations ago. Nothing has changed. We are seeing the natural world through the eyes of men who died three or four thousand years ago, and for a moment or two we succeed in entering into the minds of the dead. Or on some desolate English moorland it is even easier to feel this identity with the dead of the Bronze Age who lie near by under a piled-up cairn or under the heathery blanket of a burial mound. It is easy, too, to feel this kinship while watching the summer morning waves falling with a meditative indifference on a beach still untrodden by the human race. There are many such timeless scenes and there is an acute and melancholy pleasure in this mental game; but it is not always as easy as this. On unpeopled moorland, beside remote estuaries at dawn, or at sea approaching an historic coast, little or nothing is alien to the natural scene. We see it precisely as the first men saw it. The imagination is liberated over the scene.

But there are not many places where one can feel with such complete assurance that this is exactly as the first inhabitants saw it in 'the freshness of the early world'. Not much of England, even in its more withdrawn, inhuman places, has escaped being altered by man in some subtle way or other, however untouched we may fancy it is at first sight. Sherwood Forest and Wicken Fen are not quite what they seem. The historian, trying to enter into the minds of the first men to break into a virgin landscape, trying to envisage precisely what they saw and no more, is aware of some of the difficulties of his task, if not of all. One needs to be a botanist, a physical geographer, and a naturalist, as well as an historian, to be able to feel certain that one has all the facts right before allowing the imagination to play over the small details of a scene. For unless the facts are right there is no pleasure in this imaginative game, if we clothe the landscape with the wrong kind of trees, or allow in it plants and birds that are really only the product of some recent changes, or if we fail to observe that the river has changed its course well within historic times. We may have to make all sorts of allowances – subtracting here and adding there – before the natural landscape, still untouched by man, is recovered in all its purity and freshness. And if we succeed in recovering this buried landscape, and wish to communicate to others the pleasure it gives us, how difficult it is to do so without intruding the unpalatable jargon of the geologist or the economic historian or some other learned trade.

For what a many-sided pleasure there is in looking at a wide view anywhere in England, not simply as a sun-drenched whole, fading into unknown blue distance, like the view of the west Midland plain from the top of the Malvern Hills, or at a pleasant rural miniature like the crumpled Woburn ridge in homely Bedfordshire, but in recognising every one of its details name by name, in knowing how and when each came to be there, why it is just that colour, shape, or size, and not otherwise, and in seeing how the various patterns and parts fit together to make the whole scene. One may liken the English landscape, especially in a wide view, to a symphony, which it is possible to enjoy as an architectural mass of sound, beautiful or impressive as the case may be, without being able to analyse it in detail or to see the logical development of its structure. The enjoyment may be real, but it is limited in scope and in the last resort vaguely diffused in emotion. But if instead of hearing merely a symphonic mass of sound, we are able to isolate the themes as they enter, to see how one by one they are intricately woven together and by what magic new harmonies are produced, perceive the manifold subtle variations on a single theme, however disguised it may be, then the total effect is immeasurably enhanced. So it is with landscapes of the historic depth and physical variety that England shows almost everywhere. Only when we know all the themes and harmonies can we begin to appreciate its full beauty, or to discover in it new subtleties every time we visit it. Nor is it only a programme of symphonies that the English landscape provides. One can become satiated with magnificent views over

PLATE 3. *Prehistoric hut, probably of Bronze Age date, Kestor, Dartmoor. This is one of a number which are associated with a huge block of land over 600 acres in extent and covered by a single field system. Such a prehistoric field system is small by Dartmoor standards; the largest cover over 2000 acres.*

19

a dozen counties. There is as much pleasure to be had in the chamber music of Bedfordshire or Rutland; perhaps, one might say, a more sophisticated pleasure in discovering the essence of these simpler and smaller landscapes. This book is, then, an attempt to study the development of the English landscape much as though it were a piece of music, or a series of compositions of varying magnitude, in order that we may understand the logic that lies behind the beautiful whole.

The Pre-Roman Landscape

The English landscape as we know it today is almost entirely the product of the last fifteen hundred years, beginning with the earliest Anglo-Saxon villages in the middle decades of the fifth century. The direct prehistoric contribution to the landscape is small. It is more impressive in some parts of England than others, fascinating when studied in detail – as in the remarkable Iron Age villages of western Cornwall or the hill-forts of Wessex – but, considered as an influence on the whole landscape, of little importance. There are, indeed, some counties where it can not be ignored, but in a general survey of the country as a whole we need not linger over it.

As already noted in the Introduction, this is no longer true. The English landscape is the result of almost 10,000 years of man's achievements and failures and nowhere can they be ignored, even if they are not always easy to see.

Even in Neolithic times (2500-1900 BC), to go no further back, the maximum population of Britain was probably only about twenty thousand – about the size of a large country town, such as Bridgwater in Somerset, today. Corn-growing was still subsidiary to pasture-farming, life was more or less nomadic, and so it remained until the late Bronze

Age (1000-500 BC). The oldest recognisable corn 'fields', small irregular plots of ground associated with hut-circles on the western side of Dartmoor, date possibly from the early Bronze Age (1900-1400 BC). There are others on the western slopes of Rough Tor on Bodmin Moor in Cornwall and similar sites with small, curvilinear plots have been found on the Yorkshire moors, where they are attributed to the middle Bronze Age (1400-1000 BC). These prehistoric fields are, however, only recognisable to the archaeologist, and then only at certain times of the year, and they can hardly be said to be a feature of the landscape wherever they are. They are interesting only as the earliest known corn-plots in this country, just as the hut-circles of Dartmoor (mainly concentrated in the southern and south-western valleys) are interesting, for our purpose, as the remains of the earliest recognisable dwelling-houses, dating as they do from the early Bronze Age to the early Iron Age.

The dating given in this section is now in need of some revision. The Neolithic period is known to have begun perhaps as early as 5000 BC and to have drawn to a close about 2500 BC. The early and middle Bronze Ages would now be dated between 2500 and 15-1600 BC, the later Bronze Age between 1600 and 800 BC and the Iron Age to 800 BC to AD 43.

With the late Bronze Age, and especially the early Iron Age (from 500 BC onwards) the further development of agriculture led to the appearance of settled villages, a revolution in human life comparable in magnitude with the effects of the industrial revolution of the nineteenth century. There had been 'villages' of a kind on Bronze Age Dartmoor – as, for example, on Standon Down above Tavy Cleave – but villages as the centre of settled agricultural communities may be said to date from the centuries immediately preceding the Roman Conquest. One of these villages, or more strictly a hamlet of at least eight houses, has been completely excavated at Chysauster in the far west of Cornwall, three miles due north of Penzance. Chysauster is most exciting, even to those whose interest in prehistory is a flickering holiday affair, for here we have a village, still substantially intact, of houses built of granite dry-walling still standing to a height of several feet. The houses were built in the form of rooms opening on to a central unroofed courtyard, four houses on each side of a cobbled street. The inhabitants of Chysauster cultivated the garden-plots and small arable fields that surround the houses, and also dug and smelted tin. The village seems to have been occupied from about the second century BC into Roman times, and was then abandoned. At some later date – but precisely when it is impossible to say – a new site was occupied on lower ground about half a mile south, probably by the medieval colonist and his household who created the present farm of Chysauster. Three miles to the north-west across the moors, near the St Ives-Land's End road, is the excavated village of Porthmeor, with granite-built houses of the same type, occupied mainly between the second and fourth centuries AD. Other Iron Age village sites are known in England, but none is so revealing and impressive to the layman as these two sites in western Cornwall.

The people of the early Iron Age lived mostly in single farmsteads or in small hamlets, of which Chysauster and Porthmeor are examples. The single farmsteads are revealed in the first instance by air photography, which detects their presence by markings in the modern crops, but nothing is visible on the surface of the ground and they cannot be said to be significant for our study of the landscape. There is, however, one other relevant aspect of these Celtic farmsteads and that is the distinct possibility that a number of existing farmsteads and hamlets in south-western England (and possibly elsewhere, but of that I cannot speak) represent original Celtic farms which have been continuously occupied ever since their beginning in pre-Roman or Romano-British times. The farmstead itself in such places has been rebuilt over and over again during this long period of time, and is usually of no interest whatever to the archaeologist, but as the descendant of a Celtic farmstead on the same site it is a fascinating place to the historian.

The other visible evidences in the landscape of these early farms are the lynchets or cultivation terraces that abound on the chalk downlands of south-eastern England, though they are found sporadically elsewhere also.

Professor Hoskins' suggestion that some of the existing settlements in south-west England stand on the sites of earlier prehistoric Roman farms and villages is of considerable interest and certainly worth pursuing. In general terms there is every reason to believe that he was probably correct and that much of the pattern of dispersed settlement in south-west England, west Dorset and parts of Somerset at least is the result of Roman or pre-Roman achievements rather than of those of later periods. In the end, however, only archaeological excavation can provide the answer and digging up a working farmstead poses problems that most archaeologists have not yet faced up to.

These Celtic fields represent an immense advance on the tiny irregular corn-plots of the Bronze Age farmers, for they are more or less rectangular blocks – often approximating to a square – varying in size from half to one and a half acres. They are seldom more than four hundred feet long (usually much less), and seldom less than a hundred feet in breadth (often more). It is this great breadth which distinguishes them clearly from the arable strips of the 'open field' system that followed them in time. Such fields can be most readily seen from the air, as at Fyfield Down near Marlborough in Wiltshire, or on Windover Hill near Eastbourne in Sussex, but they are often easily seen on the ground also. On the Wiltshire and Sussex downs many square miles are covered by these fields. Immediately to the north of Brighton, an area of no less than eleven and a half square miles is still covered with the lynchets of the Celtic field system.

These ancient fields survive so clearly today because they were laid out in the smooth turf of the chalk country on a relatively dry soil, and because they were abandoned at some early date when cultivation and settlement moved down into the heavier and more rewarding soils of the valleys. In other parts of England they would be more difficult to find, especially where later cultivation has altered the field boundaries, but one can detect possible clues on the large-scale maps, in conjunction with other evidence. The present-day field pattern around the remote Dartmoor farm of Babeny, for example, is highly suggestive of Celtic farming in small square plots. Immediately below these plots flows the Walla Brook, hurrying on its way down to join the East Dart. Now Walla Brook was originally Weala Brōc, 'stream of the Welsh or Britons', a name given by the first Saxon settlers on the moorland fringes to a stream beside whose banks, far up into the Moor, scattered groups of Celtic farmers still survived. It is possible that at Babeny we have traces of one of their farms in the lay-out of the fields. Celtic farmers did not live merely upon the chalk downlands. It is only that the traces of their presence upon the landscape are more visible in that type of country. We may well seek for signs of their presence in the more difficult terrain of the West and the North, and in the lowlands of southern and eastern England.

While the description of so-called 'Celtic' fields is correct, it dwells on their detailed form and not on their often extensive nature. They formerly covered large areas of the chalk downlands. Plate 7 is a remarkable photograph with more in it than Professor Hoskins realised. It certainly does show 'Celtic' or more properly prehistoric fields, but these have been enlarged in Roman times. More interesting is that these fields have been over-ploughed by slight ridge-and-furrow clearly visible in the centre and the right-hand side. This has been dated to the thirteenth and early fourteenth centuries and is known to have been the result of temporary medieval expansion of arable into the area.

Sadly, like so much of the archaeological record which managed to survive centuries of later activity, almost all the fields near Brighton have now been destroyed by the ruthless demands of twentieth-century agriculture. They can, however, still be seen on air photographs.

Western Farmsteads and Fields

The subject of Celtic farmsteads is difficult to speak about, especially the visible evidences in the landscape. It seems likely that we shall find our surest signs in Cornwall, and above all in the far west of that county, for here the Celtic kingdom of Dumnonia subsisted until the early tenth century. Here a number of active farms continued in being and come down to us more or less intact so far as their fields and hedges are concerned. The farmsteads themselves have been rebuilt over and over again, but the network of small, irregular fields bounded by miles of granite-boulder walls was almost impossible to change once the pattern was laid down. The 6-inch maps of western Cornwall abound in this pattern, for example in the parish of Zennor between St Ives and Land's End. Bosigran farm shows perhaps the most remarkable of these patterns (Fig. 1). For the dating of these fields it is probably significant that both east and west of the farmstead Iron Age houses of the Chysauster type have been found.* At Porthmeor, not far away, the Iron Age village was occupied mainly between the second and fourth centuries AD, as we have seen; and at Treen, a little further to the north-east, another Iron Age village is known to exist (Field 831, OS 25-inch map).

Recent work in West Penwith has indeed confirmed Professor Hoskins' ideas. There is now no doubt that the pattern of modern fields, and perhaps the farmsteads as well, is certainly a Roman one and perhaps prehistoric.

Not all Celtic field-patterns are of the Bosigran type. At Castallack, in the

* H. O'N. Hencken, *Archaeology of Cornwall and Scilly* (Methuen, 1932), p.311.

PLATE 5. *Stone wall, Castallack, St Paul, Cornwall. It forms the side of a small enclosed Iron Age settlement of a type common all over Cornwall.*

PLATE 6. *This prehistoric field system on Chilcomb Down, near Winchester, Hampshire, is now sadly typical of most of those in Southern England. Modern agriculture has largely destroyed all trace of it except from the air. Even so a contemporary trackway and a long ditch, off which the fields are laid as part of a planned landscape, are visible.*

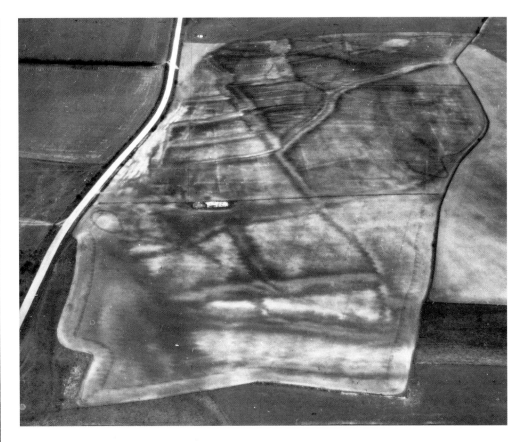

PLATE 7. *'Celtic' fields, on Fyfield Down, near Marlborough, Wiltshire.*

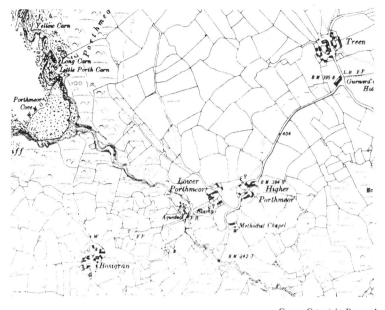

Crown Copyright Reserved

The Penwith peninsula of west Cornwall is almost entirely of this character: hamlets of the Treen and Bosigran type, and thousands of tiny fields of very irregular shape. These fields are enclosed by rubble walling of unhewn granite blocks gathered from the surface of the land and therefore almost irremovable. The fields are of the same date as the numerous 'British villages' which are dotted all over the peninsula. Only two of these have been excavated, Chysauster and Porthmeor. The latter (not marked on the above map) was discovered in 1933 near the Methodist chapel. Excavation showed that it was occupied from the middle of the first century AD until the fifth or sixth century, when it was abandoned. The present Lower Porthmeor and Higher Porthmeor represent a resettlement, probably of medieval date. The Iron Age fields retained their identity, however, because of the massiveness of their boundary walls, and were re-occupied. They form a very distinctive pattern, even more tangled and irregular than the medieval field pattern (see Fig. 8). Indeed, it is possible that the more open, but still irregular, field pattern to the north of Porthmeor and west of Treen is the result of medieval clearance, so that we have fields of two distinct periods on the above map. Reproduced by permission from the 6-inch map of the Ordnance Survey.

parish of Paul, the six-inch map reveals a continuous hedge enclosing a large squarish area roughly one third of a mile long and nearly as broad. This was later cut up into about fifteen fields with no particular distinguishing characteristics, so that the original enclosure has been completely lost sight of except to the observant map-reader. The large original enclosure was an early cattle-field, covering about sixty acres. Since a fogou, or subterranean retreat, of Iron Age date is known to have existed immediately north of Castallack farm, and 350 yards north-west lay a fortified masonry enclosure called the Roundago – probably a small Iron Age fort – we are probably safe in assuming that the enclosed cattle-field was of the same period.

At what date was this large enclosure sub-divided into a number of little fields averaging three or four acres each? I think it likely that this was done in the thirteenth century when Castallack was re-occupied. It is probable that the farm was abandoned at an early date, as we know Chysauster and Porthmeor to have been. The massive original walls of the enclosure remained, though the interior must have been completely submerged in bracken and furze. We first hear of Castallack again in a record of 1284, which suggests that it had been re-occupied not long before, and it seems fairly certain that the small enclosures within the larger one date from this time. Here, then, we have field boundaries of two widely different dates for the historian of the landscape to study.

Nowhere can we *prove* continuity of occupation from Celtic times to the present day, for no records exist to enable us to do this. It is indeed likely that a great number, perhaps most, of the farmsteads of Iron Age date have been abandoned at some date and re-occupied in medieval times under the pressure of a rising population. This may be true of such Dartmoor farms as Babeny, already referred to, where the field pattern and the stream-name both suggest the existence of Celtic farmers. On the other hand some farms may have enjoyed an unbroken occupation. The fact that Walla Brook – 'the stream of the Welsh or Britons' – cannot have been so named until the late seventh century at the earliest (when the Saxons reached Devon) is evidence for the continuance of Celtic farming along that stream (as at Babeny) at that comparatively late date, though as a name Babeny does not appear in the records until 1260. I see no reason to reject the possibility here of continuity of occupation since Celtic times, given a known survival as late as AD 700 or thereabouts.

Both here in Devon, as Professor Hoskins suggests, and in many other places in England, ancient estates, perhaps Roman or pre-Roman in origin, have now been identified. Most, like Treable, passed almost unaltered from their Roman owners to their Saxon ones and their boundaries have often survived to be recorded by detailed fieldwork of the kind described here.

Just off the northern foothills of Dartmoor, in the parish of Cheriton Bishop, is a farm called Treable for which some fascinating early evidence is forthcoming. Treable is one of the comparatively few Celtic place-names surviving in Devon: it means 'the *trev* or homestead of Ebell', a personal name corresponding to the Gaulish Epillus. Now although Treable is not recorded as a name until 1242, it can be identified quite conclusively with an estate called 'Hyple's old land' granted by King Edward to his faithful vassal Aelfsige in the year 976. Hyple is a corruption of Ebell, and the reference to 'Hyple's old land' suggests that this Celtic landowner (whose name also appears in Ipplepen in south Devon) was in possession not long before, certainly within the tenth century.* Here, at any rate, a Celtic estate – in this instance covering an area of six thousand acres – survived almost to within a hundred years of the Norman Conquest, and there is no reason to doubt the continuity of occupation of some part of it at least. A coin of the reign of Hadrian (early second century) has indeed been found in a hedge on Treable farm, but to assume continuity back to that period is hazardous.

The field pattern of Treable today shows nothing indicative of great age. The Tithe Map of 1842 – the oldest we have for this purpose – is disappointing. But there is one aspect of the estate boundary, as given in the charter of 976, which is worth dwelling upon for the light it throws on a minor feature of the English landscape. At one point on its eastern boundary, the charter takes us 'along the way to the old ditch'. Walking along this boundary, with the help of the 2½-inch Ordnance map, one finds oneself dropping down a steep hillside along a cart-track which is shut in on either side by an earthen bank several feet high, i.e., a hollow way. This hollow way – 'the old ditch' – was already 'old' in the tenth century. It can hardly be doubted that it represents the ancient boundary between the estate of Hyple and his ancestors to the west, and that of another (unknown) Celtic landowner to the east. The two hedge-banks, still enclosing the fields of today, are thus of great age – certainly pre-Saxon.

The 'hollow way' was made by each landowner digging out a ditch and throwing up the earth into a continuous bank on his own side. So we get a double ditch which forms in fact a track several feet wide and sunk several feet below the level of the fields on either side, thus:

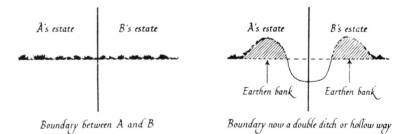

Boundary between A and B

Boundary now a double ditch or hollow way

That this is often the origin of the 'hollow way' running between two high banks is clinched by the expression in a charter of *c.* 1174 setting out the boundaries between the Abbot of Tavistock's estate at Abbotsham in north Devon and that of a neighbouring squire – Richard Coffin – at Alwington and Cockington. Here the bounds begin 'from the two-fold ditch' (*twifealda dich*). A Somerset charter of 963, relating to a Saxon estate called Manworthy in Milverton, refers to 'the hollow ditch' at one point, evidently the same construction as a two-fold ditch.

The Treable and Abbotsham charters explain the significance and origin of a puzzling feature which all those who walk across country (and do not rush in utter blindness through it in a car) must have come across at one time or another: that is the track, sometimes only a few feet wide, sometimes much broader, which begins suddenly on one side

* H. P. R. Finberg, *Early Charters of Devon and Cornwall* (University of Leicester, Department of English Local History, Occasional Paper no. 2, 1953), pp. 27ff., upon which these remarks on Treable are mostly based.

PLATE 8. *A hamlet and fields, Cape Cornwall, St Just, Cornwall. It has now been established that these irregular stone-walled fields are certainly Roman in date and may even be prehistoric. The hamlet within them is probably equally ancient.*

of a field-gate, runs between hedge-banks for several hundred yards, occasionally more, and then stops as suddenly as it began, debouching into a field and losing all identity forthwith. If we regard such lanes as trackways, they are impossible to explain, for they begin and end nowhere, so to speak. They are in fact ancient boundaries between two estates, sometimes medieval, sometimes Saxon or even Celtic, formed by the digging of a double ditch. It should be observed that this does not explain all 'hollow ways', some of which are true traffic routes, but it explains those that appear to go nowhere in particular and to peter out without reason.

There is much more to be learnt about the visible signs of Celtic estates, farms, fields and hedges, in the English countryside. I have set out above a few of the considerations that have come my way, but patient and minute topographical research – of the sort that is wrongly despised by most historians – will undoubtedly reveal to us in time much more of this distant period still embedded in the landscape around us, if only we have eyes to see, the records to follow up the visual evidence, and the imagination to read the records aright.

Roman Britain

With the spread of settled villages it is possible that the total population of Britain may have risen to something like a quarter of a million before the arrival of the Belgae early in the first century BC. The spread of the Belgae over the whole of south-eastern England and well into the Midlands, and their cultivation of the loams with the heavy wheeled plough, opened up new kinds of land hitherto considered too intractable for the light prehistoric plough, and there can be no doubt that it resulted in a further substantial increase of population. Knowing what we do of the population of Roman Britain (not much, it is true, but incomparably more than we know of the earlier periods) we cannot put the maximum population of Britain on the eve of the Roman Conquest at more than four hundred thousand – about the size of modern Bristol. When we bear in mind figures of this magnitude, and remember that for the greater part of the prehistoric period in Britain the population was less than fifty to a hundred thousand, we can readily appreciate that even the first two thousand years of agriculture from Neolithic times onwards has left little mark upon the landscape, other than a few more or less impressive isolated features. The continuous story can still hardly be said to have begun.

The population of England was probably around two million by the first century BC. The Introduction to this chapter has already pointed out that the impact of prehistoric man was far greater than Professor Hoskins believed thirty years ago. The same is true of the Roman period. There is a continuous story which can be recovered, albeit with difficulty, and which has left much in the present landscape.

Nor was the Roman contribution to the landscape, or what can be seen of it today, much more substantial. It shows itself mainly in the surviving roads, in the sites of villas, and in a few canals or dikes in eastern England, all of which remained important in their various ways well beyond the Roman period.

The network of the major Roman roads in England is fairly well known, though many gaps even in the known roads remain to be filled in. Besides the major roads, a large system of secondary roads gradually came into existence to serve local needs, and much more remains to be discovered about these. Mr I. D. Margary's *Roman Ways in the Weald* (Phoenix House, 1948) brought to light a whole network of these lesser roads in Kent and Sussex, mostly unsuspected until he wrote. East Anglia probably had an equally complex system of local roads to judge by the unrelated fragments on the present map. Most of this still awaits working out. Even so, more than five thousand miles of roads are shown on the Ordnance Survey map of *Roman Britain* (1931 edition).

The Roman road-system, both the main post roads and the local roads, was important in the history of the English landscape. Not only do many of these roads survive to this day (or

▷

PLATE 10. *This road is the modern A5, south of Milton Keynes, Buckinghamshire. It is also Watling Street, the Roman road from London to the North. The bend in the far distance is a genuine Roman one, built to allow traffic on this undoubtedly heavily used road to traverse a steep hill more easily.*

▷▷

PLATE 11. *Roman Road, Blackstone Edge, Littleborough, Lancashire. Perhaps the most remarkable surviving Roman Road in England, on the high moors above Rochdale. The central groove is said to have been cut by the friction of the brake-poles of carts descending the almost 1 in 4 gradient.*

more strictly, the line of the road) as trunk roads carrying a thunderous lorry traffic over long distances (for example, Watling Street, now the Holyhead road) or as useful secondary roads between villages in many parts of southern England, or in a more intimate fashion as bridlepaths and footpaths for solitary man and beast, but they opened up in their time whole tracts of the countryside on a scale hitherto unknown. Even the lesser local roads pushed through the forested clay lands in all directions, and crossed the high moorlands. This does not necessarily mean that these forests and moors were opened up for clearance and settlement, except perhaps in unimportant little patches. The roads cut through the woods in going from one place to another, but the bulk of settlement was still confined to the lighter and more open soils and was associated with the pre-Roman trackways rather than the Roman roads. The Weald, for instance, remained mostly unsettled and wild, except for clearings where iron mining was carried on, and the dense forests on the heavy Midland clays show very few sites of villas or native Romano-British villages. The real importance of these roads comes out in the Anglo-Saxon period, for they were, together with the larger rivers, the ready-made routes by which the English colonists penetrated more swiftly and safely into new country than if they had had to hack their way in yard by yard from the edges. There had been, of course, and there still existed, a considerable system of prehistoric trackways, along which settlers and colonists of new land had moved since Bronze Age times, and of which the Anglo-Saxon colonists also made extensive use wherever they found them; but these early trackways kept mostly to the higher and more open ground, on the lighter soils, whereas the Roman roads thrust through the heavier and more fertile soils that offered greater possibilities to the Old English farmers.

> *Apart from the deliberately constructed major Roman roads, there were lesser local roads all over England. But far from pushing 'through the forested claylands' they passed through cultivated fields as roads do today. Indeed in many instances they are the same roads. Even the Weald was criss-crossed by roads and scattered with settlements, many based on the iron indusry there which is now known to have been far more extensive than previously believed. Saxon peoples used all these roads and not just the 'prehistoric trackways' which themselves were only a small proportion of the routes used in prehistoric times.*

The Romano-British villas, of which well over five hundred are known (and many others still await discovery), represent a substantial clearance and taming of the natural landscape. Some of them, like the villa at Ditchley in Oxfordshire, were the centres of estates of a thousand acres or more. The villa was an isolated farmhouse, standing in its own large, open fields, quite unlike the small enclosed fields that surrounded the native villages. Sometimes it was large enough and elaborate enough to be regarded as a country house, with a correspondingly large estate around it. In some instances excavation has shown that a pre-Roman farmstead stood on the same site (as at Otford in Kent or at Newport in the Isle of Wight), and that the villa represents the rebuilding of an older and more primitive farmstead as some native farmers acquired wealth and a taste for Roman ways of living. Such extensive rebuildings by farmers rising in the social scale occur at later periods in English history, notably in the sixteenth and seventeenth centuries.

> *The majority of Roman villas were indeed the centres of large estates. But it is probable that many of these estates were not the result of clearance and the taming of the natural landscape, but merely the formal Romanisation of earlier estates. Excavations at numerous villas have revealed earlier farmsteads beneath them whose occupants merely replaced the wooden thatched huts by stone buildings with mosaic floors and central heating as the new Roman culture was eagerly accepted. A modern parallel is the transformation of buildings in say East or West Africa in less than a century under the impact of western 'civilisation'.*
>
> *It is unlikely that Roman villas had large open fields around them. Where they still survive, as at Barnsley Park, Gloucestershire, or are visible from the air, they seem to be relatively small paddocks.*

Most villas appear, however, to stand on new sites, though they were still built upon the lighter soils — chalk, oolite and gravel — favoured by men before them. 'They tend,' says R. G. Collingwood, 'to select a rather special type of site: a valley-slope facing south or east, not too high up, with shelter from the wind, exposure to the sun, and water close at hand.'* Though occupying in the main the lighter and more easily cleared soils, villas were also established in forest clearings, virgin sites on the heavier soils which the new wheeled plough was able to cope with. One finds such villas in the Cambridgeshire woods, on the edge of the forest in southern Berkshire, and in Wychwood forest in Oxfordshire. The attack on the forests and woods which covered the greater part of England under natural conditions, and above all on the extensive clay lands, was making headway throughout Roman times, though still only slowly and sporadically.

Besides the villas, there was a totally different type of settlement — the native villages,

---

* R. G. Collingwood and J. N. L. Myres, *Roman Britain and the English Settlements* (Oxford: Clarendon Press, revised edn 1937), p.209.

PLATE 12. *This view from Malham Cove, North Yorkshire, shows the boundary banks of late prehistoric fields stretching up the hillside. They were once almost square but were made rectangular in Roman times. Beyond, in the middle distance, are strip lynchets, which result from medieval ploughing along the contours. Overlying all these ancient fields are the stone walls of the eighteenth- and nineteenth-century enclosures.*

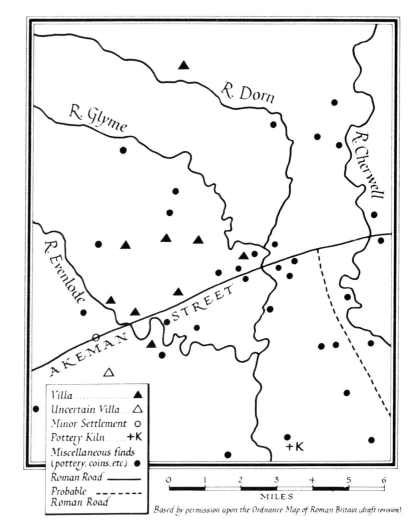

FIG. 2. ROMANO-BRITISH SETTLEMENT IN
PART OF OXFORDSHIRE

*In this comparatively small district
(only twelve miles by ten), which is
mostly upon the oolitic limestone,
there are no fewer than nine villas
(and one uncertain villa site), one
minor settlement (Wilcote), a pottery kiln, and a great number of sites
where pottery and/or coins have been
found. Some of these sites may well
prove to be native villages. The concentration of sites is particularly
notable between the Glyme and the
Evenlode. Just off the map to the west
is the important industrial settlement (iron-working) of Asthall; to
the east (off the map) is the Romano-
British temple of Wood Eaton.*

Villa .... ▲
Uncertain Villa ... △
Minor Settlement O
Pottery Kiln ...... +K
Miscellaneous finds
(pottery, coins, etc.) ●
Roman Road ——————
Probable - - - - -
Roman Road

Based by permission upon the Ordnance Map of Roman Britain (draft revision)

with their small, rectangular fields. These villages, of which a considerable number have been recognised, were simply groups of one-roomed huts: 'sometimes pit-dwellings sunk into the ground, sometimes stone-built structures standing wholly above it; they are never neatly aligned on streets or laid out on a regular plan, but clustered shapelessly, generally within some kind of ditch or fence; and although the people who lived in them used Roman pottery and coins to a certain extent, their daily life was affected by Roman ways very little, and in some cases, especially in the highland zone, not at all.'[*]

Most of these settlements were so small that they should be called 'hamlet' rather than 'village'. Only eight houses have been recognised at Chysauster in Cornwall, and the Romano-British village on Thundersbarrow Hill, near Shoreham, in Sussex, seems to have consisted of nine wattle huts scattered over an acre of ground or more.Nothing resembling a large nucleated village has been found in Roman Britain: this was to be the most distinctive contribution of the Anglo-Saxons to the landscape.

The distribution of villas and of native villages in Roman Britain is generally distinct. Certain regions, like Salisbury Plain, Cranborne Chase and the Sussex Downs between the Adur and the Ouse, were apparently occupied exclusively by villages. Such villas as occur in these districts are found on the outskirts. The villas with their large open fields and the villages with their enclosed fields seem to represent two different economic systems,

Many of the hamlets and villages of the Roman period took on the superficial trappings of Roman life. The earlier wooden huts were usually rebuilt in stone and some were rectangular in shape. Even those that remained in their old form often had painted wall plaster inside them.

[*] ibid.

PLATE 13. *One of the few places in England where Roman buildings still stand is Richborough, in Kent. The walls are the defences of a late third-century fort, one of a series constructed to protect eastern England from Saxon raiders. It began life as a protected military store base for the invasion of Britain in* AD43 *and was replaced about* AD85 *by a huge masonry monument, apparently commemorating the Roman conquest. A small settlement then grew up around it. Occupation continued until at least the fifth century* AD. *By the eighth a Saxon church existed here. Perhaps the site was never abandoned.*

existing contemporaneously. Whether they are everywhere geographically distinct remains to be seen. In the fairly closely settled region of north Oxfordshire depicted in Fig. 2 they appear to be intermingled.

In some parts of England the landscape was fairly thickly settled and cut up into fields by means of broad low banks. Of the sixty-five square miles of chalk downland between the Adur and the Ouse in Sussex, nearly fifteen square miles show signs of having been divided into fields of the Celtic type; and on this area no fewer than thirty-two occupation sites have been recognised. It now seems probable that this concentrated area of native farming supplied London with its surplus products. Already the Great Wen was going far afield for its food. In recent years areas of close agricultural settlement have been recognised elsewhere in England: in the Fenland, in the Evesham district of Worcestershire, in the lower Trent valley and on the Yorkshire Wolds near Malton.

It is doubtful whether London had more effect on producing areas of native farming than any other Roman town. Many Roman towns had villas set around them, perhaps the country residences of the urban aristocracy and merchants. Most areas of England had a very dense pattern of settlement, regardless of the proximity of the towns.

The close settlement of the Fens of southern Lincolnshire and of Cambridgeshire in Romano-British times was made possible by an extensive system of dikes or drainage channels and causeways, constructed by the Roman engineers. Aerial photography has revealed many sites of native villages and their associated fields, especially in the silt areas (as distinct from the peat) and on certain 'islands' rising above the general level. The Car Dike is the best known of these artificial waterways, and has now been shown to be Roman work. It was probably made to provide water transport between the Cam and the Ouse, but Sir Cyril Fox considers that it was also a drainage channel. In Cambridgeshire it forms a wet ditch, five miles in length, best seen near Waterbeach, on the east side of the Water-beach-Landbeach road and about four miles north-north-east of Cambridge. Through the Old West Water the Cambridgeshire section of the Car Dike is linked with the ditch of the same name and similar character on the western side of the Fens, running from the Nene near Peterborough northwards to the Witham near Lincoln, a total length of fifty-six miles with an original width of about fifty feet.

The Car Dike in Cambridgeshire may well be a Roman canal and was probably linked to numerous other canals and rivers in the southern fens. Recent research on the Lincolnshire Car Dike suggests that it was never a continuous watercourse but was a fen-edge catch-water drain to prevent the flooding of the fens. It is but one example of many that illustrates the considerable expertise of Roman engineers' work of drainage in the eastern fens and perhaps in the Somerset Levels. Again, though much altered and added to by later drainage works, a great deal of the basic framework of dikes and ditches was fixed at this time.

Long stretches of this ditch may be seen in Lincolnshire, especially just north of Peterborough; again near Bourne, where it runs parallel with the Bourne-Market Deeping road for some distance on its eastern side; and for long stretches north of Bourne. Another good stretch is to be seen from Billinghay north-westwards towards Timberland, about eight miles northeast of Sleaford. Although Roman in origin, the ditch takes its name from a Scandinavian named *Kari* or *Karr*, probably a considerable landowner in the period between the Scandinavian and the Norman Conquests, part of the ditch being in all probability a boundary of his estate. It first occurs by name as *Karesdic* in a twelfth-century charter.

Another Roman canal, the so-called Foss Dike, was probably also used for both drainage and transport. It connected the Witham near Lincoln with the tidal Trent at Torksey — a cut of eleven miles across a narrow neck of countryside — so giving direct inland communication by water between Cambridge and York. This canal was still of considerable importance in early medieval England, for by its aid the Witham trapped the agricultural and mineral wealth of the north Midlands, and it contributed to the prosperity of Torksey, Lincoln and Boston as ports between the twelfth and fourteenth centuries.

Down in Dorset, a contour canal brought water from the river Frome below Maiden

The aqueduct, for such it is, to Roman Dorchester is another good example of Roman engineering. Many towns as well as military establishments had sophisticated systems of water supply.

Newton to the Roman town of Dorchester, meandering through the country on the south side of the river. But this was an isolated feature of the landscape, of only local importance, whereas the ditches of the Fenland were important agents in the transformation of great tracts of land from natural marsh to fairly thickly scattered farms.

There was one other important Roman contribution to the landscape, and that was the town. A few towns had indeed already been founded in south-eastern Britain by the civilised Belgae, who preceded the Romans by about a century. Most important of the Belgic towns was Camulodunum (Colchester), the capital of Britain at the time of the Roman invasion. Other important Belgic towns were Verulamium (St Albans), Calleva (Silchester) and perhaps Venta Belgarum (Winchester), and there may have been others.* But the Romans founded many new towns during the second half of the first century and the early part of the second century, mostly on virgin sites, as at Exeter (Isca Dumnoniorum) which was founded about AD 50. By the second century, or the early third, most of these towns were walled around. But the towns were only small oases in a vast extent of countryside: the thirty-three civil towns together added up to only about four square miles of urban settlement. The twelve tribal capitals averaged about a hundred acres each in size, the ten smallest towns about thirty acres each. Roman London covered about 330 acres, but Roman Bath only twenty-three, and Irchester only twenty.

We have to record the appearance of towns as a new feature in the English landscape, but they were small, generally far apart, and quite foreign to the mode of life of most of the population of Britain. Possibly some 200,000 people lived in them altogether. As for the total population of the country at this period, it has been put at half a million by Collingwood, and at one and a half million by Wheeler. Grahame Clark compromises at six hundred thousand to seven hundred thousand. We do not know more exactly than this.

It might seem from the foregoing pages that in the five hundred years that elapsed between the coming of the Belgae and the departure of the Romans the natural landscape had been very considerably altered, tamed, and brought into use as farming land. Wide tracts of marshland had been drained and settled, the forests invaded by roads and by villa-estates in many places, the open downs and some of the valleys dotted with hamlets and isolated farms, nearly a hundred towns (most of them small) planted here and there all over the country, and especially south of the Trent. Over five hundred villas are known: more are discovered every year: the total may well reach a thousand in time. About seven hundred native villages are shown on the map of Roman Britain, and many more await discovery. The map of south-western England, for example, is almost a total blank: only one town (Exeter), three or four villas, perhaps half a dozen villages or permanent settlements: only this meagre sprinkling in an area of more than four thousand square miles. Moreover, this was the important Celtic kingdom of Dumnonia, which was resisting the Saxon invasions (however ineffectively) in a number of pitched battles as late as the closing years of the seventh century. It is clear that there must have been a considerable population in this part of England all through the Roman period of which hardly any record has yet reached the map, and this may be equally true of the northern kingdom of the Brigantes, where the map is almost as barren of evidence of settled life. When these parts of England have been more exhaustively explored by archaeologists, we may well have nearer fifteen hundred native hamlets in place of the seven hundred or so now known. Some twenty generations had been colonising the landscape

I give the modern names in brackets, though the sites of the Belgic town and the modern town (or village) are not quite identical.

The exact significance of the 'Belgic' invasion is now a subject of some dispute. It is more likely that the 'towns' which developed in southern England in the last few years of the pre-Roman Iron Age were the result of growing contacts with the expanding civilised Roman world on the continent, rather than of large-scale invasions. The 'towns' themselves appear to have been irregular clusters of buildings set amongst curious linear banks and ditches whose function is not clear. These banks survive around St Albans and Silchester but are better seen for example on Minchinghampton Common in Gloucestershire where no later town appeared.

Few Roman towns were on virgin sites, even though many began their formal urban life as settlements attached to early forts. Cambridge, which is an example of the latter type, has produced evidence for Iron Age occupation.

It is impossible to ascertain the population of England in Roman times. However, in view of the vast number of settlements now known, even assuming that not all were occupied simultaneously, all the previous estimates must be regarded as far too low. Perhaps four to five million people would be nearer the mark, a figure above that of early medieval times. This in itself is a measure of the impact of Roman activity in the landscape.

As already noted, there were far more settlements in England in Roman times than Professor Hoskins perceived. Certainly towards the end of the Roman period some land and settlements had probably been abandoned and towns were in decay. But in the long history of the English landscape this had happened before and was to happen again. Even in the early fifth century much land was in good heart and being cultivated, estates were still flourishing and the country still had a formal, if declining, government organisation. The withdrawal of Roman military protection and administrative control in AD 410 was to lead to a break-down in that government, economic decline and the collapse of urban life. But for the millions of people in England life had to continue albeit in reduced circumstances.

since the arrival of the Belgae, and must have made a considerable impression upon it before the Anglo-Saxons appeared upon the scene. One would have expected the back of the task to have been broken after all this activity, whereas in fact the Anglo-Saxons moved into a country that was generally still a wilderness, with almost everything yet to be done. In certain favoured regions like the Cotswolds and north Oxfordshire they may have entered a fairly civilised landscape; but in general they had to start (literally) from scratch.

There are two reasons why this should have been so. In the first place we must not overestimate the total impression made by the Romano-British generations upon the landscape. Their clearances, fields and settlements were locally important, but considered as a whole they made little impression upon the natural scene. There may have been, allowing for discoveries yet to be made, a hundred towns and some 2,500 rural settlements – villas, hamlets and single farms. It is nearly impossible to say what this rural settlement meant in terms of land cleared and under crops and grass. If we may judge by the Sussex downland already referred to, where nine thousand acres of land show signs of farming in Romano-British times and thirty-two settlements (large and small) have been recognised, we have a very rough average of three hundred acres per settlement. And if we apply this figure (which is almost certainly too high as an average for the country as a whole) to native hamlets and villas alike, we have a grand total of seven hundred and fifty thousand acres already rescued from the waste and used as arable or grassland. In 1914 the total acreage under crops and grass in England and Wales (excluding mountain pastures and heaths) was rather more than twenty-seven million acres. In Roman Britain, then, only two or three acres in every hundred capable of bearing crops and grass had been conquered from the natural waste. Such a figure can only be the roughest of estimates, but even if we doubled it – and this would certainly be too high – the Romano-British contribution to the making of the landscape remains unimpressive when considered as a whole.

Moreover, much of this cleared and tamed landscape had reverted, or was reverting, to its natural state when the Anglo-Saxons were taking over. In the fenland, the artificial drainage system of the Romans had collapsed by the fifth century and the rich farmlands were turned once more into a morass. Either there had been a general sinkage of landlevels, or the elaborate drainage system had been wrecked in the first devastating attacks of the Anglo-Saxons, or by their subsequent ignorance. Whatever the cause, the fenland went out of cultivation for many centuries, and the first Old English settlers moved through the new wastes to higher ground farther inland. On the Wiltshire downs, large tracts of arable land were being converted to sheep-walks by the latter part of the third century and the upland villages were being depopulated. Possibly, however, the displaced population was being settled elsewhere, perhaps in the fenland. We do not know. On the Sussex downs the native villages show signs of having been abandoned by about AD 400.

The idea that the Wiltshire downs were converted to sheep walks in the third century, often used as an instance of the decline of Roman life, was based on a misunderstanding of the evidence. There is now no indication that such sheep walks existed. Certainly some upland villages were abandoned, but others replaced them.

All over the country, villas and their estates were decaying well before the Saxon invasions. A few villas were violently destroyed, but most simply decayed two or three generations before the first Anglo-Saxon colonists arrived on the scene. The buildings were tumbled and weed-grown, the fields gone back to heath and scrub. We have all seen in recent years what ten years' decay and neglect can do in a bomb-damaged town. Most villa estates must have been a tangled wilderness after fifty to a hundred years of unpeopled silence, though some survived into a later generation and their land may have been taken over by the Old English without much difficulty, as we shall see in the next chapter. Much farmland went out of use in south-western England when the Dumnonii migrated in large numbers across the channel to Brittany, probably during the first half of the sixth century. It was rescued again from the waste only after many centuries, when the medieval peasant of the twelfth or thirteenth century came upon it again and called it the 'old land', for he recognised that someone had been there before him and had once tilled or grazed it. Such is the significance of farm-names like Yelland, Yellaton, Yellowland and

Yellowmead, all in Devon.

Much, then, of the work of taming and shaping the landscape by the hungry generations from the Belgae onwards had been lost in weeds, scrub and ruins by the time the Anglo-Saxon colonists arrived. The work had to begin all over again. Not quite all over again, as we shall see, but the great majority of the English settlers faced a virgin country of damp oak-ash forest, or beech forest on and near the chalk; and what was not thickly forested was likely to be cold, high mist-wrapped moorland, or water-logged wet heath, drowned marshes and estuary saltings, or sterile, thin-soiled dry heath. Studies of separate counties will correct this picture in detail, and show more clearly what survived from the wreckage of Romano-British rural life; but in the main this is what the picture looked like to those land-hungry invaders as they penetrated up the Humber rivers, the rivers of the Wash, and up the Thames, in the middle decades of the fifth century, looking for their new homes.

It is now clear that this picture is far from the truth. Whenever and however the Saxons arrived in England they found a land which was entirely tamed and exploited. Nowhere could they or did they 'start from scratch'. They merely adapted the framework laid down by generations of earlier peoples.

Chapter 2
THE ENGLISH SETTLEMENT

Introduction

In this chapter Professor Hoskins brilliantly explained the story of the Saxon settlement of England within the perceived historical background of the early 1950s. But, as with the prehistoric and Roman periods, there has been a revolution in understanding since then which has fundamentally altered our view of these Dark Ages.

Much of the new information has come from archaeologists, though the historians, geographers and place-name experts have played a considerable part. The present picture still has its dark corners and there is much that we cannot see clearly. Yet the new outlines, vague as they are, force us to re-assess the established view.

Professor Hoskins' understanding was that the early Saxons moved into a fifth-century England which was largely wild and untamed. The Saxons were thus able to create virtually a new landscape with little reference to what had gone before. They established nucleated villages of various forms on the best sites and surrounded them with common or open fields made up of a myriad of strips cut out of the all-pervading forest. From these primary villages, identifiable from their early place-names, the Saxons spread out, clearing more land and establishing other villages as well as hamlets and farmsteads whose names often indicate their secondary nature. In the north and east of England this basic Saxon pattern was then infilled from the late ninth century by villages and hamlets established by Scandinavian settlers. By 1066, therefore, when the Normans arrived and William the Conqueror ordered the compilation of Domesday Book, the basic layout of settlement and fields was established and thus recorded in that great document of English history.

Today our understanding is somewhat different. Perhaps the most important of the new evidence is that which has already been discussed; the Saxons did not come to a new and untamed country, but to a very old one which was at that time filled with millions of people living in tens of thousands of settlements and cultivating and grazing almost all the available land. It was a landscape which could only be adapted, not drawn anew.

The numbers of incoming Saxons are impossible to assess, but archaeologists have made guesses based on the numbers of known Saxon burial grounds. It has been estimated that perhaps no more than ten thousand Saxon settlers came to this country in the fifth century.

This figure is only supposition, but even if it is five or ten times too low, the fact remains that the Saxons must have been very much the minority of the population. From this point of view, the Saxon settlement looks much more like the political, tenurial and administrative take-over of a going concern rather than a new beginning. But if it was a take-over, it was not a simple one. The withdrawal of the Roman army and administration resulted in the eventual disintegration of government and protection and its replacement by a localised system of warring tribes, similar to that of the immediate pre-Roman time, which the Saxon leaders gradually took over. Even some of the late prehistoric hill-forts were re-occupied at first. In addition there was gradual economic decline, probably a deterioration of the climate and perhaps disease, though this is ill-documented and described by contemporaries vaguely as plague. There was almost certainly a dramatic decrease in population, perhaps by as much as a third or even a half with the possibility of there having been only two or three million people in England by the seventh century. One result of this may have been a regeneration of certain areas of forest such as the Weald in Kent, Sherwood in Nottinghamshire and Wychwood in Oxfordshire amongst others. It is against this background that we now have to redraw our picture of the Saxon landscape and to take account of other, perhaps startling, evidence. First, though many Roman settlements were deserted, and perhaps particularly those on the higher moors, dry chalklands and formerly drained marshes, modern excavations have shown that many places continued to be occupied, albeit in reduced circumstances. At a number of Roman villas it has been shown that though the main buildings were abandoned, wooden huts and shacks were erected in the ruins and at the great villa at Rivenhall in Essex, for example, a major Roman building was re-used as a great Saxon hall. At many of the small Roman farmsteads occupation also continued, with the simple huts replacing Roman houses.

This later occupation is dated to the post-Roman period by crude pottery called by archaeologists 'Saxon'. But this term does not imply that it was made by Saxons. The commercial pottery industry of Roman times had collapsed and everyone, whether a true Saxon or a descendant of the Romano-Britons, made and used this 'Saxon' pottery. It thus tells us nothing of the racial origins of the occupiers of these settlements, only that the settlements themselves continued.

More significant is the archaeological evidence for numerous 'Saxon' settlements. Much of this has come from the recovery of crude pottery from ploughed fields, as a result of modern cultivation. This indicates that far from there being early 'Saxon' villages there was, over much of England, a dispersed pattern of hamlets and farmsteads creating an arrangement very similar to that described by Professor Hoskins in Devon and Cornwall and called by him 'Celtic'. One example, far from the south-west, must suffice. In the parish of Brixworth, Northamptonshire, no less than nine small 'Saxon' settlements have been found in this way, and as much of the land in the parish is not available for examination, it is probable that the true figure would have been nearer twenty.

Air photography which shows the remains of early Saxon huts where they existed on light soils also indicates that the landscape was dotted by small areas of occupation sites every half mile or so in some areas.

Excavations have been carried out on a number of these settlements. They have shown without any doubt that large Saxon villages did not exist in the fifth, sixth and seventh centuries. The work has produced evidence of well built timber structures, but scattered in groups with no clear plan, no 'greens', no neat streets, often on geographically poor sites and with no indication of 'early place names' associated with them. Chalton in Hampshire is one, situated on a wind-swept chalk hill and comprising a group of timber huts. Catholme near Burton-on-Trent, Staffordshire, consisted of five or six farmsteads grouped together along a lane. At West Stow the 'village', lying on the dry heathland of the Suffolk Breck, was made up of six timber houses and associated huts with no coherent plan and no streets. Other evidence indicates that there was indeed early Saxon occupation on the sites of many of our existing villages, but as far as we can see, it was always on a small scale and more importantly it has no direct relationship to the plan or form of the village that is there now.

The overall pattern of 'Saxon' settlement, as it is being recovered, seems to be much more akin to that of Roman and prehistoric times rather than that of the medieval and later villages.

If this is so it is also doubtful whether the open or common fields, traditionally said to have been brought in by the Saxon settlers, could have existed at this time. It is much more likely that the small Roman enclosed fields continued to be used.

Where then does the English village and its strip fields come from? They cannot be of early or mid-Saxon date. Yet certainly by the twelfth century most were in existence, probably with shapes or arrangements that we can still identify in the present century. And when were the early Saxon hamlets and farmsteads abandoned, leaving their traces for modern archaeologists to discover? Most of the latter seemed to fade out in the sixth or seventh centuries, but many of these were in turn replaced by similar later Saxon settlements, sometimes on different sites.

Yet, somewhere between the eighth and twelfth centuries, over parts of England villages appeared, together with their open fields. Exactly when and why did this happen? The short answer is that we

still do not know, but clearly what we have is the second great revolution in the English landscape. For it is some time in this period that much of England took on the form that existed until the eighteenth and nineteenth centuries and which still can be recognised today. The evidence for the first revolution, in the later Bronze Age, indicates that much of it was the result of a consciously planned reorganisation on a vast scale. The same is true of this revolution.

The date of the traditional English villages with their neat greens, continuous building lines and regular gardens and paddocks has now been established through numerous excavations. All these show that although there has been, sometimes but not always, continuous *occupation* of the sites from Roman, early to mid-Saxon, or even late prehistoric times, the beginnings of the actual arrangement of the settlements as they have come down to us, belong mainly to the ninth to twelfth centuries. It seems that quite suddenly, over large parts of England, villages appeared within the space of three hundred years or so. No invasion of conquerors or new peoples can explain this, for it occurs all over the country and was taking place both before and after the Norman Conquest. Nor can any climatic change be invoked. The population of England may have been increasing again, and certainly the older Saxon tribal organisation had been replaced by united kingdoms, eventually the Kingdom of England itself. Economic life had also revived. It may be that general political, demographic and economic conditions made it possible to instigate changes, but in the end these changes came about by deliberate and specific human actions.

If we look at the villages themselves we can get some idea of what happened. Many villages and especially those belonging to Professor Hoskins' 'haphazard' type if looked at carefully can often be seen actually to be made up of separate small nuclei. Middle Barton (Fig. 5) is one such place. A village like this did not come into being as a result of individual squatters on common pasture or in a clearing in a forest, but probably the growing together of a group of earlier Saxon hamlets as population rose. Such villages can thus be reasonably interpreted as the spontaneous response to an increasing population.

Far more important are the villages that indicate many of Professor Hoskins' 'green' and single-street village types. By far the greater proportion of these, if examined in detail either on the ground or through early maps, prove to have a regularity of form that can only be explained by formal planning. That is, perhaps the majority of English villages, all of which appeared between 900 and 1200, were deliberately created, sometimes on already occupied sites, but often on completely new ones. The creation of villages was thus not the work of early Saxons, but of medieval people six hundred years later. Who were these people and why did they do it? Historians are uncertain. Some believe that it was the result of individual peasant communities deciding to remodel their landscapes for the economic benefit and with the acquiescence of their lords. It seems far more likely, however, that it was the lords themselves who were the instigators. In some places this seems certain. Institutional lords, for whom the long-term economic benefits of reorganisation were an obvious attraction, certainly replanned villages. The Cambridgeshire village of Spaldwick was given a neat green and a regular plan soon after 1209 when it was acquired by the Bishops of Lincoln, while Cerne Abbas in Dorset, for example, was probably replanned by the adjacent Benedictine abbey in the twelfth century. The Bishops of Durham were responsible for the wholesale replanning of many of the villages they held in north-east England.

Secular lords too were clearly involved in the planning of villages. In Lincolnshire the Bardolf family not only created a new village at Castle Carlton in the Lindsey marshlands, but also laid out Riseholme in West Lindsey, both around 1166. In the north of England the 'Harrying of the North' by William the Conqueror seems to have led to the subsequent planning of hundreds of villages but planned settlements of this period have been identified all over England.

It was not merely villages that were re-arranged at this time. The medieval open or common fields were either introduced for the first time, or more likely, having evolved slowly and piecemeal during the sixth to ninth centuries were now torn apart and laid out anew, often on a vast scale. In numerous parishes the open fields were arranged so that the pattern or strip holding was in the same order as the peasants' dwellings in the associated planned villages. Evidence comes from as far apart as Durham and Northamptonshire. Elsewhere, new strips, up to a thousand yards long, were laid out across the countryside in a way which totally ignored local topography. Again this has been recognised in Northamptonshire, as well as in Cambridgeshire, North Yorkshire, Holderness and elsewhere.

The vast reorganisation at this time is the mark of the second landscape revolution. But massive though this reorganisation was, it did not affect the whole of England. In many places the older pattern of settlement survived. Professor Hoskins recognised this in Devon and Cornwall, areas which he knew well, but it also accounts for similar areas of dispersed settlement in, for example, north Essex, Kent, west Dorset and much of the west Midlands. In north Essex and Hertfordshire, for example, the population was always higher than in adjacent Cambridgeshire, but in contrast to Cambridgeshire few villages were ever created. The existing pattern of small hamlets and ancient farmsteads there has been proved to have early Saxon, Roman and even earlier origins. No lords ever remodelled these settlements. Likewise the curious pattern of tiny open fields with no real regularity of form, size or operation and inextricably mixed up with hedged fields, remained intact in this area until the nineteenth century.

Even in what may be termed 'village' England, recent work has suggested that, up until the fourteenth century and sometimes even later, there was a sub-stratum of minor settlements of hamlet proportions, about which almost nothing is known. They are regularly discovered by archaeologists combing the fields for pottery, but they are rarely even mentioned in medieval documents and in most cases their names are unknown. There is still much to learn about the origins and development of early medieval settlements.

The beginning of this period of the second landscape revolution coincides roughly with the Scandinavian invasions. The numerous Scandinavian place-names in the east and north-east of England have led scholars, including Professor Hoskins, to suggest that the Scandinavian settlers created many new settlements at this time. It now seems unlikely that this happened. Professor Hoskins was astute enough to recognise that 'perhaps in many instances' the newcomers took over an existing place and gave it a new name. This certainly seems to have happened in most cases, though the excavations needed on deserted villages with pure Scandinavian names, that Professor Hoskins rightly saw as necessary, still have not taken place. The material collected from various Lincolnshire examples, destroyed by modern ploughing, has shown that either these villages started life as small hamlets or farmsteads in early Saxon times or that occupation did not begin there until the twelfth century. Either way the villages cannot be Scandinavian in origin.

This evidence seems to call into question the validity of the Scandinavian place-names and perhaps all early place-names where settlement origins are concerned. In fact the study of place-names is complex and specialised and the results from it have too often been applied to settlement history without care or concern for other evidence. Further, as with all academic disciplines, the study is a developing one and what was assumed to be the truth a few years ago is no longer accepted today.

Certainly the former idea that some habitation names ending in -*ingas* or -*ingaham* were early and that their distribution thus marked the areas first occupied by the Saxons in the fifth century is no longer tenable. In general the earliest place-names are now thought to be the topographical ones; those which refer to specific natural features or areas of land. Nevertheless whatever early name is now attached to a settlement, it does not necessarily mean that the name always referred to a settlement on that site. There are good reasons to believe that settlement names were carried around from one settlement to another. Many of the relatively late villages may have been given names originally belonging to settlements elsewhere in the locality.

Professor Hoskins rightly stressed the importance of Saxon estates and indicates both the interest and value of tracing their boundaries. In the final analysis it is these estates which are the real framework of England. Some were perhaps prehistoric in origin, many were certainly Roman. They passed into the hands of the Saxon kings and aristocracy still largely intact. Within their boundaries, settlements whether Iron Age, Roman or Saxon lived and died, moved or remained static. Fields changed from small enclosed paddocks to open strips, but the estates remained well into Saxon times. Only as part of the second landscape revolution were many estates broken up or amalgamated. Even so many remained intact. Subsequently the medieval pattern of parishes and townships, tithings or vills, the name varies from one part of England to another, emerged to give added stability to the basic framework of the landscape.

PLATE 14. *Westcott Barton, Marwood, Devon. This isolated farmstead is recorded in Domesday Book in 1086, but its actual date is unknown. Its fields were probably small hedged enclosures from the beginning.*

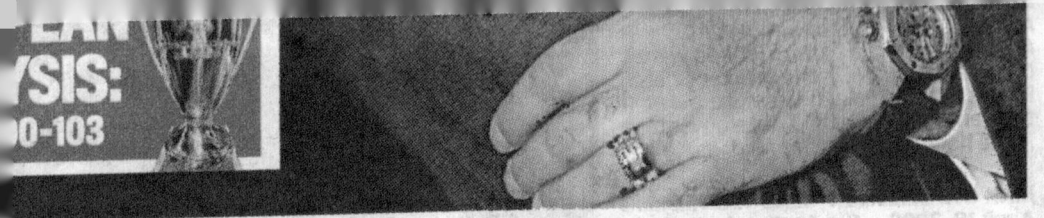

AN ERA
d heading for Old Trafford exit

6,229

as (2,4)
e (7)

ent
- (5-2)

t (5)

uld like to hear it now, call 0906 651 3583. Calls cost
Services Helpline: A&N Mobile & TV – 08000 141 178

Thoughtless. 7 Free. 8 Maudlin. 9 Rib.
r. 19 Rampage. 20 Iron.
Gambit. 4 Trust. 5 Eclipse. 6 Sangria.
na. 15 Remote. 17 E-mail.

Crossword grid answers: CROSSES, EXPERT, VAGRANT, CUTS, RING, DEBACLE, PALAVER, EACH, SHED, GRADUAL, EL PASO, DUCHESS

The Mail is published by ANL, 2 Derry St, London W8 5TT.

21-DEC
57 - 2811 - 0931

END OF

Scholes, Giggs and Ferdinar

By IAN LADYMAN
Northern Fo… …respondent

PAI… …s to retire once and
f… …season as Man-
… …ir Alex Fergu-
… …mer shake-

…s that he
…e will

stil…

But h… …
ble. Last …
so minutes a…
on and beat Em…
around on the floo…
to be an injury of gro…
and exchanged blows with…

'It is always exciting one wa…
when Chico is around,' says b…
Muela. He is a friend and part of…
agency that has looked after Chico…
affairs since he was a 16-year-old.

'Ever since he was a boy in football, he
has been like this.'

Chico, as he is simply known, was born
Jose Manuel Flores Moreno in Cadiz in
southern Spain to a family with no great

…ester players
… put the
…Robinson to be to
…d fan like it was
…at it what the
…land Rooney advice to
…ne van Persie o
…and Robin for advice
…gby Robinson for advice
…side question to
…ey robinson
…with Robinson
…ney',
…nartline@dellymallo.co.uk and twitter.co…
…c.sales@dellymall.co

2

THE ENGLISH SETTLEMENT

Villages and their Fields

The Anglo-Saxon settlement was spread over some twenty generations between about 450 and 1066. During this time England became a land of villages. Historians used to draw a contrast between the small, scattered settlements – hamlets and single farmsteads – of the north and west, where Celtic life continued, and the more or less compact and nucleated villages of central, eastern and southern England, where the Old English swept all before them and built and planted afresh. But this picture is much too simple and does not square with the facts. Even in Cornwall and Devon, in the far south-west, the large compact village can be found all over the map and is found at the time of the Norman Conquest; and hamlets and isolated farmsteads of great antiquity can be found dotted about the midland and the eastern counties.

The village can be found everywhere in England. In certain parts (in the Midlands, above all) it is the predominant – and at times the only – form of settlement, while in the northern and western counties we find a thoroughly mixed pattern of settlement, of villages, hamlets and single farmsteads. Here the village is only one form of settlement among several, all of considerable antiquity.

Compact villages, of varying size, are to be found in all counties, dating for the most part from Anglo-Saxon times. Everywhere they were accompanied originally by the open-field system. It used to be thought that open fields had never been imposed upon the landscape in the peripheral regions of England – in Kent and Essex, Devon and Cornwall, Lancashire and the north-west. In fact they were introduced into all these regions, but they disappeared from them long before the period of parliamentary enclosures in the eighteenth century. Indeed, they had gone even before the Tudor enclosures of the sixteenth century, so long ago that it was rashly assumed that they had never existed. It seems likely – though we know too little to generalise – that in these peripheral counties the open fields were being enclosed into the hedged fields that we know today during the course of the thirteenth and fourteenth centuries, at a time when records of the process are hard to come by.

Nor is much known of the nature of the open-field system in the Anglo-Saxon period. In its simplest form it probably consisted of two large fields – one on each side of the village, and often called the East Field and the West Field, or the North Field and the South Field. Each field covered perhaps a few score acres to begin with, but every decade and generation added to their area by clearing the woodland and other wild ground around their circumference. It took many centuries for villages to reach the limits of their territory, and for the fields to reach their maximum extent. Not until the end of the thirteenth century, or the beginning of the fourteenth, was this generally achieved.

Most people are now familiar with the fact that the unit of cultivation was the *strip*, which varied in area, and in length and breadth, according to the nature of the soil and the lie of the land. The standard or 'normal' size of one acre – 220 yards long by 22 yards wide – was only rarely found in most parts of England. Strips of half an acre or even one third of an acre were probably the most usual. A bundle or parcel of strips, all running in the same direction, made up what was known as a *furlong* (or *cultura* in contemporary documents), so that the field (or *campus*) – the largest unit of all – was made up of scores of furlongs of varying shapes and sizes, and hence of several

Much is still unknown about the nature of the open fields even in the late Saxon period. Certainly we can no longer assume that there were simple two- or three-field systems then. Nor had they necessarily been cut from the all-pervading woodland. Though more woodland existed by mid-Saxon times than had perhaps been there in the Roman period, England was probably still relatively treeless except in certain restricted areas.

Professor Hoskins here describes the classic open or common field system as it existed over much of central England in late-medieval or post-medieval times. Such a system was not to be found everywhere and there were many regional and local variations. Nor can we be sure that such fields actually existed until the twelfth century in most places.

FIG. 3. WEST FIELD AND WESTWOOD COMMON, AT LAXTON, NOTTINGHAMSHIRE, IN 1635

FIG. 3. WEST FIELD AND WESTWOOD COMMON, AT LAXTON, NOTTINGHAMSHIRE, IN 1635
The common lies to the west of the arable field. The individual strips are grouped in blocks (furlongs), clearly seen on the map. The broad green balks or occupation roads are also very conspicuous. Reproduced by permission from C. S. and C. S. Orwin, The Open Fields *(Oxford: Clarendon Press, 1938).*

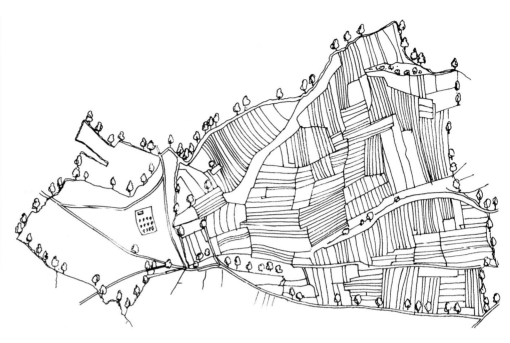

PLATE 16. *Ridge-and-furrow at Crimscote, Warwickshire. The ridges mark the general arrangement of the medieval open strips, though in detail the strips themselves comprised groups of ridges. This old photograph shows scrub invading the by then old grassland, the result of neglect during the agricultural depression of the 1930s.*

Ridge-and-furrow actually only represents the pattern of agriculture at the time that it was last ploughed. Most ridge-and-furrow was only abandoned in the eighteenth or nineteenth centuries, while only on rare occasions can it be earlier than the fourteenth or fifteenth century. Thus while there is still much to learn about late and post-medieval agricultural practices from ridge-and-furrow, its study will probably never tell us anything about Saxon fields.

Sadly, the old Great Central line has long since gone, together with much of the ridge-and-furrow alongside it. Most of this ridge-and-furrow has been photographed from the air, but scholars can hardly be said to have begun to understand it, except at the simplest level. There is much to learn about its detailed form.

hundred strips. A map (Fig. 3) will make the picture clearer than a good deal of description.

There may have been some Anglo-Saxon villages with three fields instead of two. When the records became numerous and more informative about village fields, in the last decades of the twelfth century, we find both two-field and three-field villages. It is possible that the three-field system evolved out of the two-field, as we know happened in some places in medieval times.

This is no place to describe in detail the agricultural arrangements of the open-field system. So far as the open fields are concerned, we can see the kind of landscape they produced in a few places to this day – at Haxey in the Isle of Axholme, at Laxton in Nottinghamshire, or at Braunton in North Devon. It also survives in many parts of the Midlands where the arable strips of the open fields were fossilised, so to speak, under grass when the extensive sheep and cattle pastures were created between the fifteenth and seventeenth centuries.

The up-and-down ploughing of the long narrow strips, with a certain type of plough, threw the soil towards the centre of the strip, so producing a high ridge. Each strip was separated from its neighbour by a double furrow (in some districts by an unploughed grass balk), so that the ancient pattern of the medieval and Saxon open fields is perpetuated by the ridge-and-furrow which is so conspicuous an element in the Midland landscape today. One sees particularly widespread and interesting patterns of ridge-and-furrow from the train on the former Great Central line in the country to the south of Rugby. Much of this ridge-and-furrow disappeared with the intensive ploughing-up of pastures during the Second World War, but a good deal remains. This should be mapped and photographed from the air while there is yet time. In certain places it is very likely that one has the complete lay-out of a medieval open-field system. The more we can discover of these arrangements the better, for 'strip maps' are relatively uncommon and there is much yet to be discovered about the agrarian arrangements even of the recent past. Not all ridge-and-furrow is of this antiquity; some is of comparatively recent origin and of no historical significance. We need the local historians

and topographers to distinguish carefully between the two types.

The Anglo-Saxons covered the whole of England with their villages, more thickly in some parts than others. In Leicestershire and Lincolnshire, for example, they were often less than a couple of miles apart, and the Scandinavian settlement later added to the 'congestion'; but in Devon and Cornwall they were half a dozen miles or so apart, especially to the west of the Exe, probably because Celtic hamlets and farmsteads survived in not inconsiderable numbers and occupied much of the intervening country.

Villages were not new to England at the coming of the Anglo-Saxons. A considerable number, as we have seen, had existed in Romano-British times, but most of these were probably deserted by the fourth or the fifth century. It yet remains to be proved that there is any village in England

Some ridge-and-furrow was first created in the late nineteenth century by the break-up of the upland moors or former woodland by steam ploughing. There is also a type of very narrow ridge-and-furrow which is of late eighteenth- or early nineteenth-century date. The seventeenth- and eighteenth-century water meadows of southern England also look superficially like ridge-and-furrow, while in East Anglia a natural geomorphological phenomenon known as stripes produces patterns that look like ploughed out ridge-and-furrow. Further confusion has recently been added by the discovery of areas of extremely narrow cultivation ridges on the hills of Northumberland. This is certainly pre-Roman and is probably of Bronze Age date.

PLATE 17. *Here at North Bishopstone, Wiltshire, the hillsides are lined with plough terraces or strip lynchets, produced by medieval farmers. Many of them continued to be cultivated until the early nineteenth century.*

It is very difficult to prove with certainty that villages have been occupied since prehistoric times. Nevertheless there is a growing amount of evidence that many villages may have been, though what constitutes continuity is something that scholars have argued about at length. Discovery of prehistoric and/or Roman pottery, for example, within an existing village does not prove either ancient origins or continuity. Given the ten thousand years of man's activity in England, with settlements being established everywhere and later abandoned, there is hardly a square yard of England where there is probably not some evidence of human activity. Archaeologists continually prove this, for whatever they excavate, they usually find something earlier underneath it.

Ashmore is a fascinating village both in its form and its position. While there is no proof that it has been continuously occupied since Roman times or perhaps earlier, it does seem very likely. The village sits on the end of a south-facing promontory of the downs; almost every known late prehistoric or Roman settlement in the surrounding area is in a similar situation.

which has been continuously inhabited since Celtic times. Most of our villages are certainly on new sites – along the river valleys for the most part, which earlier village-dwellers had ignored – selected by the Old English, the Danes and the Norwegians, between the fifth century and the eleventh. Yet there are, here and there, certain exciting clues which suggest that a few villages may have been continuously inhabited since pre-Saxon times. Though such villages may be only a small minority, they are all the more worth pursuing.

Hill-top villages are particularly suggestive of a great antiquity. High up on the edge of Cranborne Chase, on the borders of Dorset and Wiltshire, stands a village with the good old Saxon name of Ashmore (Plate 19); but it has probably been continuously lived in since Romano-British times. Not only does it stand on a hill-top, in country that is thickly strewn with evidences of early man, including several Romano-British villages, but it is built around a big embanked pond which gives the village its Saxon name – ash-mere, 'the pond of the ash tree'. Crawford, in a highly interesting essay on ponds,* shows that these embanked ponds go back in some instances to the beginning of the Christian era or a little earlier, and that the upland villages which take their names from such ancient ponds or *meres* 'have either been continuously occupied since pre-Saxon times, or . . . were re-occupied, after abandonment for a period, by early Saxon settlers'. Buttermere (in Wiltshire) is another such village.

Crawford also shows that when the Old English settlers occupied the valleys and marked out their boundaries, certain upland areas were left untouched and native (Romano-British) villages went on untroubled. Where the uplands took the form of narrow ridges, the settlements in two adjoining valleys had a common frontier down the middle of the intervening ridge of downland; and the ancient upland villages, where they still survived, were squeezed out of existence. But Ashmore lies in one of those upland areas too far from the valleys to be touched. Its Saxon name may be misleading: that may well have been bestowed by the Old English down in the lowlands, for the great majority of place-names must, from their

* *Archaeology in the Field* (Phoenix House, 1953), pp. 123-31.

PLATE 18. *Medieval open fields, Isle of Portland, Dorset. A rare survival now. On the right of the road is a series of open strips, separated by low lynchets. On the left, the former strips have been partly enclosed by low banks, though some still remain. Note the deeply hollowed lanes leading through the enclosed fields to the stone quarries along the cliff. The quarries themselves have cut through the former fields.*

PLATE 19. *The large embanked pond in the centre of Ashmore in North Dorset was the ancient nucleus of the village, and gave it its Saxon name: the pond of the ash tree. The village lies on the highest point of upland country on the edge of Cranborne Chase, which is thickly studded with villages and settlements of the Roman period. Ashmore may well be a Roman village which has survived without a break to the present day. The parish church lies some distance from the pond on the outskirts of the village, as we might expect, if it is so much later in date than Ashmore itself.*

nature, have originated with neighbours and not with the inhabitants themselves. We know, for example, because we happen to have the necessary early records, that in Somerset certain Celtic place-names were changed by the newcomers. In a charter of 1065 relating to the village of Biddisham near Axbridge, we are specifically told that its proper name is *Tarnuc*, an earlier Celtic name. Similarly, the Celtic *Lantokai* ('the church of St Cai') is now the prosaic Leigh near Glastonbury.* The Saxon name of Ashmore, then, is no argument against its possessing a pre-Saxon antiquity.

Seebohm, in his neglected and under-valued book *The English Village Community*, has a dozen fascinating pages on local evidence of continuity between Roman and English villages. He gives several examples of possible continuity in the Hitchin district, in north Hertfordshire, of which it will be sufficient to cite one (see Fig. 12, p. 168). At Litlington, near Ashwell, 'the church and manor house . . . lie near together on the west side of the village, and in the adjoining field and gardens the walls and pavements of a Roman villa were found many years ago. At a little distance from it, nearer to the Ashwell Street, a Roman *ustrinum* and cemetery were found, surrounded by four walls, and yielding coins of Hadrian (to) . . . Magnentius.'

The problem of changing place-names is one which has not been given the attention it deserves. Many place-names were changed, not by Saxon newcomers but by Saxon-Norman people of the sixth to twelfth centuries, and not necessarily from Celtic to Saxon. In Dorset, for example, over ten per cent of all the settlement names are post-Norman Conquest personal names added to -ton. They presumably all had different names only a short time before.

As already noted, the discovery of a Roman villa at a village such as Litlington does not necessarily mean continuous occupation. Litlington has a complex form which probably results from a whole series of changes during its life. It perhaps developed from a group of small nuclei of which four can still be identified. Whether they have any relationship to the Roman villa is problematical.

At Woodchester in Gloucestershire, the parish church, the mansion-house and a Roman villa all lie close together; and there are other very suggestive sites in the Cotswold region which was rich in villa sites and to some extent in Romano-British village sites also. Ditchley in north Oxfordshire has produced a villa site that continued in use possibly into the fifth century. At Eynsham, about six miles to the south, the evidence for continuity of occupation on a native village site is very suggestive. Here various finds of pottery and coins show occupation from the first century AD to the fourth; and in the year 571, Eynsham was one of the places captured by the Anglo-Saxons as a result of the battle of Bedford. Quite clearly it was a living village at that date. There are not a few places in southern England where the evidence for continuity of life calls for a new examination.

Large villages and open fields are and were certainly rare in Cornwall. Whether the villages are all of eighth-century origin, following the final Saxon political take-over there, is questionable. It is more likely that they date from a much later period.

In Cornwall, the Old English conquerors in the eighth century seem to have taken over places with Celtic names and to have transformed them into large Teutonic villages. They certainly seem to have introduced their open-field agriculture in such places.† The east Cornish village of Callington bore the Old Cornish name of *Celliwic* ('village by a grove') to which the English added *tun* when they took over. Kilkhampton, in the north of the county, and Helston, in the west, are other examples of villages with Old Cornish names, where a Saxon termination was added at a later date and Saxon open fields were introduced. Such villages as these have conceivably had a continuous existence since Romano-British times.

Hamlets

Even for the Old English, the village and the open field was not the only form of human settlement. 'No single type of settlement,' says Sir Frank Stenton,

can ever have prevailed throughout the whole, even of southern England. On heavy lands, and, indeed, wherever there was a prospect of a steady return to co-operative agriculture, ceorls tended to live together in villages. But as late as the eighth century life for perhaps a quarter of the English people was a struggle for existence against unprofitable soil and a scrubland vegetation which would spread again over cultivated fields on any slackening of effort. It was by individual enterprise that these poor lands had been brought into cultivation, and innumerable isolated farm-steads bearing Anglo-Saxon names remain as memorials of the process.§

PLATE 20. *West Auckland, County Durham. Typical of one of the huge northern 'green' villages, now known to have been planned in the late eleventh or early twelfth centuries.*

* Turner, 'Some Aspects of Celtic Survival in Somerset', *Proc. Somerset Arch. and Nat. Hist. Soc.*, XCVII, 1953, pp. 148-51.
† See W. G. V. Balchin, *Cornwall* (Hodder & Stoughton, 1955).
§ Sir Frank M. Stenton, *Anglo-Saxon England* (Oxford: Clarendon Press, 1943).

51

PLATE 21. *Here, set among the rolling Devon hills at Cheriton Fitzpaine, are the scattered farmsteads whose origins still remain unknown. Most were certainly there at the time of the Norman Conquest. But how much older are they?*

Ancient hamlets and isolated farmsteads do indeed cover much of England and real villages have a very restricted distribution. Some of these hamlets and farmsteads were created by the clearance of the wastes and forests both in Saxon times and later. But it is perhaps unwise to see them all as a result of clearance or indeed to over-emphasise the importance of woodland clearance in Saxon times. Professor Hoskins, probably correctly, saw much of the dispersed pattern of a prehistoric and Roman pattern. The same is perhaps true of similar settlement patterns elsewhere. While forest clearance was certainly necessary and was indeed taking place in the ninth and tenth centuries it was perhaps on a limited scale except in certain areas such as Kent.

The place-names adduced for evidence of clearance are amenable to a variety of interpretations. Wood could be burnt in various ways both naturally and by man and not always for agriculture. The description of a burnt clearing, if 'ley' does indeed always mean 'a clearing', does not tell us when it was burnt or for what purpose. Much semi-woodland or scrub was burnt off every twenty or thirty years as part of an infield-outfield system of agriculture which may well have been a practice in early or mid-Saxon times.

Such an isolated farmstead of Saxon origin may be seen at Queen Hoo Hall, in Hertfordshire, among the winding lanes three miles east of Welwyn. This is recorded in a Saxon charter of *c.* 1060 as *Quenildehaga*, signifying 'the enclosure of a woman named Cwenhild', clearly a farm with separately hedged fields that formed no part of the open fields of the older village of Tewin from which its first founder had probably come. There are other farms, not far away, such as Roxford (in the parish of Hertingfordbury) and Epcombe, which Domesday Book shows were cultivated on their own, quite outside the co-operative agriculture of the village fields. The counties of Devon and Cornwall are full of such isolated farmsteads, founded in small clearings in the woods, and recorded in Anglo-Saxon charters or at the latest in Domesday Book.

The clearance of the woodland was, indeed, the greatest single form of change in the natural landscape, especially in the early stages of the Old English settlement before there was any thought of draining the water-logged fens and marshes or the estuarine flats, or of reclaiming the high, stone-strewn moorlands. The Old English have left us with almost no word at all about the kind of landscape they found on arrival, that they set out to reclaim from the natural wilderness. They had no eye for scenery, any more than other hard-working farmers of later centuries. But the 'lives' of the Celtic saints, missionising in the south-west of England between the fifth and eighth centuries, and founding small monastic communities in isolated places, give us some idea of the work that was involved. In the life of St Brioc, the fifth-century Welsh saint who travelled through Cornwall and Brittany, we read that the brethren 'gird themselves to work, they cut down trees, root up bushes, tear up brambles and tangled thorns, and soon convert a dense wood into an open clearing . . . Some cut down timber and trim it with axes, others planed planks for the walls of their houses, many prepared the ceilings and roofs, some turned up the sod with hoes. . . .' This is one side of the picture, of zealous men joyfully clearing the ground for their monastic home; but the lonely pioneer without the burning zeal of an intense faith must have felt more like lamenting in the words given to Adam in the ancient Cornish drama *The Beginning of the World*:*

> *Strong are the roots of the briars,*
> *So that my arms are broken*
> *Working at them again and again.*

The smaller trees, bushes and undergrowth were cleared by the axe, the mattock and the bill-hook, but no family or village community could have survived long enough without crops if this were the only way of clearing the ground. There is evidence that the forests were set on fire and rapid clearances effected in that manner. A number of place-names testify to this. Swithland, a Leicestershire village on the edge of Charnwood Forest, means 'the land cleared by burning'; and this is the meaning of the place-name Sweden, often found in the northern counties. Barnet was a considerable district on the wooded borders of Hertfordshire and Middlesex where the ground was similarly cleared by burning, and Brentwood in Essex is 'the burnt wood'. Brindley in Cheshire is 'the burnt clearing'.

There is evidence that Neolithic man cleared woodland by burning: layers of charcoal occur at Neolithic level in the bogs of Denmark. All the English examples quoted above are late in date (twelfth and thirteenth centuries), showing that this method of clearance was being employed in medieval England; but some of the laws of the Anglo-Saxon kings show that it was a recognised method in pre-Conquest times. Among the laws of Ine (688-94) is one penalising anyone who destroys another man's trees by fire: 'he shall pay sixty shillings because fire is a thief.'

The axe was probably the most important method of clearance, for the large and small

Timber was certainly too valuable a commodity for woods to be left as wild waste. In fact woodland had been carefully managed, including being coppiced for hurdles and fences, from the Neolithic period. It continued to be so until relatively recently. Woodland was usually looked after with almost as much care as arable or meadowland and probably much more carefully than pasture, throughout prehistoric, Roman and medieval times.

PLATE 22. *Collapit Farm, West Alvington, Kingsbridge, Devon. One of over a dozen similar farms in the parish. Most were in existence by the eleventh century. Whether they originated from new colonisation in the late Saxon period or are much older remains unknown.*

* Quoted by Pounds in 'The Ancient Woodland of Cornwall', *Old Cornwall*, Dec. 1942, pp. 523-4.

PLATE 23. *Situated in the middle of the Blackmoor Vale, Dorset, Blackrow Farm, Lydlinch, is one of a large number of superficially similar farmsteads which seem to date from the seventeenth or eighteenth centuries. All are first mentioned in documents of the fourteenth century but they are certainly older than this and perhaps mark the sites of twelfth-century farms set up as the surrounding forest was being cleared. On the other hand they may be of Saxon date, established by a much earlier group of farmers. It is even possible that they relate to a Roman or prehistoric phase of settlement.*

timber was needed for a multitude of purposes. Timber played the part played by steel, concrete and coal in the modern economy, in the building of houses, ships and churches; in the making of farming implements, household tools, and in repair work of all kinds; and in supplying domestic fuel. Fire must have been regarded generally as a rather desperate expedient, to be employed in a frontier economy and not after the establishment of a settled community. A third powerful agent in the rapid clearance of the forests was the grazing of animals, who by consuming the seedling trees in large numbers as they roamed in the woodlands round their homesteads prevented the natural regeneration of the forest, and the replacement of its losses from old age, and eventually reduced it to more or less open clearings of the nature of park-land. This process may be seen at work today round the frontier homesteads of northern Norway.

The Shape of Villages

The axe, fire and animals combined to reduce the dense and continuous woodlands of Anglo-Saxon England. By the middle of the tenth century, says Sir Frank Stenton, charters prove 'the existence of innumerable villages, each known by a permanent name and maintained by a territory of which the boundaries could be described in minute detail'. Nearly every village on the map of England today – except in certain industrial districts – existed by the eleventh century and is described in Domesday Book. Some go back in date to the fifth and sixth centuries, as we know from the clues afforded by their place-names or from the archaeological evidence of heathen cemeteries; many more are recorded in the surviving charters of the seventh to the tenth centuries. The work of colonisation went on generation after generation, century after century, and it is impossible to give even an approximate date to the foundation of most villages. Even a place called Newton ('the new *tun*') may be recorded in Domesday Book, though we might be fairly safe in assuming that it was then of comparatively recent origin and possibly dated from the tenth or the early eleventh century.

As he goes around England, the observant traveller will notice the variety of plan, of general shape, in all villages that have not been swamped by twentieth-century building, and this is brought out, too, on the earliest detailed maps of villages that we possess, those made in the late sixteenth century and the early seventeenth. There are three great types into one of which most villages fall: the village grouped around a central green or square, the village strung out along a single street, and the village which – though noticeably a conglomeration of houses – consists of dwellings planted down almost haphazard, with no evident relationship to each other or to any visible nucleus. There are innumerable examples of all three types, but it is sufficient to cite such examples as Finchingfield (Essex) or Easington (Durham) among the 'green-villages'; Long Melford (Suffolk) and Henley-in-Arden (Warwickshire) among the 'street-villages'; and Middle Barton (Oxfordshire) as an example of the 'fragmented village'. It is possible, of course, to distinguish well-marked varieties even within some of these types. The 'green-villages' of county Durham, for example, have been studied in detail and classified by Mr H. Thorpe, and Mr Conzen has done likewise for the whole of north-eastern England. There are mixed types also, possibly the result of later changes, and there is finally a comparatively small number of planned villages (mostly of eighteenth-century date) such as Milton Abbas in Dorset or Blanchland in Northumberland.

Almost every village in England may have existed by the later eleventh century but not necessarily with the shape it has now. Many villages were replanned in the following century and a half. Nor are these villages described in Domesday Book. This, the greatest of our historical documents, lists land holdings not settlements. The latter were totally irrelevant to the clerks and medieval civil servants who compiled Domesday Book. They were concerned with what value the land and its people had, not where villages were.

Finchingfield is a splendid example of the myths which surround the origin and names of English villages. The name does mean 'the feld of Finc', but how are we to interpret that? Certainly not as the village green in a forested country, for 'feld' is perhaps best translated as 'extensive open land'. It is much more likely to be all the land held by Finc or his people, that is, the parish of Finchingfield already 'open', that is cleared of forest by early Saxon times. Likewise the village green itself looks very much as if it is a secondary feature to an earlier village. There is a small irregular green and a regulated, probably planned, settlement attached to the east side of the churchyard. What we see in Plate 24 may be the result of additions to Finchingfield in the twelfth or thirteenth century.

PLATE 24. *Finchingfield, Essex, is an apparently ancient village built around a large green, with the parish church overlooking the whole site. In fact the reality is much more complicated and the present form of the village is the result of many changes, most unrelated to its Saxon history.*

The variety of plan among the villages of England, besides affording one of the most delightful characteristics of the countryside, is profoundly interesting – and tantalising – to the historian of the landscape. It is interesting because he realises that this variety of forms almost certainly reflects very early cultural or historical differences, and it is tantalising for two reasons. First, because we cannot be sure that the present plan of a village is not the result of successive changes that had been completed before the earliest maps are available: we cannot be sure we know what the *original* shape was in many instances. And secondly, even if we are sure of the original shape of a village, we are not yet in a position to say – for the subject has been so little studied in this country – what the various shapes and plans mean in terms of social history.

Though the village green is popularly supposed to be the essential attribute of the rural scene anywhere in England, it is in fact found predominantly in the Lowland Zone of eastern England and rarely in the Highland zone to the west. It is particularly characteristic of north-eastern England, where a typical green-village has been described in these words:

The homesteads form a compact block bordering the green and their frontages face on to it so that in some cases, as at Heighington and Easington, the flanks of the greens have been taken in as front gardens for some of the houses. Of the dwellings fronting the green, many are still farmsteads, complete with farmyards and outbuildings, all strikingly divorced from their fields; their status within the village differs markedly from peripheral dwellings in that grazing rights for cattle, sheep, and horses (pigs are usually excluded), as well as for the homely goose, are restricted to homesteads which face the green . . . The backs of the houses and farmsteads usually lead on to a 'Back Lane', which may be continuous around the settlement and which often separates them from newer houses . . . This back lane, which reflects the shape of the village green, has clearly developed from the link-up of old cart-roads and drove-roads leading from the ancient common fields and pastures to the outbuildings of the farmsteads.*

* H. Thorpe, 'The Green Villages of County Durham', *Proceedings of the Institute of British Geographers*, 1951, pp. 160-1.

PLATE 25. *Milburn, Cumbria, like many northern villages, has a remarkably regular plan with its houses arranged around a great green. It was not laid out like this in Saxon times but was deliberately designed in this form probably in the twelfth century. The long narrow fields that surround result from the enclosure of former open-field strips.*

The green almost invariably contains two features which are contemporary (or almost contemporary) with it: a well (usually now covered by a small stone building and disused) which represents the primeval water-supply without which the community could not have come into being at all, and the church, which stands on the green or to one side of it. In later centuries, the school and the smithy were sometimes permitted on the green, but no other building was allowed.

Although village greens are rare on the western side of England, it seems likely that the compact villages built around the perimeter of a large square or rectangle, such as may be found in Devon and elsewhere, represent the same type as the 'green-village' of eastern England. The plan of Ugborough in south Devon or of Bradworthy in west Devon suggests this clearly. In many other Devonshire villages the open square or rectangle has been partly built over at a later date and the original plan obscured (as at Thorverton, Fig. 4), just as hundreds of original 'green-villages' have lost their greens at some more or less distant date, or at the parliamentary enclosure.

It seems likely that these villages built around the perimeter of a large green or a square represent enclosures for defensive purposes, like the native villages of some East African tribes today. Here the huts are grouped around the perimeter of a circular pound, with narrow openings between them which are closed at night by thorn-fences and which it is an obligation upon the householder to keep in repair. Into these pounds the livestock are driven at night for fear of the lions. In the villages of Saxon England, the necessity for protection from wolves in forested country may have led to the same plan being adopted, though any obligation to keep in repair the entrances to the green or square dissolved long

Certainly we are still at an early stage in the understanding of village shapes. Most of them are the result of continuous changes that make it extremely difficult to be sure what the original pattern actually was.

Professor Thorpe's description of the northern 'green-villages' has not been bettered. Yet it misses what is the most important fact, their incredibly regular layouts which show that they were planned. Work in Durham has shown that many date from the late eleventh and early twelfth centuries and represent part of a total reorganisation of the landscape at that time.

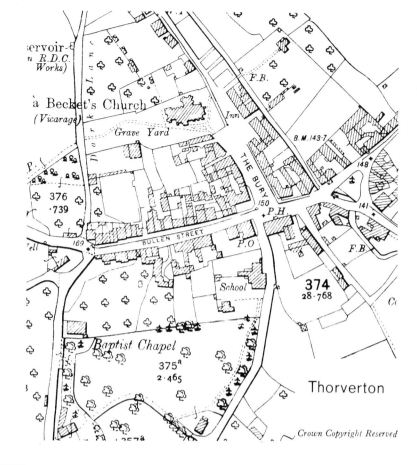

FIG. 4. PLAN OF THORVERTON IN EAST DEVON

Thorverton is a village of Saxon foundation, first settled in all probability in the seventh century. The original nucleus was the large rectangular open space beside the stream, with the significant name of The Bury (from the Saxon word burh, *meaning 'a fortified place'). The reference must be to the Saxon earthwork or other fortification which formed the original nucleus, as there is not the slightest trace of any Roman or pre-Roman fort here. This significant name is also found on a similar site in the neighbouring village of Silverton, founded at the same date. The parish church lies at one end of the* burh, *again a very characteristic position. The original large space has been halved in area by the encroachment of domestic building on its eastern side, probably in medieval or sub-medieval times. Reproduced by permission from the 25-inch map of the Ordnance Survey.*

Crown Copyright Reserved

Thorverton, Devon is another instance where an entirely different interpretation is possible, and indeed more likely. The neat rectangular 'bury' into which all streets run looks much more like a formally planned market place or green added to an older part of the village. The name may also reflect this purpose – in the sense of borough or market. The shape of Thorverton may rather be the result of a failure of a medieval town than a flourishing Saxon village.

It seems very unlikely that village greens were defensive in any real sense, nor indeed that any villages were designed with defence in mind by the tenth to twelfth centuries. The common name Stockton probably means that either the settlement belonged to or lay near a holy place ('stock') or possibly, a settlement with buildings made out of logs ('stocc').

ago with the disappearance of the larger predatory animals. Still, the ancient plan remains, with the church, the public well, and the lanes and roads leading into the central space from all points of the compass; and such names as Stockton may well commemorate the original stockade of wooden posts that surrounded the original settlement.

Though some of these green- or square-villages go back to the early days of the Old English settlement, we cannot assume from this defensive shape that they are necessarily the oldest plan. A life of St Cuthbert (*c.* 634-87) gives us one of the rare descriptions of an early village, an unidentified place that was in danger of being burnt. It is apparent from the account that this seventh-century village was strung out in an east-west direction along a single street. Some 'street-villages' are therefore of great antiquity; though many of them can be shown, on the other hand, to have developed along a busy main road in early medieval times, and not before.

As for those villages that are neither grouped around a central space nor along a street, where the houses are dotted about singly or in pairs, and joined together by a network of lanes and paths, we shall probably be right in seeing them as the result of individual squatting on the common pasture or in a clearing in thickly wooded country. Such squatters had no concerted plan and no leader with a small com-

PLATE 26. *In late Saxon times Spaldwick, Cambridgeshire (Huntingdonshire), was part of a great estate, centred on the neighbouring village of Stow Longa and held by the Abbey of Ely. In 1109 this estate was transferred to the Bishop of Lincoln in partial compensation for the loss of Lincoln's jurisdiction when the diocese of Ely was established. The Bishops of Lincoln transferred the centre of the estate to Spaldwick, constructed a great palace there, built or rebuilt the church, and laid out a new planned village at the gates of the palace. The palace has long since disappeared, but the broad open space, formerly a green, in the centre of the village remains to mark this major twelfth-century estate reorganisation.*

58

59

Middle Barton in Oxfordshire is a settlement without any nucleus or discernible plan. Houses lie scattered at all angles to each other and usually detached on their own little plots of land. Some are evidently eighteenth-century cottage encroachments on the roadside, but most probably occupy medieval sites. The village is first recorded by name in 1316, but the water mill (marked A on the map) was in existence in 1279 and this was possibly the origin of the village. It lay within the manor of Steeple Barton and probably grew up on the common pasture on the western edge of the manor. The roads and lanes of the village suggest an origin in paths and tracks across open land.

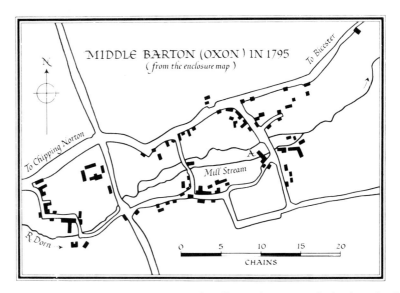

MIDDLE BARTON (OXON) IN 1795
(from the enclosure map)

Some villages which have no clearly defined shape may have indeed originated as the result of squatters establishing houses on common land, or in a clearing in a forest. But most are either the result of the growing together of much older foci, or are settlements which originally had quite different forms and which have been altered out of all recognition as a result of later changes.

Professor Barley was certainly correct in pointing to the rectangular nature of many Lincolnshire villages. Recent detailed work on these in the western part of Lindsey has indicated that this recurring form is the result of deliberate planning or of planned extensions during the tenth to thirteenth centuries.

munity around him, as in those numerous early villages the name of which embodies some Old English personal name. They acted individually and built wherever they had cleared a sufficient space, though always in close proximity to their neighbours. They were not building isolated farmsteads in the depths of the woods, but a loosely-framed village covering a considerable area (Fig. 5). Possibly this type of village is later in date than those created as a whole by a community led by one man, as at Peatling in Leicestershire, which means 'Peotlas's people' and suggests a concerted effort in clearance and building. A great number of the village names ending in -*ing*, -*ingham* and -*ington*, which are numerous all over southern and eastern England, fall into this class, and are among the earliest villages to be founded. Certainly this is true of -*ings* and the -*inghams*.

In Lincolnshire, the green-village is uncommon, but Mr M. W. Barley observes that 'often the village plan is rectangular, and the area enclosed by the lanes, and given up now to cottages, farmhouses, and the home paddocks, was originally the first furlong of arable laboriously cleared and ploughed by anxious and toiling pioneers'. There are scores of Lincolnshire villages with this rectanglar lay-out, of which Mr Barley cites Mareham le Fen, Goulceby in the Wolds and Scotton as good examples. In these open-field villages, dependent on a co-operative agriculture from the start, room was found in the back lanes for another cottage whenever required, and the ancestral village slowly swelled in size. In the fens, on the other hand, there was no open-field agriculture, and young men dispersed into the marshes and made new hamlets and farmsteads on their own from late Saxon times onwards. So the pattern of settlement is different: the ancestral village lies on the silt ridge, but roads run out from it in all directions to its daughter hamlets and its lonely farms down towards the sea. The map of the fenland parishes is dotted with their names and laced together by winding roads, while the map of the open-field parishes shows the ancient village at or near the centre, with few or no names outside it, only empty fields. Such farmsteads as there are in these parishes, and they are always few if there are any at all, date from the parliamentary enclosure of the parish in the eighteenth century.

Many English villages have suffered considerable changes in plan since they were first founded, and it requires some practice to see the Anglo-Saxon bones beneath the later growth. But one can still come across remote villages where one feels oneself in the presence of remote antiquity, a parental type, such as Bygrave, two miles to the north-east of Baldock in Hertfordshire (Fig 12, p. 168). The late William Page called it 'one of the most interesting survivors of a primitive self-contained settlement in England'. It stands in the midst of the 1,620 acres of its territory, just off the Icknield Way which forms the entire southern frontier of the parish. The site of the manor house and the church, which stand on the highest ground in the parish, is enclosed by a moat, and the minute village lies along the street to the west. There is not a single outlying farm in the parish, which looks exactly the same on the map of 1950 as it did on the first edition of the Ordnance Survey map in 1834. It is first recorded in a Saxon charter of 973 – 'the place by the ditch' – and it retains all the essential characteristics of a small community founded a thousand years ago. Even the Saxon open fields of Bygrave disappeared within living memory. There are more of these primeval villages left than we might imagine, and it is one of the pleasures of the traveller on foot in England to come across one he had not known before.

Some Anglo-Saxon Estate Boundaries

The villages have undergone great changes in appearance since they were founded by the Anglo-Saxons, but there is at least one feature in the countryside which is of Saxon origin and often remains more or less intact. I refer to the boundary banks of large Anglo-Saxon estates, which one learns to recognise by laboriously tracing the points named in the surviving charters. This exercise gives one a truer and more detailed knowledge of the English countryside than any other pursuit, not excluding fox-hunting. By the time one has scrambled over hedges, leapt across boggy streams in deep woods, traversed narrow green lanes all but blocked with brambles and the luxuriant vegetation of wet summers, not to mention walked along high airy ridges on a day of tumultuous blue-and-white skies with magnificent views of deep country all round – by the time one has done this, armed with a copy of a Saxon charter and the 2½-inch maps, the topography of some few miles of the English landscape is indelibly printed on the mind and heart. And at the same time, one has the constant intellectual exercise of fitting the frequently obscure landmarks of the charter to the ground one is traversing, and the mental excitement of making some unmistakable identification and of revealing to oneself the age of some ordinary feature of the scene – a ditch, a hedge, a piece of marsh, a pond, or what you will.

Between 925 and 939 King Athelstan gave to the abbey of St Mary and St Peter at Exeter one 'mansa' at Monkton (*Munecatun*), an estate of about four thousand acres about six miles north-north-west of the city, in the beautiful New Red Sandstone country rising to the Raddon Hills. The whole of the southern boundary, some three miles long, is marked by an ancient road ('herepath') from the Exe to the Creedy, about which there can be no doubt; and a small stream demarcates the entire western boundary. The eastern boundary of the estate also presents no problem for the greater part of its length; but it is when one comes to work out the northern and the north-eastern boundary on the ground that one makes discoveries.

This is no place to speak of the details of the northern boundary, which has several points of interest. But perhaps the most interesting of all is the high earthen bank (called the *dic* in the charter). On the map a narrow lane, quite unfit for wheeled traffic, winds around the end of the Raddon ridge. There is nothing about it to suggest great antiquity or any special interest; but one's attention is drawn to it, as mine was for years, by the fact that it obviously serves no modern purpose. In fact it is the north-eastern boundary of this tenth-century estate and, when one sees it, it runs like a rampart-walk cut half-way up the side of a high, steep bank.

Even if one did not know of the existence of a Saxon estate here, and were merely

▷

PLATE 27. *A typical sunken lane near Thorverton, Devon. It originated as a boundary between two ancient estates perhaps even in prehistoric times. By the tenth century it divided the king's land of Silverton and an estate of Exeter Abbey. A double ditch was dug out and the earth thrown up to form hedge banks on each side. The 'two-fold ditch' thus becomes a sunken lane running as far as the Saxon boundary required.*

▷▷

PLATE 28. *This Saxon boundary bank on the Raddon Hills, Thorverton, Devon defines the north-east part of the Monkton estate which belonged to Exeter Abbey by the seventh century (see plate 27). The sunken lane has here become an open path running half-way up the side of the great bank. The monastic estate marched along the lands of a private landowner, probably the Cada who gave his name to the adjoining parishes of Cadbury and Cadeleigh and to a stream called Kidlake, now a farm-name.*

Professor Hoskins' enthusiasm for the tracing of Saxon estate boundaries comes to anyone who undertakes a similar task. There is always something of value and interest to find, as there was for a group of students in southern Northamptonshire. Climbing the side of a broad ridge they found a battered boundary bank and ditch which, in 943, marked the edge of a great Saxon estate and which even then was the 'old dike'.

walking along it for the pleasure of exploring a new piece of country, one could not fail to notice the construction and course of this bank. It is the charter which reveals, with the aid of painstaking fieldwork, that the bank is the boundary of an estate which goes back to the early tenth century, and conceivably back to the seventh century when Exeter Abbey was founded. The fact that the estate was called Monkton when Athelstan granted it to the abbey in 925-39 suggests that his charter was a confirmation of a grant of land already called after the monks of Exeter, and originally given to the abbey at its foundation.*

A casual exploration one evening near Somerton, in the heart of Somerset, revealed a similar construction, undoubtedly a boundary-bank of an estate for which no charter survives. This may be seen by taking the lane that runs around the north and north-western side of Bradley Hill, one and a half miles north-west of Somerton. This lane is a sort of rampart-walk along the top of a high bank, similar to that already described; and the estate boundary clearly follows the line of ground a few feet above the edge of the levels, then mostly water-logged and useless.

Somerton was a royal estate; so, too, was Monkton before it was given to Exeter Abbey. It may be that these massive ramparts, for such they are at times, could only be constructed by kings and magnates with the command of unlimited slave-labour, and therefore that where they are found they represent the boundaries of the more important estates. Here, too, a great deal of fascinating fieldwork awaits the historically minded explorer of the English

---

* Too much weight cannot be put on this evidence, however, for the extant charter is itself a later reconstructed text.

landscape. One would naturally work most profitably from specific Anglo-Saxon charters, but if one felt like a casual evening walk any piece of narrow lane which appears from the 2½-inch or 6-inch map to have no particular objective – especially if it is followed by a parish boundary, always a sign of antiquity – is worth looking at carefully. One may draw a blank, but there is so much of this field-history waiting to be discovered in England that one is bound to be fortunate sometimes.

A remarkable survival of a Saxon landmark may be found at Alton Priors, on the northern edge of the Vale of Pewsey in Wiltshire.* In the year 825 King Egbert granted to the church of St Peter and St Paul at Winchester an estate at Alton, covering the greater part of the present parish. At one point the boundary ran, so the charter tells us, 'to a stone in Woncumb in the lower part (of which) on the upper side is a hole'. This stone, a sarsen with a hole right through it, was found by the party working out the bounds of the charter, still where the Saxon 'surveyors' saw it more than eleven centuries ago.

The Scandinavian Settlement

From the late ninth century onwards the Scandinavian conquest of a good deal of England resulted in a great number of new villages being founded. How many we do not know, for though many hundreds bear pure Scandinavian names (those names ending in *-by* are the most easily recognisable), we have reason to know that sometimes – and perhaps in many instances – the newcomers took over an Old English village and gave it a new name. Thus Wigston in Leicestershire was called 'Viking's *tun*', after some local Danish leader, and might be supposed to be a foundation of the Scandinavian period. But at the close of the eighteenth century an Anglo-Saxon cemetery of the heathen period was discovered just outside the present village. There can be no doubt from the contents of this that Wigston had existed, under another name, for nearly three hundred years before Viking and his men appeared on the scene. We know, too, that Derby formerly bore the Old English name of Northworthy, indicating a settlement founded in the Old English period.

Nevertheless, the demobilised Danish soldiers, bringing over their families, also founded a great number of new villages in country which still lay uncleared and untilled by the Anglo-Saxons. In some parts of eastern England they greatly outnumbered the native English. The Scandinavian partition and settlement of Yorkshire began in 876; that of the east Midlands (Mercia) in the following year. By 919 Mercia had been reconquered for the English, so that Scandinavian settlements in this part of England can be dated for the most part between 877 and 919; but north of the Humber a Scandinavian kingdom lasted much longer. And in the tenth century there came waves of Norwegians who settled in the north-western counties of England and left characteristic traces of their presence in the place-names of this region – e.g., the numerous *thwaites* of Cumberland and Westmorland.

This is not, however, a history of England. Here we are concerned with the changes brought about in the landscape by this fresh wave of settlers, and these seem to be mainly two: first, a great intensification of the work of forest-clearance in districts still relatively untouched by Old English settlers, and the establishment of new village communities; and second, the establishment of isolated hamlets and farmsteads away from the villages, some of them the result, apparently, of the drainage of marsh and fenland.

As to the first, we do not know whether the Scandinavian settlers brought with them any peculiar and distinctive village type. There is nothing we can recognise in those parts of

Professor Hoskins was correct here. In most instances it seems that the Scandinavian newcomers merely gave existing settlements a new name.

It is unlikely that the Scandinavian settlers cleared any more forest than their Saxon predecessors. Few villages are probably truly Scandinavian in origin and certainly there is no characteristic feature that could remotely be said to indicate a Scandinavian settlement. A number of villages with Scandinavian names which were later deserted have been examined after modern destruction. Most seem to have started life in early Saxon times or even earlier. Their medieval lay-out appears to be of the twelfth century. Either way the Scandinavian input was negligible.

* I owe this information to Mr G. M. Young, to whom the original discovery was largely due.

eastern England that were intensively Scandinavianised, that suggests that the Danes of the ninth and tenth centuries built villages to any plan fundamentally different from those built by the Old English. This failure to recognise any distinction today may, of course, be due to the modifying changes effected in villages during the course of the past thousand years, changes which may have gradually obliterated any original differences of plan. It may be that when we come to excavate villages of Danish foundation that were abandoned at an early date (e.g., Revesby in Lincolnshire), before important changes of plan had taken place, we shall learn more about this subject; but in the landscape as we see it today there is certainly nothing that stands out as a distinctively Scandinavian contribution. Nor did the Scandinavian settlers introduce any new field system. In the open-field parts of England they, too, established open fields of their own; and in those districts that did not lend themselves to such large-scale co-operative agriculture they established hamlets or farmsteads with small fields enclosed and worked like the farmers' fields of today, just as the Old English had done in similar country.

Domesday Book shows scattered hamlets and homesteads, in the broad plains of eastern England, founded by Scandinavian settlers. Stallingborough, on the edge of the Lincolnshire marshland, near Grimsby, consisted of a central village and three scattered homesteads occupied by five sokemen (of Danish descent) and three villeins. There were only one to three households in each settlement, and the eight households had only one plough between them. Many other examples of isolated homesteads may be found in the Lincolnshire marshland, some of which date back to the ninth and tenth centuries, and others to the eleventh. Here was 'a very different economy from that of the ancient open fields. The inhabitants lived not in village streets but in dispersed dwellings, supporting themselves on their small enclosures of meadow and marsh.'* The very scattered settlement of many Norfolk parishes goes back, in part at least, to the intensive Danish partitioning of the land in this period. At an early date we find in these parishes homesteads well away from any village, and small compact farms quite unlike those of the open-field regions; and later we find the phenomenon of two churches (or even three) within one vill and sometimes within one churchyard. This is undoubtedly a reflection of the peculiar social structure and social history of the region, the precise effects of which still need working out.

Stallingborough illustrates the care needed to look at every aspect of the landscape before attempting to interpret it. The present village consists of a main central part and two or three hamlet-like nuclei set around it. But these are, or actually were before modern destruction, linked together by continuous spreads of earthworks indicating former settlement. Stallingborough has a very complicated history of development and its present form cannot be easily understood.

The Lincolnshire marshlands are indeed dotted by isolated farmsteads and a similar pattern extends south into north Cambridgeshire and north-west Norfolk. But these settlements are not of Scandinavian origin nor of the ninth to eleventh century. Intensive field walking on the Lincolnshire marshlands has indicated that there was a dispersed 'Saxon' settlement pattern here even by the sixth century. Most of these settlements were later abandoned and what survives is probably in part the remnants of this Saxon pattern. Other farmsteads and hamlets are of a much later date.

The scattered occupation in parts of Norfolk also has nothing to do with the Danish settlers there. It seems to be the result of a long drawn out process of settlement movement, decay and expansion beginning in early Saxon times and continuing up to the present day. The exact details are still beyond our comprehension.

* D. M. Stenton, *English Society in the Early Middle Ages* (Penguin Books, 1951), p. 125.

Chapter 3
THE COLONISATION OF MEDIEVAL ENGLAND

Introduction

This is one of the most coherent and apparently convincing chapters in this great work. Here Professor Hoskins drew together the great mass of evidence which indicated to him that much of England was finally reduced to cultivation in the centuries between 1066 and 1349 and that, as a result, the fields, farmsteads, churches, roads and towns all emerged in a little under three hundred years. It is thus with considerable trepidation that any writer attempts to re-assess the development of the English landscape in these few centuries.

Yet it has to be done, and in the end, it must be indicated that this period was perhaps not the one during which the colonisation of England took place but only the well documented last phase of a series of processes which had begun centuries before.

There is no doubt that much colonisation and reclamation work did indeed take place in these years. The evidence which Professor Hoskins puts forward is only a minute fragment of what actually survives in the documentary record. Yet two important factors have to be taken into consideration. The first is the new evidence for prehistoric and Roman occupation of England which, as has been indicated, shows that most of England had been colonised, settled and cleared long before even the Roman Conquest. In addition it is necessary to appreciate that, despite the considerable fall in the population of England in immediate post-Roman times which led to the abandonment of much previously cultivated and occupied land, the second landscape revolution between the ninth and twelfth centuries had led to a new wave of reclamation and settlement before the detailed documented colonisation which Professor Hoskins records began. Another important factor is the nature of the documentation itself. The mass of detailed records which tell us of forests being removed, dikes dug and new homesteads established is, at least in part, the result of an administrative revolution in medieval government in the mid-twelfth century.

For the first time in English history a new 'civil service' was in existence and developing its own practices. We today know only too well what happens when bureaucrats and administrators are given their heads, for we are all now in danger of being swamped by forms, statistics and reports. A similar situation developed in twelfth-century England. The Norman kings needed and thus encouraged the development of judicial and administrative systems which, once established, were extended not only right through national government but downwards to local government and estate management. The result was the great collection of national and local documentation which fills the Public Record Office and local record offices and which are the bread and butter of historians. But this documentation was largely unrelated to what was, and more importantly had been, taking place in the real world outside the confines of the offices of medieval clerks. No such detailed records exist for early to mid-Saxon times and very little at all until after the Norman Conquest. Yet archaeological evidence indicates that the landscape was being torn apart and remodelled for centuries before the new civil servants came on the scene to record what was happening.

Thus the colonisation which Professor Hoskins so brilliantly summarised from the written record was not just a feature of the twelfth to early fourteenth centuries but more likely the last fling of a much larger and more extensive process that had been going on for hundreds of years.

Certainly between 1100 and 1350 the population of England rose rapidly, though perhaps the actual numbers of people in 1086 was somewhat higher than earlier scholars of Domesday Book believed. Professor Hallam, for example, has suggested a late eleventh-century population of between 1.5 and 2 million rising to between 5.4 and 7.2 million by the end of the thirteenth century. But the population had been rising from a presumed immediate post-Roman trough for some time and indeed this may in part have led to the second landscape revolution of the ninth century. This being so, it is impossible now to see, as Professor Hoskins did, that at the time of the Norman Conquest 'vast areas remained in their natural state, awaiting the sound of a

PLATE 29. *The Marshlands, south-east Lincolnshire. The period when these rich lands were reclaimed is not known exactly. It was probably between the eighth and the fourteenth centuries but it is difficult to be more precise.*

human voice'. The great forests did not extend from shore to shore. They existed, but in clearly defined areas, marking the places first given up by the post-Roman farmers and not yet reclaimed. Even then much of this woodland was carefully managed for timber and for deer, or dotted with swine and cattle pastures.

The fens and marshlands had certainly been abandoned after the massive drainage works of the Roman period. Indeed much of the eastern fens was given up in the third century AD as the climate deteriorated. But they were still criss-crossed by the lines of ancient ditches, scoured for wild fowl and exploited for fish, reeds and peat. The uplands too were grazed by sheep and even in places cultivated sporadically as part of an infield-outfield system of agriculture whereby marginal land was continually cropped for a few short years and then abandoned to recover. What did occur in the three centuries after the Norman Conquest was the further intensification of this exploitation as most of the last remnants of the forests were removed and an improved climate allowed renewed reclamation of the marshes and the upland moors. It is this process which is so well documented, but it was the tail-end of the second revolution, not the revolution itself. Much more important, in coping with the millions of new mouths to feed, was not the clearance of marginal lands and the colonisation of the wastes, but the intensification of the use of the land that was already settled.

Oddly this work is much less well documented than the direct colonisation, though it certainly took place. Perhaps it would be fairer to say that historians have failed to look at, and indeed understand the documents that do undoubtedly exist.

Almost all the villages of England seem to have expanded in size after 1100. Often there are direct signs of this expansion, elsewhere we can infer it by the evidence of later reduction. Many of the old villages, made up of separate foci, grew until the foci lost their individual nature and produced irregular conglomerations of houses and lanes. The result is, of course, that it is often now very difficult to identify the original nuclei. The late planned villages too were greatly enlarged. Greens were infilled, ribbon development extended along former open ways and back lanes were built up. Perhaps of more interest were the planned additions which lords added to villages, often as part of a deliberate policy of tenurial fragmentation. Dr Ravensdale has shown how, at the Cambridgeshire fen-edge village of Cottenham, the original planned late-Saxon nucleus had at least two regularly laid out additions made to it, associated with new fees or sub-manors created by the Norman bishops of Ely who held the village in the early twelfth century.

Most villages, at least in the southern part of England, were probably changed almost out of recognition by these alterations. But perhaps the relatively new or at least newly reorganised open fields were also expanded greatly. This expansion was effected not only by cultivating the wastes but also by dividing existing enclosed fields, perhaps prehistoric or Roman in origin and still in use, into strips. This process would account for the ditches found below and along the edges of medieval open field furlongs and which contain Roman pottery.

It was also at this period that most of the parish churches of England appeared, at least in the form which we see today. Yet here too our vision may be clouded by the visual impact of these magnificent structures and we tend to forget that they had long and complex histories of development and often humble beginnings, not all of which can be seen immediately without considerable research.

It is now likely that most of the first churches, established some time after the re-conversion of England in the early seventh century, were the so-called minster churches. These were organised on a semicollegiate basis, usually located at old estate centres and were set up for political as much as religious reasons by Saxon kings and lords. These were, perhaps from the beginning, large buildings, whose priests ministered to the inhabitants of the estate and even more extensive areas.

The location of some of these churches can be identified by the names subsequently given to their associated settlements. Iwerne Minster, Sturminster, Charminster and Wimborne Minster in Dorset are examples. Others can still be recognised by their location within former Saxon estates and by their more than average size and complex plan when compared to normal parish churches, even if, as is usual, there is no architectural dating evidence. King's Sutton in Northamptonshire is an instance of this type.

Subsequently a number of developments took place. Sometimes the 'old minsters' spawned 'new minsters' which took over the work of ministering to parts of the great *parochia*. Elsewhere the minsters developed dependent chapels or field churches in the new and replanned villages, over which they attempted, often without success, to retain control. In yet other places individual lords established what are termed proprietorial churches, within their own lands and for their own use and the use of their tenants. Not all these secondary churches survived and one of the most remarkable advances of modern ecclesiastical archaeology has been the discovery of timber and stone churches which came and went in a relatively short time. One such small stone church has been discovered at Raunds, Northamptonshire, established around 875-900 and abandoned in the twelfth century.

Gradually during the later Saxon period, the smaller village church became the norm, the old minsters declined in status and influence, and the ubiquitous parish church appeared, built by the twelfth century to an almost standard plan. In the thirteenth century many were rebuilt or greatly enlarged, partly to accommodate the increasing congregations, but also to reflect local wealth and to vie with neighbours. The results were those which Professor Hoskins describes so well.

Professor Hoskins suggests that the major development of towns took place in this period soon after the Norman Conquest. We now know that this is not true and that the development of urban life began long before 1066. Any discussion of this however must be left to Chapter 9.

Curiously, Professor Hoskins has little to say about castles. True, the development of military architecture from simple Norman mottes, through rectangular keeps, bastioned walls and concentric curtains to the first structures designed for artillery is a somewhat specialised and technical process which may not be of interest to everyone. Nevertheless castles have much in them which is rewarding to the landscape historian. At one level their mere existence as centres of estates led to the growth or planning of many settlements associated with them, as Professor Hoskins suggests. Of equal interest is the way castles changed their plans and forms, not merely for military reasons, but more often because of the need to make the castle an administrative

centre and a home. The chapels at Ludlow, the great hall at Oakham, the chimney breasts and window seats at Rochester all show that castles were more than fortresses. Also of interest is how the castle as an institution declined and was transformed into totally new directions. Its military function was, with the development of artillery, taken over by the bastioned forts of the sixteenth century, many of which still lie along the south coast as at Falmouth, Deal and Walmer. Its domestic and administrative functions were gradually acquired by country houses. By the fifteenth century castles were almost country houses. They still had crenellated towers, arrow slits and machicolations from the past, but also broad windows and decorative moats. Bolton-in-Wensleydale, Bodiam in Sussex and Tattershall in Lincolnshire are examples of this type.

3

THE COLONISATION OF MEDIEVAL ENGLAND

The Landscape in 1086

Though Domesday Book is so full of factual information, much of which still awaits excavation from its pages, it does not tell us directly how much of each county had been colonised and populated, and how much was still 'waste' of one sort and another. But we can obtain a fairly good idea of the extent to which England had been colonised during the six hundred years since the first Old English landings by looking at the Domesday population of different parts of the country. The total population of the country was possibly about one and a quarter million, of whom about one in ten lived in the 'boroughs'. Only six counties had more than fifty thousand people each. The most populous county in England was Norfolk, with some ninety-five thousand people, rather fewer than the city of Oxford today. Lincolnshire had about ninety thousand people, Suffolk and Devon about seventy thousand each. Essex and Somerset each had between fifty and sixty thousand people. A group of four southern counties – Kent, Hampshire, Sussex, and Wiltshire – had between forty and fifty thousand people each. Yorkshire, which had suffered great devastation since the Norman Conquest, had considerably fewer than thirty thousand people all told, about the same number as modern Redcar or half as many as modern Wakefield. Over the whole of northern England it is doubtful whether there were, on an average, more than about four persons to the square mile. Even in the east Midlands, one of the more populous parts of Norman England, the whole of Northamptonshire contained fewer people than modern Kettering, Leicestershire had about as many as modern Coalville, and Nottinghamshire – least colonised of all in this region – had only twenty thousand people altogether, fewer than the little borough of Newark today.

East Anglia was the most thickly settled part of England at the end of the eleventh century, with an average of between forty and fifty people to the square mile. But there were wide variations even here from district to district. In Norfolk, for example, the density of population ranged from about eighteen to the square mile in the western marshland and twenty in the Breckland, to eighty or more in the coastal parishes north of Yarmouth and the inland parishes to the south of Norwich. The parishes in the latter districts are remarkably small, as we should expect with this high early density of population, whereas in the marshland, fenland and Breckland – all down the western side of the county – they each run to several thousand acres. Feltwell, down in the fens, runs to more than fourteen thousand acres, Methwold to over thirteen thousand; but some parishes to the south-east of Norwich, such as Sisland and Ashby St Mary, have fewer than five hundred acres and many have less than a thousand.

The counties of Lincolnshire and Essex had about thirty-five people to the square mile on an average, but again with a very wide variation from district to district. Only two parts of England at this date had an average of more than thirty people to the square mile: a large block of eastern England from Lincolnshire down to Essex, and another block of three counties in the south Midlands – Oxfordshire, Wiltshire and Berkshire. Somewhere between these two extremes of four persons per square mile in the north and rather more than forty in the east, lay all the other counties of England. Even after six hundred years of colonisation much of England was still only thinly settled.

Though most English villages had made their appearance by the time of the Norman Conquest, and indeed many others which have since perished, vast areas remained in their natural state, awaiting the sound of a human voice. In many regions, like the extensive

As already noted, the estimate of 1.5 million for the population of England in 1086 is perhaps too low. England was not the empty land Professor Hoskins suggests.

forest of Andred in Kent and Sussex (*Andredes Weald*) or the great Midland forests, the primeval woods were still 'shedding and renewing their leaves with no human eye to notice, or human heart to regret or welcome the change'. Elsewhere, along the Sussex and Kentish coast, in the deep fens of eastern England, in the Somerset Levels, and in patches all over the lowlands, much of the landscape was populated only by great wading birds. Inland, especially in the far west and north, there still remained millions of acres of stony moorland haunted only by the cries of the animal creation, where the eagle and the raven circled undisturbed. The villages of Earnwood in Shropshire and Yarnscombe in Devon commemorate a former 'eagles' wood' and 'eagles' valley'; while far up in the West Riding of Yorkshire the limestone crags above Littondale provided eyries for these noble birds, and in due course the Old English village of Arncliffe took its name from the 'eagles' cliff'. Over some inner fastnesses there reigned, except for the wind and the rain, an utter silence. Carrington's description of the central waste of Dartmoor in the early nineteenth century would have been true of most of the higher moors of Norman England:

> Nothing that has life
> Is visible; – no solitary flock
> At will wide ranging through the silent Moor,
> Breaks the deep-felt monotony; and all
> Is motionless, save where the giant shades,
> Flung by a passing cloud, glide slowly o'er
> The gray and gloomy wild.

This poetic description of the emptiness of England in the late eleventh century is far from the truth. Large parts of England may not at this time have been intensively exploited, but almost all of it was extensively used. Even today the casual visitor may regard, say, the Cheviot Hills as a wild uninhabited place. Yet the farmers who live there know every foot of it and by grazing their sheep there are exploiting the land to the full.

Further, most historians have been conditioned to believe that such settlement as existed on the upland wastes and elsewhere must be late and date from the twelfth to early fourteenth centuries, as the documents suggest. It comes as a shock to some that, when excavations are carried out on the sites of these upland farms, they prove to be much older than this. The medieval farmstead of Hound Tor, high on the eastern edge of Dartmoor, has been estimated to have begun life not in the twelfth century but in the eighth and to have remained in use until the thirteenth century. Likewise an abandoned farmstead high on the Pennine hills at Ribblehead, near Ingleborough, Yorkshire, looked for all the world like the site of a medieval habitation set at the limits of the thirteenth century colonisation. Excavation revealed that it had probably been established in the late ninth century. Though it was only occupied for a short time both it and Hound Tor indicate that the process of 'colonisation' was a much longer one than most people have believed.

Since Saxon times the clearance of the natural woodlands had been the greatest single change in the landscape; by the time of Domesday the attack on the moorlands was just beginning and that on the marshland and the fenland was well advanced. In Devon, for example, where there was much high moorland, a close examination of Domesday Book reveals that the late Saxon farmers had reached a height of about nine hundred feet on the western and wetter edge of Dartmoor, and of twelve hundred feet on the drier eastern side. On Exmoor one or two farmers had also reached a height of twelve hundred feet above the sea. These isolated farms were the spearheads of the attack: one can sometimes see fields on such frontiers shaped precisely like this, thrusting a blunt point into the waste. But in general the frontier of cultivation was probably much lower than this. How high it had been drawn on the Yorkshire moors and on those of north-western England we have yet to discover.

In south-eastern England, where there was much marsh, there is evidence that it was being used for pasturage as early as the seventh century. In the year 697, for example, Wihtred, king of Kent, gave to the monastery at Lyminge pasture for three hundred sheep in Romney Marsh. Sir Frank Stenton observes that 'the local names of the Kentish weald and marsh are, in general, of an ancient type, and prove that the intricacies of these regions had been familiar from a very early time'. The Romans indeed had settled on parts of Romney Marsh and shown what could be done to reclaim valuable pasture land. The water-table was lowered by the making of ditches, and banks were constructed to keep out the sea. Such ditching and embanking was costly and possible only on a piecemeal scale. It gives us therefore relatively small enclosed fields, instead of the large-scale open fields, in which the ditches not only serve as drains but also as the boundaries of the newly reclaimed land.

The 'inning' or reclaiming of the Pevensey Levels in Sussex dates in part from pre-Conquest times. A charter of 772 by which king Offa gave land at Bexhill to the see of

It is notable that the four examples of pre-Norman exploitation and drainage of marshland all come from pre-Conquest abbeys. As perpetual institutions they were far more careful of their records at this time than either individuals or even the Crown was. We therefore get the impression that such early work was only carried out by institutions such as these. But the similar colonisation by individuals, which must have been going on, was never recorded.

Strictly the name Powderham need only mean that it was a settlement near or within polders. The polders themselves could have been much earlier.

FIG. 6. THE EARLY COLONISATION OF THE LINCOLNSHIRE MARSHLAND
The early Anglo-Saxon villages (and North Thoresby, which is Danish in origin) are marked thus: . The probable course of the sea dike constructed by these villages before the Norman Conquest is indicated by a broken line. Daughter villages founded on the dike are shown thus: and the earliest reference to them is indicated by a date in brackets. The marshland between the parent villages and the dike had been reclaimed from the sea by the eleventh century for the most part; and the earliest settlements of the dike were probably of huts occupied in the summer months only (as is suggested by the name Somercotes, 'summer cottages or huts'). Beyond the dike lie no villages but only single isolated farms of varying dates from medieval times onwards. The parent villages were all founded between twenty and forty feet above sea-level.

Selsey refers to a number of ditches in the levels, some already of great age and therefore possibly Roman. In Somerset, Glastonbury Abbey had begun the draining of the water-logged 'moors' by the tenth century, and there is some reason to believe that the great Dunstan, when he was abbot about the middle of the century, had been responsible for much work of this kind. A certain bridge and a ditch were still named after him in the thirteenth century. Down in mid-Somerset the foundation of Muchelney abbey before the end of the seventh century probably initiated drainage of the wet 'moors' in this district, and we find it still going on centuries later.

In the levels of east Yorkshire, a number of place-names in Holderness and near the alluvial Derwent suggest wide-spread drainage activities before 1066, for example the village names of Catfoss, Fangfoss, Wilberfoss and Fosham. In Devon, where there was not much marsh except in local patches, a village name like Powderham (*polder-ham*) reveals successful reclamation of marsh before the Norman Conquest. All over England, in patches both large and small, one finds this evidence of the successful attack on fen and marsh begun well back in Saxon times. Many of the embankments of the Fenland proper, most notably the so-called Roman Bank near the Wash, will prove upon detailed examination of the evidence to be of Anglo-Saxon origin, or the work of Scandinavian settlers (Fig. 6).

Even so, a vast amount remained to be done. Though Offa's charter speaks already of ditches in the Pevensey Levels, Domesday Book shows us that three hundred years later the tide-water still flowed freely over most of the Sussex marshes, and so it was everywhere else near the sea. Though the beginnings had been made so early, we have always to remember that (in the words of Eric Gill) 'it was a hand-made world throughout, a slow world, a world without power, a world in which all things were made one by one . . . a world dependent upon human muscular power and the muscular power of draught animals.' Unless we keep this continually in mind, and think ourselves back imaginatively into such a hand-made world, we shall never understand the immeasurably slow process by which the English landscape, down to the nineteenth century, came into being, and

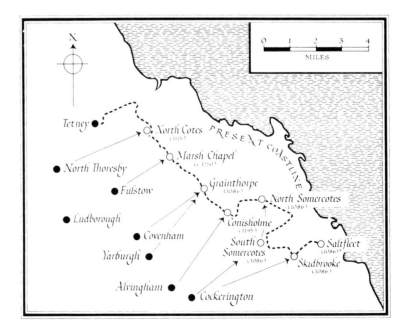

much of the beauty and fascination of its detail will for ever escape us.

It is not entirely true to say that it was a world without power. The water-mill had appeared in England by the eighth century and spread steadily all over eastern England and the Midlands during the next three hundred years. About six thousand mills are recorded in Domesday Book. In Lincolnshire about one village in three possessed a mill, in Norfolk and Suffolk about the same. But as one went westwards the number of water-mills fell rapidly, despite the greater number of suitable streams. In the west and north the ancient method of the hand-quern was still practised. Thus Somerset had 371 mills, but Devon only 98, and Cornwall only six.

Such water-mills were very small, generating perhaps the same horse-power as a small car today, and were driven by streams which now look as though they could hardly propel a minnow, so clogged have they become with rushes and weeds. Nearly all rivers were originally much wider than they are today. A few mills recorded in Domesday Book are still working, but they are rare in all parts. With the modern development of large-scale milling in the coastal ports the great majority of local mills have ceased to work. Many had ceased work in earlier centuries, with the conversion of old arable lands to pasture, and their very sites are now difficult to locate. One sometimes comes across a little water-mill lying derelict far from any habitation, and realises yet again the hand-made scale of that early world. These derelict mills, though they may now contain nothing of great antiquity, stand upon ancient sites that often go back to Saxon times. Once a site had been selected and a stream diverted or dammed, it would tend to continue in use until the end of local corn-milling. All the mills recorded in Domesday Book are water-mills for grinding corn. Neither the windmill nor the fulling mill for stamping cloth by water-driven hammers had yet made its appearance in England. They appear simultaneously towards the end of the twelfth century.

Besides the water-mill, another building had made its appearance on the scene by the time of the Norman Conquest – the country church. From the sixth century onwards, even a little earlier perhaps in some places, Christian churches had been built. By 1086 there were several hundreds in existence, possibly a few thousand, for it is quite certain that Domesday Book (which had no particular concern with churches) does not attempt to record all those that existed at that date. In the regions where good building stones were available, some of these churches were stone-built and large (as at Brixworth and Earls Barton in Northamptonshire), but over most of England they were incon-spicuous little log-huts, roofed with thatch, which have long ago been replaced, except at Greenstead in Essex. The church was usually as incon-spicuous in the scene as the water-mill. Towers were exceptional, and that very characteristic English view of the church spire rising from the tufted trees or piercing the quiet autumn skies in a wide view had yet to be seen. The earliest spires were built at the end of the twelfth century or the beginning of the thirteenth, and we find them first, as we should expect, in the great limestone belt of Northamptonshire and its adjacent counties.

Nearly every village we know today had appeared on the scene by 1086. The chief exceptions are the villages of the north and Midlands that were created by the Industrial Revolution, but here and there in the still densely wooded districts of England a few villages had to wait for their foundation until the twelfth or thirteenth century. Around nearly every village stretched its open fields, either two or three in number, each covering a few hundred acres, but hardly anywhere had these fields reached the frontiers of the village territory. If one walked half a mile, a mile at the most, out from the village, one came to the edge of the wild, to a wide stretch of moory or boggy ground that formed a temporary barrier, or the

The splendidly simple interpretation of the seaward expansion of late Saxon and medieval colonisation shown in Fig. 6 is now known to be at variance with the facts. Recent work along these Lincolnshire marshlands produced numerous Roman sites, a few early Saxon occupation areas and considerable numbers of middle Saxon settlements. What the real development sequence is is now by no means clear, but it was certainly more complicated and spread over a much longer period than is suggested by this diagram.

Not all mills described in Domesday Book were neces-sarily water-mills. Many may have been quite small and powered by animals. As such they have left no trace in the landscape.

It is certainly true that many of the first proprietorial churches may have been wooden structures though that at Raunds, Northamptonshire, built in the late ninth century, was of stone. By the early eleventh century things were very different. Inevitably, as a result of later rebuilding, most of the late Saxon churches no longer exist, but from the relatively few that do it is clear that highly developed stone-built parish churches were not uncommon. Brigstock, Northamptonshire, is a good example. Even more important were the old minsters. By the tenth century and probably long before these were huge stone churches which completely dominated the landscape. Stow, in Lincolnshire, is perhaps one of the best instances of this. Even today it still towers over its surrounding village.

massed tree-trunks of the primeval woods still awaiting the axe. Every village had its own frontiers, probably as yet ill defined in upland country and the subject of disputes with neighbouring communities when they began meeting in no man's land; and at the time of Domesday perhaps half the land of the village territory (the ecclesiastical parish to be) still remained to be rescued from the natural wilderness.

Over a good deal of England, especially in the west and north (but sometimes in the heart of the Midlands also), one found few villages but a scattering of hamlets and single farmsteads in remote clearings, settlements so remote that they betrayed their presence only by the smell of woodsmoke among the trees. Around the larger hamlets, open fields may have been laid out like those of a village but on a smaller scale. One finds records of these miniature open-field systems in Devon and in Oxfordshire, and no doubt they were to be seen in all counties. But often the hamlets, like the single farmsteads, were surrounded by small fields, usually of very irregular shape and enclosed by massive earthen banks that betrayed their piecemeal reclamation, acre by acre, by pioneering households rather than the large-scale clearing operations of the village lands. Fields were small, often barely an acre in extent, because of the nature of the tools with which they were created and because the need for more land was desperate. Every acre was brought into use as quickly as possible.

Long before 1066 boundaries of the territory of settlements had been fixed. Many had been established in Roman times or even earlier. But certainly by the eighth and ninth centuries, as numerous late Saxon land charters testify, England was very definitely divided into clearly defined territories with boundaries which were well-known and jealously guarded.

There is no argument that such fields existed by the eleventh century and, as Professor Hoskins says, this is best seen in Devon and Cornwall. But how old these fields are is more problematical. It is likely that they are not the result of late Saxon colonisation, but were merely reused and modified by Saxon farmers. Their origins are perhaps irrecoverable.

Small fields of irregular shape were, and are, characteristic of the more difficult regions of England, especially those with slopes too steep for the plough or those where the surface was thickly strewn with stones. In such rocky districts boulders were often so huge that it was not worth while to shift them, and they were incorporated in the line of the hedgebank to save trouble and to render them harmless. Frequently the extreme irregularity of the course of an early hedgebank was due to its going around or taking in a large tree or a massive boulder in this way. One finds this illustrated best of all in the granite regions of south-western England, but it is generally true of all regions where the rock lies near or on the surface.

Elsewhere, the shape of fields depended very largely on the kind of plough that was customarily used in the region. In south-eastern England it has been shown that the plough with a fixed mould-board produced long, narrow strips. These, grouped in parcels or *furlongs*, formed the basis of the open-field system as it is generally understood. On the other hand, the one-way plough, with shifting ear or turn-wrest device, could produce either strips or square plots, and either of these shapes could be associated with open-field agriculture. Kent shows both types of 'field' at an early date.

It is no longer certain that the shape of fields depended on the type of plough in use. The technical aspect of ploughing is a difficult subject, with relatively little hard evidence on which to base any conclusions. One can only endorse the statement that there 'is still a great deal we do not know about field shapes and their origins'.

The prevalence of square plots in Kent, perhaps more convenient for grazing cattle, meant that it was easier to consolidate and to enclose plots with hedges so as to produce what we regard as the typical modern pattern. Hence the very early enclosures of Kent, where the open fields probably disappeared well before the end of the Middle Ages.* The same considerations may well apply to the early enclosure of the open fields in Devon, which we know was taking place in the thirteenth and fourteenth centuries, and where we find hints of squarish plots as well as of elongated strips on the maps. There is still a great deal we do not know about field-shapes and their origins in different parts of England, and only the patient work of local scholars will enable us to add to our knowledge.

The landscape of 1086 was not entirely rural. The town had made its appearance – or re-appearance in some instances – in a rudimentary form. Some towns of Roman foundation had struggled through the Dark Ages to a new life, or had been revived on the same site after a period of desolation, and the Saxons had added more towns, especially in the ninth and tenth centuries. Such 'towns' were small and hardly distinguishable from villages,

PLATE 30. *Orford, Suffolk. When the great castle was built by Henry II in 1165-7 it was to a totally new design with a polygonal keep. The decayed medieval town that nestles beneath it has a regular market place and street plan. It was also laid out anew in the 1160s.*

* Michael Nightingale, 'Ploughing and Field-shape', *Antiquity*, XXVII, 1953, pp. 20-26; and 'Some Evidence for Open Field Agriculture in Kent', unpublished Oxford thesis, 1952.

except that they might have around them (or partly around them) an earthen rampart such as we can still see at Wareham in Dorset or at Lydford in Devon. Only five towns had more than a thousand burgesses in 1086: London, Norwich, York, Lincoln and Winchester.

Wareham and Lydford were two of a ring of deliberately planned fortified Saxon towns set up by King Alfred to defend Wessex against the Scandinavian invaders. Both of them, and indeed most of the others in the defensive ring such as Shaftesbury, Dorset, and Cricklade, Wiltshire, certainly had earthen ramparts. But they also had a deliberately created street pattern. Wareham has a grid of streets, set within its rectangular defences, in a fashion similar to Roman towns. Lydford, on a restricted and narrow peninsula, has a less complex but equally artificial street plan, much of it now reduced to hollowed lanes.

Excavations at Newbury have confirmed the date of the beginnings of the town. The first occupation, overlying former arable land, has been dated to the eleventh century.

At the other end of the scale, many Domesday boroughs had minute populations: St Albans and Pershore, which had grown up at the gates of monasteries, had only forty-six and twenty-eight burgesses respectively. St Albans had been founded about the year 950 by abbot Wulsin, but even after four or five generations it had fewer than 150 to 200 people. Elsewhere in Hertfordshire, Westminster abbey had founded a borough at Ashwell before 1066. Only fourteen burgesses are recorded here in 1086, and no recognisably urban life ever developed here. Stanstead Abbots, on the Lea, was even smaller and soon faded out as a borough.

All over England we find these little towns planted in a landscape that was predominantly green country. Some, like Exeter, still had their impressive Roman walls, and a cathedral within, but most were mere collections of huts and houses surrounded by an earthen bank, and many were destined to fade out altogether during the course of the next century or so. A few towns were brand-new at the time of Domesday: Newbury in Berkshire is first heard of about the year 1080, and Okehampton in Devon had but four burgesses and a market at the time of Domesday – evidently newly born. And all over England towns that are historic today were as yet empty sites: Newcastle, Hull and Liverpool in the north; Boston and Kings Lynn in the east; Portsmouth and Salisbury in the south; Plymouth and Ludlow in the west. In Midland and eastern England scores of little market towns were still unborn – Woodstock, Market Harborough and Newmarket – and scores of others were still mere agricultural villages, like Stratford-upon-Avon and Burton-upon-Trent.

With an average of only about twenty-five people to the square mile, England at the end of the eleventh century was greatly under-populated. Thousands of square miles were still untouched by plough or beast, thousands more only half used in a shifting cultivation of out-field. The rich natural resources of mineral wealth had hardly been scratched. Great tracts of forest, of moor and heath, marsh and fen, lay awaiting reclamation by pioneers. England was still in an early colonial stage of development, and it is in this light – of pioneers, frontiers and forests – that we must look at the tremendous activity of the eight or nine generations between the making of Domesday Book and the coming of the Black Death, which put a decisive end to the first great wave of medieval colonisation.

The Clearing of the Woodlands

Much of England was still thickly wooded, even in districts that had long been settled. Generally it was a thick oak and ash forest, especially on the clays that were to be found in most parts of the country, but on the chalk and limestone uplands (or rather on the extensive patches of clay that capped them in places) the beech woods extended for miles. In the lowlands the elm, the maple and the lime were all familiar trees, and on the hills, where the forests thinned out, the silver birch grew as it does today. Most of the trees we know were familiar to our Saxon and medieval ancestors, but there were two important differences from today. The first was that the oak was so much more common in medieval England: there were tens of thousands to be seen in places where we now see a few hundreds. And secondly, one of our very characteristic trees, especially around upland farmsteads, the burnished sycamore – so familiar to Wordsworth and Matthew Arnold – was nowhere to be seen. It was not introduced into England until the closing years of the sixteenth century.

From rising ground England must have seemed one great forest before the fifteenth century, an almost unbroken sea of tree-tops with a thin blue spiral of smoke rising here and there at long intervals. Even after twenty generations of hacking at the waste, the frontiers of cultivation were rarely far away from the homesteads. At Lawling, in the eastern marshes of Essex, we have a place-name of an archaic type suggesting very early settlement by the Old English, possibly as far back as the fifth century. Nevertheless, we find extensive woods eight hundred years later. A survey made in 1310 shows that more than six hundred acres of woodland had been cleared in recent assarts (a word derived from the Old French *essarter*, 'to grub up trees'), and there were still more than five hundred acres left untouched. Essex as a whole was a heavily wooded county in the eleventh century, even more so in the west than in the east. In the west we find villages with woods capable of feeding a thousand or two thousand swine.

Most of this woodland was cleared and turned into arable land or pasture by individual peasants in the twelfth and thirteenth centuries, who thereby created new fields and new farms out of the waste. But sometimes we hear of new villages being founded in this way. In the deep woods of

PLATE 31. *That the tradition that medieval farmers always cleared woodland is a myth is seen here at Tawmead Copse, Alton Priors, near Pewsey, Wiltshire. It was actually planted in 1250 and has been carefully managed almost continuously ever since.*

In the following pages Professor Hoskins gives many examples of evidence for the massive clearance of forest as seen in the written record. To redress the balance somewhat it is worth looking at Whiteparish, Wiltshire, where there seems ample documentary material for the assarting of the forest there in the thirteenth century. In fact the documents, full though they are, actually record the assarting of 155 acres of land between 1255 and 1330. Yet the actual area of land apparently cleared from woodland in the parish at some time before the early fifteenth century can be estimated with a fair degree of accuracy as just under a thousand acres. When therefore were the other 850 acres cleared? Surely not all in the following seventy to eighty years. It is much more reasonable to suppose that the clearances took place over a longer period of time and that they had already begun in the Saxon period. On the other hand it is possible to turn the whole argument upside down and ask if most of these fields are the result even of Saxon clearance. Deep in the surviving woodland to the south there is an Iron Age fort. It is now covered in and surrounded by trees, but it cannot have been thus in Iron Age times. It may be that it was the centre from where late prehistoric people cleared the forest here and created the existing fields.

PLATE 32. *Bradgate Park, Leicester. This great deer park created in the mid-thirteenth century has remained virtually unaltered to this day. It was enlarged in 1499 when Thomas Grey built a house there but that disappeared in the early eighteenth century.*

the Midland clays, we hear of Woodhouse Eaves in Leicestershire for the first time between 1209 and 1235. The name means 'the houses in the wood'. Numerous Woodhouses appear in the Nottinghamshire forests in the same period. So, too, does Woodhouse, now a suburb of Leeds, which we first hear of in the year 1208, and Woodhouse, now a suburb of Sheffield, first recorded between 1200 and 1218. Scores of English place-names, from Yorkshire down to Devon, reveal the importance of this post-Conquest clearance of woodland, most of them first recorded in the twelfth or thirteenth century – the Woodcotts, Woodmancotes, Woodhalls, and the like. Numerous Newlands and Newhalls date from the same period. These all became villages, or at least parishes with their own church serving a community of scattered farmsteads and cottages, but thousands of other woodland clearings were never more than isolated farmsteads, such as all those in Devon whose name embodies the element 'wood' or 'beare' (from the Old English word *bearu*, 'a wood'). Such a farm is Woodland, on the steep and still-wooded sides of the Torridge valley near Great Torrington, which we first hear of as *La Wodelond* in the year 1302. It had probably come into existence only a few years before this. One could find scores, if not hundreds, of similar examples of this type of colonisation in south-western England in this period.

The *Red Book of Worcester* shows us forest-clearance on the western slopes of the Cotswolds, near Cheltenham. Bishop Roger of Worcester (1164-79) had granted a tract of woodland at Bishops Cleeve to one Girold for an annual rent of one mark, and we are told that Girold had succeeded in adding no less than 170 acres to his holding, though some of the woodland still remained to be cleared. Here the cleared land was not enclosed in separate little hedged fields, but was added to the existing open fields of the village for purposes of communal cultivation, half to one field, half to the other. Not far away, however, the name of Woodmancote, first recorded in the *Book of Fees* in 1220, suggests that a new hamlet had also been founded. At Lawling, in the survey of 1310 already referred to, it seems clear that separate little fields were being created. We read, for example, that John de Wycumbe has a certain holding called *Heggelond* for which he pays a rent of 4s. 1d. a year, and elsewhere within the manor he has a parcel of land 'newly assarted, lying within his enclosures' for which he pays only a penny a year at Michaelmas. The difference in rent possibly arises to some extent from a difference in acreage, about which we are given no information, but in the main it probably springs from the fact that Hedgeland was an older enclosure and now under profitable cultivation, while the new assart in *Danegris* had yet to be brought into full use as farmland.

Elsewhere in the forested parts of England we find both types of landscape coming into being: old villages enlarging their open fields, and new hamlets and farmsteads being created at the centre of islands of small irregular fields enclosed by earthen hedge-banks.

Much of England was 'forest' in a more technical sense in the centuries following the Norman Conquest, that is, country set aside as royal game preserves and subject to special law – the forest law. The Anglo-Saxon kings had had their parks for hunting, large tracts of natural woodland and open country which were surrounded by a fence or a bank and ditch and jealously guarded against poachers and trespassers. Such a royal preserve was Woodstock, near Oxford, which we first hear of about the year 1000, though it may well go back to Alfred's time. It was not difficult to find considerable tracts of uninhabited country in Saxon England, but the Norman kings were not content with this. They introduced their forest and onerous Forest Laws into settled and cultivated country, and extended them to a great part of England. The making of the New Forest by William the Conqueror, which involved the destruction of a number of villages and many farms, is the best known example of this process, but other forests were much larger. The whole of Essex lay under forest law, and the whole of the Midlands from Stamford Bridge in Lincolnshire south-westwards to Oxford Bridge, a distance of eighty miles. By the thirteenth century a great belt of forest extended from the Thames by Windsor through Berkshire and Hampshire to the south coast.

The royal forest reached its greatest extent under Henry II, when it may have covered as much as one third of the whole country. It had the effect, because of its severe penalties against poaching and trespass, and the fact that it was periodically hunted over, of greatly hindering the farming of occupied lands and of impeding the colonisation of new land, but we must not exaggerate its importance in these respects. It was probably no more irritating to settled farmers than the equally crude behaviour of the hunting squires in our own day, with their trampling of crops and breaking down of fences, and the depredations of their sacred game. Similarly, the existence of Forest Law over wild, unsettled country did not entirely stop peasants from making clearances in places and paying a fine for doing so. The Pipe Rolls of this period are full of references to such fines for making assarts in the king's forest, but these are to be regarded rather as payments for licences to do so. Medieval men were as licence-ridden as we are, and they were accustomed to paying for every licence. Once the assart was made and the fine or licence-money paid, the peasant was left alone to make what he could of the new land, which, however, still remained subject to Forest Law.

In the year 1184-5, for example, we read of Richard Fortescue, a small landowner in South Devon, paying a fine of one mark for 'waste of forest', almost certainly the result of clearing and enclosing new fields out of the woodland. But in the same record we find one Jacob of Mountsorrel (a Leicestershire place-name) fined no less than £12 3s. 8d. for his activities in the royal forest, the equivalent of possibly twelve or fifteen hundred pounds today. It is highly likely in this instance that Jacob had been attracted all the way from

The fact that in making the New Forest William the Conqueror had to clear villages and farms shows that even royal forests were not uninhabited woodland. Forest Law itself is no indication of the actual extent of trees. It was a convenient legal ploy to retain tighter control over land and its inhabitants than was allowed by Common Law. Large parts of Essex, the east Midlands and south Derbyshire, though technically forests, were densely inhabited in the eleventh and twelfth centuries as a multitude of documents testify, yet the actual woodland in these areas was relatively small.

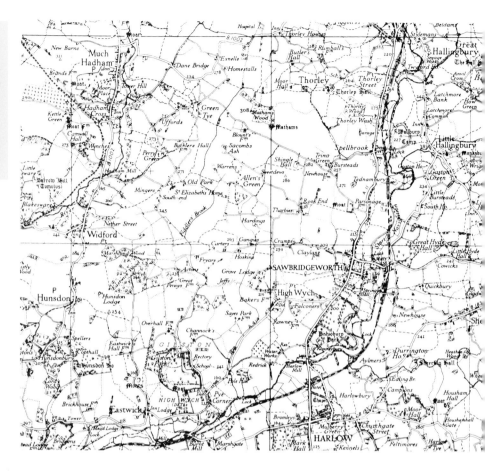

This map of Hertfordshire certainly looks as if the landscape it depicts was created by forest clearance and a twelfth- to thirteenth-century date seems acceptable. However, Dr T. Williamson, working in an identical area immediately to the north, has shown that it had already been cleared by Roman times and that even in the Saxon period there were small hamlets and farmsteads scattered all over the landscape. It may be that the differences between the landscape here and that in Fig. 12 (p. 168) owe more to the variations in tenure, population density and social structure than anything else.

FIG. 7. SAXON VILLAGES AND MEDIEVAL DISPERSION IN HERTFORDSHIRE

In the river valleys lie the Saxon villages of Hadham, Widford, Sawbridgeworth and Harlow (Essex). Between them lay a forested upland of heavy clays which was opened up and colonised in the twelfth and thirteenth centuries. The tangle of narrow lanes and paths winding from one isolated farmstead to another, the score or more of farms named after medieval owners or occupiers, the numerous 'greens', and the still-frequent remnants of woodland, are all deeply characteristic of country enclosed direct from former forest. Notice, too, the 'lost' villages of Thorley and Gilston, where only the church and a 'hall' survive in each instance. Gilston itself is a late settlement (twelfth century), and Thorley ('thorn clearing') was probably settled late in the Saxon period. Reproduced by permission from the 1-inch map of the Ordnance Survey.

As a result of the work of Professor Cantor we now know that there were thousands of deer parks all over England, only a very few of which continued as country house parks. Nor were all in areas of heavy clay soils or forested land. One of the largest, Blagdon in north Dorset, covered nearly five thousand acres of high downland, although including many copses developed on the clay-with-flint and gravel soils there.

Leicestershire to Devon by the tin boom of these years – in which the Jews probably played a prominent part – and that he had been prospecting on a considerable scale in the royal forest. Indeed, the search for minerals – chiefly coal, tin and lead – in the twelfth and thirteenth centuries all over the upland regions of England must have led directly to the opening up by prospectors of country so difficult that it might otherwise have waited for decades or generations for settlers.

Nevertheless, the existence of royal game preserves on this scale must have discouraged new settlement and made existing farming difficult, and the steady disafforestation of large areas by Richard I and John, in return for lump sums of ready money, gave a strong impetus to new colonisation in the waste lands. That it was felt to be a heavy burden is borne out by the size of the payments made by the working population to be free of it. The men of Devon paid John no less than five thousand marks in 1204 to have the whole county, except Dartmoor and Exmoor, disafforested. In terms of modern money this is somewhere between £300,000 and £400,000.

Less burdensome and extensive were the private parks which were the game preserves of certain feudal magnates. In many instances these represent the beginnings of the country house parks as we know them today. Thus Knowsley, now the largest park in the north of England, is first heard of in 1292 when we are told that Sir Robert de Latham had 'a wood which is called a park'. The word *park* meant originally no more than 'an enclosure'. It is used in this sense in several languages, and also in many field-names, especially in south-western England. Knowsley begins as a piece of

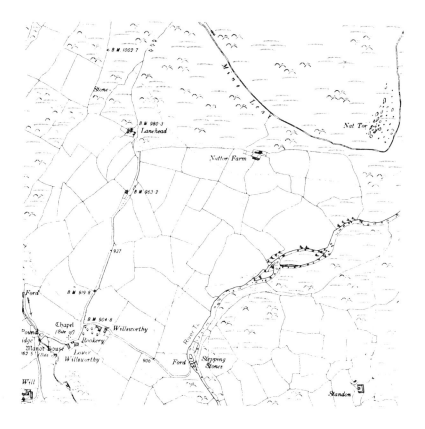

FIG. 8. MEDIEVAL FIELD PATTERN IN DEVON

The area shown on the map lies on the south-western edge of Dartmoor. Willsworthy ('Wifel's farm') is recorded in Domesday Book and is a farmstead of late Saxon origin. There was a small amount of arable in 1086, and a large extent of pasture (two leagues long by one league in width). The farm was worked by four slaves for Alured the Breton, who took over from Siward, the Saxon owner, in 1066. Standon ('stone hill') is first recorded in 1242. The fields around this farm were probably first made from the rough moorland pasture recorded in Domesday, at some date in the twelfth century, and are typical of piecemeal enclosure direct from the waste – very small and very irregular in shape. Nattor Farm is first recorded in 1340. No early reference to Lanehead has been found, but it is almost certainly of medieval origin like all the outlying farms in this district. The medieval frontier of cultivation is well brought out on this map. Reproduced by permission from the 6-inch map of the Ordnance Survey.

natural woodland enclosed from a larger area by means of a live hedge or a bank and ditch. Thirty years later it is described as 'a park with herbage'. It is evidently evolving into more open country in places, but there is a long way to go before it becomes a park as we visualise the word.

Similarly, the beginnings of Hatfield Park in Hertfordshire have to be sought in the thirteenth-century woodland. Hertfordshire was naturally a densely wooded country, and the manor of Hatfield had been given by King Edgar (959-75) to the monks of Ely in order to secure ample wood for their building activities. By the middle of the thirteenth century two parks had been enclosed out of the manorial woodland, one of them – the Great Park – containing about a thousand acres, the other about 350 acres. Not until the nineteenth century were these two ancient parks united to form the present Hatfield Park. The well-known park at Ashridge, on the northern slopes of the Chiltern Hills, is also first heard of in the thirteenth century, though large additions were made to it, as to many other notable parks, at a later date. Bradgate Park, in Leicestershire, still largely in a natural state of bracken, rocks and water, existed in the year 1247 when Roger de Somery made it over, 'with the deer-leaps then made in it', to the Earl of Winchester in return for hunting rights in the Earl's forest all around.

Where a medieval park was enclosed by means of a bank and ditch it is possible to follow this boundary for great distances and even, in some cases, to restore the complete original boundary to the map. Mr O. G. S. Crawford demonstrates this of the large twelfth-century park at New Buckenham in Norfolk and at Hampstead Marshall near Newbury, in Berkshire, where the original boundary-bank can be traced for several miles.* The bank along the south side of John of Gaunt's deer-park in King's Somborne (Hampshire) is still twelve feet high, with a ditch on the outside, and many others of these medieval boundary-banks

* *Archaeology in the Field* (Phoenix House, 1953), pp. 189-96.

are massive earthworks, rivalling in size (as Mr Crawford says) such defensive earthworks as Offa's Dyke and Wansdyke. But not all are as impressive as this, and the explorer of these forgotten boundaries must be prepared to look for much smaller banks and ditches at times. The reconstruction of medieval parks and their boundaries is one of the many useful tasks awaiting the fieldworker with patience and a good local knowledge.

Marsh, Fen and Moor

There are certain sheets of the one-inch Ordnance Survey maps which one can sit down and read like a book for an hour on end, with growing pleasure and imaginative excitement. One dwells upon the infinite variety of the place-names (and yet there is a characteristic flavour for each region of England), the delicate nerve-like complexity of roads and lanes, the siting of the villages and hamlets, the romantic moated farmsteads in deep country, the churches standing alone in the fields, the patterns made by the contours or by the way the parish boundaries fit into one another. One dissects such a map mentally, piece by piece, and in doing so learns a good deal of local history, whether or not one knows the country itself.

Such an exciting map is that of the country around the Wash, particularly the country on the western and southern sides – the Lincolnshire and Norfolk marshland. One can no more do justice to this beautiful map in a few lines than programme notes can convey the quality of a symphony. The very names like Bicker Haven and Fleet Haven, now many miles inland; or Moulton Seas End and Surfleet Seas End and Seadyke Farm, all far back today from the shore-line; the so-called Roman Bank twisting across the open levels, and the chapels far out on the salt marshes – all these matters of observation set the mind working at once about the past history of this piece of country. One observes also the intricate tangle of the road and lane pattern between Boston and Wainfleet, along the western side of the Wash, in marked contrast to the great open spaces of the fen behind where the roads are few and straight, or to the marsh in front where they fade out altogether and give us a landscape of nothing but scores of drains running straight ahead to the mud-flats and the sea and sky beyond. The belt of tangled roads and lanes is only a mile or two wide for the greater part of its length and is thickly sprinkled with dispersed farmsteads and a few hamlets. At intervals of every few miles one finds a considerable village. And one notices one other remarkable thing – that the main road from Boston to Wainfleet is as full of bends and corners as any of the little lanes that lie on either side of it: it must be the most difficult main road in England for motorists. It runs roughly parallel, so far as anything is parallel to anything else in this irregular landscape, to what the map calls the Roman Bank and the Old Sea Bank, and roughly parallel also to a string of lanes. By now we are convinced that this piece of country, like that along the southern side of the Wash which it so much resembles, has had an exceptional history: and so indeed it has. It is a landscape of a few ancient villages and of centuries of reclamation from the marsh on one side and the fen on the other; a landscape created largely between the seventh century and the seventeenth, where many of the winding lanes represent successive frontiers in the conquest of the salt marshes from the sea.

The first settlements in this landscape were the nucleated villages. Although the one-inch map does not show it, these all lie along a belt of silt

As already noted in the Introduction to this chapter, the reclamation and colonisation of the eastern marshlands now seems to be more complicated than Professor Hoskins indicates here. His suggested phases of expansion may well have occurred, at least in general terms, but much of it took place within a framework of a perhaps abandoned Roman landscape and certainly well before the twelfth to thirteenth centuries. Many of the sea-banks were probably merely repaired and extended at this time. The great 'sea-bank' along the western side of the estuary of the River Nene in northern Cambridgeshire has been examined and much that is new has been discovered. It is now known to have had ramparts or breakwaters projecting from its seaward side to reduce the force of high tides striking it. It is thus a major earthwork raised against a threat from the sea. Its date, in Cambridgeshire at least, now seems to be firmly established by radio-carbon dating to 1250 plus or minus ten years.

Within the southern fens of Cambridgeshire there is also good evidence of reclamation which, at first sight, suggests it took place on a huge scale in the twelfth and thirteenth centuries. Yet where it has been related to the actual landscape and compared to the post-medieval reclamation and drainage it can be seen to be on a relatively small scale. For example, at Burwell, Cambridgeshire, the actual fenland of the parish covers just under two thousand acres. By the mid-seventeenth century only about four hundred acres had been reclaimed and this seems to be a larger area than elsewhere.

which itself lay between the fen and the marsh and several feet above both. On this dry, firm foundation the first Old English settlers made their homes, possibly in the seventh century and not earlier. There is not a single early place-name in all this region between Steeping, on the edge of the Wolds, and Spalding, far up the Welland, and not a single cemetery of the heathen period.

Into this thinly peopled and somewhat unattractive landscape came the Danish conquerors, soldier-settlers of the tenth century for the most part, as evidenced in village-names like Skirbeck and Wrangle. But most of the village names are English. The narrow band of silt was embanked both against the fen behind and the sea ahead. As the population grew, the pressure on the available land became acute, and we begin to hear of banks being constructed further out in the fen and marsh in order to bring in new land.

Despite the name Roman Bank, which appears in half a dozen places on the map of this district, there is no evidence that the Romans carried out any embanking in this region around the Wash. Much of what is called the Roman Bank is known to be as late in date as the sixteenth or seventeenth century, especially that section to the east of the Boston-Wainfleet road. But the old bank, so far as it can be traced now, is certainly pre-Conquest in date, and its line is probably represented by that of the main road from Wainfleet as far as Benington. When we regard this road as originally the causeway along the top of an ancient sea-bank, and as the result of a gigantic piecemeal effort by hand-labour, we begin to understand the extraordinary number of corners and curves in its course. Beyond Boston (which did not then exist) the bank swept miles inland to run around Bicker Haven, which was at that time open sea. This haven is known to have silted up soon after the Norman Conquest, so giving us a terminal date for the construction of the bank; and the fact that certain Domesday villages lie upon it (e.g., Wrangle) clinches the argument for a pre-Norman date. Beyond that we cannot go at present.

The marshland villages were still few and small at the end of the eleventh century,* the marshland and fen hardly touched. It is between about 1150 and 1300 that we get abundant evidence of the construction of banks and ditches in both fen and marsh.

Rainfall may have been more moderate then. At any rate the Crowland abbey chronicle speaks of the fen drying up in this period, so that it was not difficult to make fen-banks on a large scale and to take in wide tracts of new arable land. To the south of the Wash, the men of Holbeach, Whaplode and Fleet were hard at work from about 1160 onwards. We hear of the Saturday Dike by about 1160-70, Hassock Dike by 1190-95, Asgardike in 1203-6, and the Common Dike in 1241. All these dikes represented successive advances into the fens, so that in the space of eighty years no less than fifty square miles were added to the arable and pasture of these townships. Of this some seventeen or eighteen square miles were added by the last great intake between 1206 and 1241.†

This fen-reclamation was carried out by whole communities, mainly by the hundreds or double-hundreds of the Danelaw, and the newly won land was divided into bovates, each of which carried with it the obligation to keep a certain length of the dikes and ditches in repair. In the village of Walsoken, for example, every acre of land repaired four feet of sea-bank in the marshes, and one foot of Podike in the fen. At West Walton every acre repaired six feet two inches of sea-bank and one foot of Podike. What might happen if a single man neglected this duty was illustrated on 19 January 1439. One Thomas Flower, despite the warning of the dike-reeve, failed to repair his section of the Wisbech fen-dike, the floodwaters pouring down from the Midlands broke through, and in a short time between twelve and thirteen thousand acres of land were under water. On another fenland manor in 1331 we are told that nearly a thousand acres were under water; and at Terrington and West Walton in 1316 'a great part of the lands are submerged in the sea.'

Simultaneously with the embanking in the fens, there was an advance from the village towards the sea. The action of the tides around the southern end of the Wash especially was raising up the salt marshes, so that there came a point at which they could be enclosed

* See the population maps in H. C. Darby, *The Domesday Geography of England* (Cambridge University Press), vol. I: Eastern England, 1952, p. 116.

† I am indebted to Professor H. Hallam for the substance of this paragraph. See the Select Bibliography for this chapter.

and protected from the tides by a sea-bank. Salt marsh became fresh marsh after a few seasons, and some of the fresh marsh eventually became fertile arable. We get therefore a series of sea-banks of different dates between the villages and the sea today. For example the men of Holbeach and Whaplode built a town dike outside the Roman Bank in the year 1286.

Many of these dikes were high and wide enough to carry a road. When the Old Podike fell into disrepair and a new dike was to be raised by all the townships of marshland and by Wiggenhall, we are told it was to be five or six feet high, eighteen feet wide at the base, and twelve feet wide at the top. Elsewhere we read that the dikes between the townships of a certain hundred were to be sixteen feet high to keep the waters of one vill from another vill. Many of these ancient fen-dikes and sea-banks carry secondary roads today and this helps to explain their peculiarities, both their frequent and abrupt bends and the fact that they often extend for several miles in what is obviously a continuous line despite the frequent changes of direction. In north Lincolnshire, near Grimsby, we are told in a survey of 1595 that what was then the main (and only) street of the hamlet of Marsh Chapel was in former times the old sea-bank. As early as the twelfth century we find villages and hamlets strung along this bank, which can be traced on the map from Tetney down to Saltfleet (Fig. 6). One or two of the villages on the bank existed at the time of the Norman Conquest, so that here again we have a communal reclamation of marshland going back to pre-Conquest times.

Not only do we find this reclamation of marsh and fen going on throughout Lincolnshire and the adjacent counties, carried out by monastic houses in some cases, by feudal magnates in others, by whole villages in other places, and no doubt by individual peasants at times, but we find similar activity in all the marshland regions of England – in the Somerset Levels (where the Abbeys of Glastonbury, Muchelney and Athelney were busy), in the Kentish marshes (where Canterbury Cathedral Priory was foremost from the twelfth century to the late fifteenth), and in Holderness. The reclamation of marsh and fen brought hundreds of square miles of new land into cultivation, and produced a characteristic landscape of willow-lined ditches, rich green pastures that carried thousands of sheep, and scattered farmsteads. We can generally distinguish the work of the medieval centuries by the irregular pattern it makes on the map: winding ditches, frequent abrupt bends in banks and consequently in the roads upon them, a thick powdering of dispersed settlement, all in contrast to the long, ruler-straight lines of later drainage and the wide, empty spaces between infrequent farmsteads.

Again while much of the Somerset Levels may have been reclaimed in the medieval period it is possible that it was only a redraining of an older landscape. Work on the South Wales marshes, just across the Severn estuary, has shown that almost the entire layout of the existing ditched fields is probably Roman and it has been suggested that the same may apply to the Somerset Levels.

The reclaimed pastures of the marshlands were not the only ones to carry large flocks of sheep. There is evidence from the eighth century onwards to suggest that the chalk and limestone downlands had much the same aspect as they have today of open and rolling sheep-pastures. The nuns of Holy Trinity abbey at Caen had a flock of seventeen hundred sheep grazing on Minchinhampton common in the Cotswolds early in the twelfth century; and in the south Wiltshire village of South Damerham and its hamlet of Martin over four thousand sheep were grazing on the chalk downs in 1225. We do not know when the pastures of the limestone and chalk downlands were first exploited in Old English times, for Domesday Book gives us no information about livestock in these parts, but casual evidence from Saxon charters suggests that the value of these upland pastures was well known at that time. When I visited recently some outlying fields of my own Oxfordshire parish, on the oolitic limestone, to discover the whereabouts of *Rammadene* – the rams' valley – mentioned in a charter of 958, there on the open sunny slopes were hundreds of sheep grazing, precisely as they must have grazed a thousand years ago when their numbers gave a name to the little dry valley. It was an immemorial scene. We cannot doubt, I think, that the landscape of the Cotswold uplands and the Wiltshire downlands was even in late Saxon times much as we know it today. The numerous Shiptons and Shipstons in the

PLATE 33. *In 1250, somewhere close to this spot near Lyng on the Somerset Levels, the Dean of Wells met the Abbot of Athelney in an attempt to settle a dispute over land here. Some of it was being drained and enclosed at that time, but much more seems to have been reclaimed long before.*

PLATE 34. *The complete medieval landscape, Widecombe in the Moor, Devon. The village lies huddled around the church. The great perpendicular tower is traditionally said to have been paid for by wealthy tinners. Above lies the old farmland of the parish with, beyond, the open moor.*

Cotswold country are further testimony to the existence of large flocks of sheep on the uplands at the time of Domesday and earlier. Shipston-on-Stour owes its name to a sheep-wash which existed here in the eighth century. Shipton-under-Wychwood is also recorded in a charter of the eighth century, and Shipton-on-Cherwell in the first years of the eleventh. Indeed, the discovery of a considerable fulling establishment in the Roman villa at Chedworth, a few miles south-east of Cheltenham, takes large-scale sheep-farming on the Cotswolds back to the third or the fourth century.

Unfortunately the alleged fulling-mill at the Chedworth villa has been shown by the late Sir Ian Richmond to be merely part of the Roman baths there.

In the medieval period the monasteries, above all the Cistercian houses from the early twelfth century onwards, were responsible for many changes in the landscape: the large-scale drainage of marsh and fen, the clearance of woodland, and the extension of sheep-farming on their ranch-like granges, especially in the Yorkshire Dales and in Wales. Usually they settled in a wilderness and brought it into cultivation, but occasionally the Cistercians had to create an artificial wilderness for themselves by wiping out settled villages and farms. In the Midlands, Combe Abbey destroyed the hamlet of Upper Smite in 1150, and Garendon Abbey wiped out the village of Dishley and made a grange of it where, centuries later, Robert Bakewell carried out his revolutionary experiments in stock-breeding. In Lincolnshire, Revesby Abbey in 1142 reduced three small villages to ruins so effectively that their very sites are now hard to discover.

Many monastic granges were created for arable farming, especially in lowland areas like the Vale of York, but most of them were created for sheep-farming on a large scale, above all on the chalk and limestone uplands of Yorkshire and Lincolnshire. Without doubt the monastic sheep formed the largest single flocks, but the peasant flocks, taken all together, often greatly outnumbered them, as the evidence from south Wiltshire shows. In many places the peasant had been exploiting the upland pastures before the monasteries appeared on the scene.

On the true moorlands, the monastic contribution was less evident. The transformation of moorland into little pastoral farms was mainly the work of peasant households, sometimes working as a single household, sometimes apparently in small groups, so that we get either a single farmstead or a small cluster of three or four – a hamlet. We notice this in the re-colonisation of Dartmoor from the middle of the thirteenth century onwards, after an almost total abandonment since the Iron Age. Of the thirty-five 'ancient tenements' of Dartmoor, some, like Riddon, consisted of a single farm; others, like Babeny and Pizwell, each consisted of three farmsteads grouped together on one site. The remains of some of these medieval farmsteads, built of enduring granite, can still be seen on Dartmoor, as at Yardworthy, Challacombe and Cholwich Town. In most instances it was the individual peasant household that laboured among the bracken and the rocks to make a new farm, such as Fernacre ('bracken land'), far up the De Lank valley on Bodmin Moor, or Wortha in St Neots parish, which we first hear of in 1241, and numerous other farmsteads in all the parishes adjoining the Cornish moorlands.

In the north of England the frontier of cultivation was similarly being pushed higher up the hillsides. Along the western slopes of Cross Fell we hear of the small village of Milburn for the first time in the year 1200; and the late Norman work in the parish church supports the view that it was the result of moorland reclamation in the twelfth century. Not far away we see pioneers at work well into the thirteenth century, as on the moors of south-western England: Kirkland is not heard of until about 1230, Murton ('moor *tun*') in 1288, and Dufton in 1289. All these are hamlets, but the single farmstead is also found, like Brackenthwaite ('bracken clearing') and Outhwaite. Beyond a certain height, however, the high moorland was not worth reclamation. It was incapable of supporting even the hard life of a medieval peasant family, and it was left to the curlews and the mountain sheep. Even so, it was not a no man's land. It became the subject of dispute when villagers in adjoining dales met on the high watershed with their flocks and accused each other of trespass over an

PLATE 35. *Wasdale Head, Cumbria. In the heart of the Lake District the small scattered hamlet of Wasdale Head is surrounded by a complex pattern of stone-walled fields. Though Professor Hoskins thought the fields were the result of the thirteenth-century clearance of the waste, they are in fact the result of the enclosure of a single large medieval open field, some time in the seventeenth or eighteenth centuries. In the sixteenth century eighteen farmers held strips in this field which must have originated as the 'infield' or the permanently cultivated land of the hamlet with 'outfield' or intermittently cropped land beyond. The origin of both hamlet and field system may lie in prehistoric times.*

invisible line in the rough pastures. The tenants of Fountains Abbey on the Kilnsey Moors, above Wharfedale, and those of Salley Abbey on the Arncliffe and Litton Moors to the west, were at loggerheads until, in the year 1279, a boundary was marked out with great stones, each stone marked with a cross. On Malham Moor the abbeys of Fountains, Bolton and Salley were erecting miles of limestone walls to clear up boundary disputes. Such walls have doubtless been repaired many times since then, but they are still substantially walls of medieval origin, representing the climax of the colonisation movement high up among the cotton-grass and the cold mists.

Buildings in the Landscape

By the eve of the Black Death the population of England was about three times that of Domesday. It is impossible to be very precise about such statements at this period, but it has been estimated that at the peak, just before the first outbreak of the Black Death (1348), there may have been nearly four million people in all. Hundreds of thousands of acres of new land had been won from the waste and the water, and settled, though still thinly, in the ten generations that had elapsed since the Norman Conquest. Many new towns had appeared, a number of new villages, and some thousands of hamlets and isolated farmsteads had been brought into being. There were now far more buildings to be seen in the landscape than ever before.

In certain parts of the country, monastic buildings – some of them on a grand scale – were a common sight. There were in England as a whole between five and six hundred monasteries. In Yorkshire alone there were sixty-six, in Lincolnshire fifty-one. Somerset, Kent and Gloucestershire were similarly rich in great abbeys and priories. The abbey churches of some of them resembled cathedrals (Plate 38), set in the depths of the countryside or towering above a medieval market place.

Much more numerous than the monasteries, and generally less grand, were the parish churches, of which several thousands had been built since the Conquest, most of them perhaps in the hundred years between 1150 and 1250. It was in this period that the division of England into ecclesiastical parishes was completed (at least until the rapid expansion of the northern and midland towns during the industrial revolution) and the parish church arose as a visible symbol and centre of a new community. Many of these parish churches were small and unpretentious structures, a simple nave and chancel built of rubble masonry from a local stone-pit, built with peasant labour and peasant materials, as at Honeychurch in deepest Devon. Sometimes the lord of the manor paid for most of the fabric, and the result is a handsome and more sophisticated village church, like Stoke Golding in Leicestershire. But not all peasants were poor by the

Most of the parish churches of England which appear to date from 1150-1250 are probably older and were merely rebuilt at this time, partly because of the rising population, partly for status and partly for fashion. The parishes too were now fixed, but only as units of ecclesiastical jurisdiction and finance. Most were much older township units or, and especially in the north, groups of ancient townships.

PLATE 36. *Deerhurst church, Gloucestershire. Despite the additions of aisles in the late twelfth century and the inevitable later windows, the body of this church is early ninth century in date. It was not only the site of a Saxon monastery but was also situated at the centre of a large estate covering what later became nine separate parishes. It was therefore also an early minster church.*

▷
PLATE 37. *Now oddly situated in the centre of a modern housing estate, Escomb church, County Durham, is a rare survival of an almost complete Saxon church. Yet like all churches it has been continually altered. It has lost a two-storey Saxon western annex, the tall narrow chimneys are of the thirteenth century, the porch is of the fourteenth century and the large window is nineteenth century.*

▷▷
PLATE 38. *Rievaulx Abbey, one of the most beautiful of the Cistercian abbeys of Yorkshire. Rievaulx was founded in Ryedale in 1132. Like all the other abbeys of the order it colonised the wilderness around, and established its outlying ranges. Arable farms were created in the valleys and extensive sheep-walks on the limestone hills above.*

early fourteenth century. There were certain parts of England with a considerable population of wealthy peasants, as for example the marshland and fenland parishes of south Lincolnshire and western Norfolk, and here we find a splendid constellation of parish churches without a break for mile after mile. Many of these superb churches have spires, which first appear in the early years of the thirteenth century; and so we get what is often regarded as a typical English scene: church spires rising from clumps of trees or piercing the fenland skies all around the horizon. The spire is in fact particularly characteristic of a broad belt of country running diagonally across England from Lincoln down to the north coast of Somerset, along and near the belt of fine oolitic building stones. Elsewhere, towers considerably outnumber spires, but it is not entirely a matter of geology.

In the rich little county of Rutland, which had about twelve or thirteen thousand people at the most, there were more than fifty medieval churches, one to every 250 people. Most of the Rutland churches are handsome, some of them are large and strikingly beautiful (Plate 39). In the neighbouring county of Lincolnshire, Cobbett reckoned that one could count a hundred parish churches within a six-mile radius of Horncastle. Parishes in such parts of England as this were generally very small: some near Norwich, as we have seen, had fewer than five hundred acres. But up in the moorland parts of Yorkshire and Lancashire medieval churches were few and far between, and parishes ran to enormous sizes. The old parish of Halifax ran to nearly seventy-six thousand acres; in Lancashire the mother-parish of Whalley was, even in the nineteenth century, still about thirty miles in length and fifteen miles wide. It had included, in medieval times, nearly fifty townships.

Two new kinds of mill made their appearance almost simultaneously towards the end of the twelfth century – the windmill and the fulling-mill. The earliest windmills are recorded in the reign of Richard I, after which they spread rapidly, especially in southern and eastern England. Greenwood and Pringle's survey of Essex in the early nineteenth century marks 212 mills in the county, while the earliest large-scale map of Kent shows

PLATE 39. *Ketton, Rutland (Leicestershire). As the farmlands and sheep pastures of eastern England reached their first great period of prosperity during the thirteenth century, one of the consequences was the rebuilding of parish churches on a grander scale. The early English churches of Rutland and Northamptonshire are particularly notable. Here is the suave beauty of Ketton tower and spire unsurpassed even in its own countryside. Yet the church has an even longer history. It was originally perhaps a late Saxon minster of considerable size, rebuilt around 1190.*

seventy-eight and that for Sussex shows sixty-six. Windmills are still a conspicuous feature of the landscape in these counties, but the vast majority have long since ceased to work and stand or lie in various stages of dereliction. As for fulling-mills, which we first hear of about the year 1185, they were more highly localised and have all disappeared without a trace, though here and there a derelict corn-mill represents a former fulling-mill.

Towns were a more important and enduring element in the landscape. It is remarkable how many English towns have come into existence since the Norman Conquest, most of them as a result of 'the fever of borough creation' in the twelfth and thirteenth centuries. All classes of landowners shared in this fever of speculation – the king himself, bishops and abbots, lay magnates, and even small local landowners. It was Henry II who founded the town of Woodstock in Oxfordshire, at the gates of the royal park, and its dependent origin is revealed to this day in the fact that this pleasant and thriving little town is still technically a chapelry of the mother-church at Bladon, an inconspicuous village a mile off. It was

FIG. 9. THE MEDIEVAL PLAN OF SALISBURY
Salisbury (New Sarum) retains its original grid-iron plan, laid out in 1220-5. The bishops of Sarum possessed rich meadow lands beside the Avon, two miles to the south of Old Sarum, and upon these Bishop Richard le Poore laid out a city to the north of his new cathedral. Straight streets, with streams running down them, cut the site into rectangles or chequers. Inside each chequer the individual house-plots were also marked out, with a standard size of seven perches by three, each plot paying a ground rent of twelve pence yearly to the bishop. A large market-place was laid out, with a guildhall on one side and the chief parish church on the other. Though the burgage tenements or house-plots have long ago lost their perfect symmetry, the original street-plan survives, for the later city grew on the western and eastern sides and left the thirteenth-century nucleus intact. Reproduced by permission from the 6-inch map of the Ordnance Survey.

Richard I who founded the town of Portsmouth in the year 1194, to take the place of the more ancient town of Porchester, now becoming silted up; and it was King John who gave to the growing village of Liverpool in 1207 its first charter setting up a borough.

Great ecclesiastics were prominent among the borough-founders. Plymouth was the creation of the priors of Plympton in the middle years of the thirteenth century; the Abbot of Eynsham in 1215 laid out a piece of his demesne, on the edge of the old village, as building-plots for his new burgesses. At Stratford-upon-Avon the bishop of Worcester in 1196 similarly laid out, on the edge of the Saxon village (now called Old Town), a piece of his demesne covering 109 acres. This was marked out in building-plots twelve perches in length and three and a half in breadth (roughly one third of an acre each) and six streets were planned, three running parallel with the river and three at right angles to it, a piece of clementary town planning such as one finds on a far larger scale in the bishop of Salisbury's creation of New Sarum a few years later (Fig. 9). Stratford, like Salisbury, was an immediate success. A survey made in 1252 records 'some two hundred and forty burgage tenements, besides about fifty plots of land, various shops, stalls, and other holdings'. An area of 109 acres with three houses to the acre would have held about three hundred houses, allowing for the streets and other open spaces, so that within two generations probably all the available area at Stratford had been taken up and built upon. Great lay lords also created boroughs, like the Grenvilles at Bideford or the Berkeleys at various places in Gloucestershire, with varying degrees of success.

Some of these boroughs were created on entirely new sites, others were an enhancement in status of an agricultural village. Some grew successfully

The 'new towns' developed much as Professor Hoskins described (but see Introduction to Chapter 9). However much research is still needed to understand them in detail. Salisbury (Fig. 9) for example has a very distorted grid, for all its careful planning. Why should this be so? Analysis of the topography there and a re-assessment of its early documented history indicate that the Bishop's planners had to take account of the main Winchester-Wilton road which crossed the site from east to west, now Milford, Silver and Bridge Streets crossing the River Avon. Another road running north to south, partly now High Street, crossed the east to west road at the Bridge Street-Silver Street junction. The first parish church of the town and its new market place lie at this junction. Even more important was the need for a system of channels to provide water for both household and industrial use. These channels ran down the centre of the new streets. In order to ensure that the water flow was on a gentle and continuous gradient the streets had to be carefully aligned to respect the natural topography. The result of all these factors produced the rather irregular grid at Salisbury.

PLATE 40. *St Thomas's Church, Winchelsea, Sussex. Winchelsea is the archetypal medieval planned town, set up on a previously bare hill-top by Edward I in 1288 and given an almost perfect grid plan. Yet it is also a failed town. Its grid was never fully built up, it was damaged by French raiders in the fourteenth century and finally destroyed as an urban centre by the silting up of the River Brede and the retreat of the sea. The church mirrors this history. It was clearly intended to be a lavish building commensurate with the aspirations of the new town. With its churchyard it entirely filled one whole block of the grid. Yet the nave was perhaps never built and the transepts and tower have been pulled down. Only the chancel and its side chapels remain.*

The tree being removed in the foreground is one of the losses of the great storm of October 1987. A reminder that nature too changes the landscape.

into market towns; many failed to develop any urban characteristics, for a royal or a seig-norial charter was not in itself any guarantee that people and trade would follow. About half the boroughs set up in Devon failed to come to anything, and about the same proportion in Cornwall. Some of the new towns were laid out on a simple grid-iron plan from the beginning, like Salisbury, Stratford, Ludlow and Eynsham; but the great majority were just left to grow anyhow within the specified area.*

The towns of medieval England were, by the early fourteenth century, a common feature in the rural landscape (most of them remained small and half-rural in any event) and their successful growth between the twelfth and fourteenth centuries affected the nature of communications throughout the country. The creation of hundreds of little market towns, each serving a radius of three to five miles, perhaps up to ten miles in the remoter parts, brought into existence, or perhaps we should say solidified, a great number of main roads for the first time, and led to the erection of hundreds of bridges. These main roads joined town to town, and some became of national importance.

Various roads called Port Street in pre-Conquest charters constituted early through-roads from one town to another, and there are many such roads in the southern half of England. Even so, the period between 1066 and 1348 saw hundreds more come into existence, mostly by the linking together of already ancient inter-village paths, and where necessary filling in gaps in the direct line by treading out a new stretch. Simultaneously, we find most of our ancient bridges appearing for the first time in the records.

The importance of bridges had been well recognised in Saxon times, when their repair was regarded as among the 'three necessary duties' of all landowners. A certain number of English bridges go back to Saxon (and even Roman) times, but over most of the country fords or primitive plank bridges were the usual means of crossing rivers. Stone bridges were sufficiently rare in the twelfth and thirteenth centuries to be recorded as such in charters of the period. They were naturally commoner where good building stone was available, as along the oolitic limestone belt. In counties such as Devon, where suitable

* See also Chapter 9 on 'The Landscape of Towns'.

stone was unobtainable, even important bridges like those at Barnstaple and Bideford were built of timber when they were first erected in the closing years of the thirteenth century. The twelfth-century bridge at Exeter was of timber, but had been replaced by a stone bridge before the middle of the thirteenth century.

Most bridges that are well known today first appear in these years of growing internal trade and prosperity. The Trent was bridged at Nottingham as early as 924, but this was the only crossing, other than by ferry, until one arrived at the upper reaches. We hear of Wichnor bridges in the reign of Henry III, of the bridge at Burton-upon-Trent in 1175 and, at a few miles below, of the important Swarkeston bridge (much of which can still be seen) in 1204. Kelham bridge, near Newark, is first heard of in 1225; and Muskham bridge, the lowest medieval bridge over the river, was a going concern in the year 1301, when it was known as 'hay bridge' – that is, one capable of bearing a load of hay. Thus nearly all the important bridges over the Trent came into existence in the twelfth and thirteenth centuries, and we should find that the same is true of most of the larger English rivers.

Castles made their appearance in England in the late eleventh century. Before long nearly every important town had one towering over it, considerable numbers of houses being demolished to make room for it in many old towns. In many places where a great castle was built on a strong and strategic site an entirely new town grew up beside it, to supply its daily needs and to enjoy its protection. Such towns were Ludlow, Launceston, Newcastle-upon-Tyne and Devizes, among others. Castles were to be found all over England by the early fourteenth century, but were by no means uniformly distributed. Thus Kent had about forty castles; the large county of Devon had only eight.

PLATE 41. *This windmill, at Rolvenden, Kent, is strictly a postmill. Though not of great antiquity, having been rebuilt on numerous occasions, it is an example of the type of windmill that was in use in medieval times over much of England.*

Though many bridges were built in the twelfth to thirteenth centuries to replace earlier fords, the lack of early documentation, already referred to, is also a problem here. Many bridges probably existed in Saxon times but we have no record of them until they were rebuilt much later on. A minor country lane between the village of Great Everdon and the now deserted village of Fawsley, in Northamptonshire, crosses a tiny stream on a magnificent fourteenth-century bridge. There is no obvious explanation for this. But there is a Saxon land charter of 944 AD whose bounds at this point note 'the stone bridge'. Even more significant, the charter itself is recording part of the slow break-up of a former royal estate which earlier had covered most of north-western Northamptonshire and the adjacent part of Warwickshire. Fawsley was the administrative centre of this estate and also probably had a great minster church. No wonder the lane had a stone bridge, for it was the main approach road to Fawsley in mid-Saxon times and later.

Chapter 4
THE BLACK DEATH AND AFTER

Introduction

The Black Death of 1348-9 is usually said to mark a clear break between the great expansion of the English landscape and the subsequent period of retrenchment and later regrowth.

Yet although the plague had an immediate and devastating impact on the landscape and an appalling effect on the people of England, in the wider view it was only one event in a period of general economic decline which in the end was perhaps more important.

For as much as half a century before the onset of the Black Death the country was stagnating economically or perhaps even in decline. The population which may have reached seven million by the end of the thirteenth century levelled off and probably began to fall. Marginal land in the more remote parts of the country was abandoned and there was a general reduction of arable farming. The establishment of new towns largely ceased. Of the few towns that were founded, most failed within a short time. Not every part of England was affected to the same degree but there is no doubt that the long period of expansion had finally come to an end.

As today, people then did not understand the complex economic changes that were taking place and tended to put the blame on other, more obvious factors. For example, in the fenlands of Cambridgeshire, much reclaimed land was given up in the mid-fourteenth century. In 1356 several hundred acres of land were said to be valueless because water had covered the fens and destroyed everything. Yet there had been disasters and floods earlier which had not ended in abandonment. Now, with an economic recession setting in, it was no longer worth keeping land drained and so the floods prevailed. With the fall in population, settlements began to fail and a reduction of arable land took place. These early fourteenth-century desertions do not appear to be very numerous but they certainly took place, widely scattered over the country.

On the other hand it has to be remembered that abandonment of settlement is a constant feature of all periods. Prehistoric and Roman settlements were, of course, eventually abandoned in their thousands. The archaeological evidence for countless early to mid-Saxon settlements only exists because most were abandoned within two or three centuries of their foundation. Villages were cleared in the twelfth century by the new Cistercian abbeys, mainly in the north of England,

but also elsewhere. Thus the village of Pipewell, Northamptonshire, was removed to make way for the abbey there in the twelfth century. At Legsby, Lincolnshire, the tiny settlement of Caldecotes had already been abandoned by 1322 when the houses there were described as being in ruins. Thus, to see a major period of universal expansion followed by universal decline is to over-simplify the real picture.

Nor did the Black Death have the devastating effect on villages and other settlements that has often been claimed. Only a handful of villages actually seem to have disappeared as a direct result of the plague. In Northamptonshire for example where there are over eighty known deserted villages, only one, Hale, in Apethorpe parish, is a certain Black Death desertion. Even where a village was completely deserted as a result of the plague it was often resettled soon afterwards. Cowsfield, in Whiteparish, Wiltshire, was said to be valueless in 1349 'on account of all the tenants being dead from the plague'. Yet three years later new tenants had arrived and the village lives on, albeit very small, even today.

The main effect of the Black Death was that it weakened those settlements already in decline or which had always been tiny, and thus allowed them to be more easily depopulated in the following two and a half centuries. Over most of England the plague merely exacerbated what the general economic decline had already begun.

By 1400, therefore, the population of England was perhaps down to three and a half to four million, labour for arable farming was in short supply and land began to revert to pasture in the previously intensely cultivated areas. The process was particularly significant in east Yorkshire, Lincolnshire and Norfolk as well as over large parts of the Midlands.

In addition to these factors, certainly from 1450 onwards, and despite a renewed growth in population, pastoral farming, instead of being merely the alternative to arable, became the most profitable form of agriculture. There was now a demand for wool and its price rose as both home consumption increased and an export market developed. As a result arable land was converted to pasture and, where it was possible, villages were removed, their inhabitants evicted and the land turned over to sheep or cattle. A great deal of the ridge-and-furrow that still survives in the Midland counties was last ploughed in

PLATE 42. *The Street, Chilham, Kent. The village was almost certainly replanned, probably in the late eleventh century. Its present appearance, however, dates from much later. The timber-framed building on the right is a so-called Wealden house. It was built in the late fifteenth or early sixteenth century and then consisted of an open hall in the recessed centre with two-storey end blocks. It was undoubtedly the home of a rich farmer. It has been altered in later times.*

the late fourteenth or early fifteenth century and certainly the majority of the now deserted villages in Leicestershire, Northamptonshire and Warwickshire were finally swept away at this time and their inhabitants driven out. Such actions cannot be condemned outright as the work of uncaring, rapacious, and wealthy landowners. Not only were many of the desertions carried out by relatively minor tenants, but these people were operating in a society whose rules and philosophy were very different from our own and whose aim was, in many cases, merely to prevent themselves from going bankrupt.

Nor must we make too much of this apparent universal conversion to grass and clearance of settlements. The process was largely restricted to a broad zone running north to south across northern and midland England. Even there most villages survived, together with their open fields, for another three hundred or so years without any large-scale changes. Over much of England and especially on the upland areas where pastoral farming had always been important, there was not only relatively little arable but also still plenty of room to expand grazing.

Indeed over large parts of England, often at a very local level, the former process of expansion continued even if it was in a different direction than earlier. Professor Hoskins himself indicates this in the following text. The new fishing villages in the south-west of England set up in the fourteenth and fifteenth centuries are but one example. Certainly by the sixteenth century in the Cumbrian dales population growth had led to the communal reclamation of former wastes on a large scale and even the development of more open fields.

The fifteenth century also saw a veritable rash of new and improved churches as Professor Hoskins discusses at length. It is curious that at a time when the upper classes of English society were engaged in almost continuous civil war and when the political history of England was one of apparent chaos, the countryside was filled with builders, carpenters and masons, busily engaged in erecting some of the finest and most beautiful buildings of all time. Yet even this is not always fully understood. The great Perpendicular churches of the West Country, the Cotswolds and East Anglia such as those at Huish Episcopi, Northleach, Lavenham, Long Melford and Sall, reflect the great wealth of both individuals and communities engaged in the woollen industry. They are rightly admired, as are those of the rich tinners of Devon and Cornwall. But, in addition, it has to be remembered that there is hardly a medieval church in England that was not up-dated at this time by the insertion of new Perpendicular windows, the raising of a fifteenth-century clerestory or the heightening of a tower. Much of the work is not necessarily of high quality and in the end it can be regarded as somewhat repetitious and dull. Yet collectively it represents an enormous input of individual and communal wealth. This wealth was sometimes, but by no means always, the result of new developing industries such as wool, mining and even fishing. But it also reflects increasing wealth countrywide. It was the result of a change of religious and social attitudes. In earlier years gifts of money and land were poured into monastic houses. Now money went to individual parish churches, sometimes to found chantry chapels where the souls of the benefactors were to be remembered and prayed for, but more often to enhance the look of a building, to rival or outstrip neighbours or, in the final analysis, to give visual expression to deeply held religious beliefs which were increasingly concerned with the individual.

Alongside the enlargement and beautification of churches went the appearance of new secular buildings. The concept of the Great Rebuilding is dealt with in a later chapter, but in many places the fifteenth and early sixteenth centuries saw the start of a massive improvement of houses which has continued ever since. Prior to the fifteenth century, while the upper classes occupied their castles and the more elaborate manor houses the majority of the population lived in fairly squalid huts of somewhat primitive form. But the increasing wealth of the fifteenth century was acquired by a new class of society which had largely not existed before. It was made up of newly rich tenant farmers who often became independent 'yeomen', as well as merchants involved in the new industrial and commercial development. Such people were able to build more substantial houses for themselves and these often still exist. Their houses, incorporating, as

they usually did, a hall emulated the great houses of the upper classes. Areas such as the Weald of Kent, which produced a particular form of late-medieval house known as the Wealden type, as well as parts of the north-west Midlands, are notable for the survival of dwellings of this kind.

Professor Hoskins rightly pointed to the many late-medieval bridges which survive in parts of England. There were other improvements to transport at this time. Roads on the whole, apart from bridges, remained poor and hazardous. River transport, always important for the movement of bulk cargoes, was further improved and the first real canals since the Roman period were constructed. The earliest post-Roman canal was that between Exeter and Topsham which Professor Hoskins describes in a later chapter. A slightly later one was that at Stamford in Lincolnshire which was meant to improve the navigation of the River Welland. It was begun in 1570 but it had a haphazard construction. More work was carried out in 1620-1 but it was not completed until 1673. It was abandoned in 1863 but its earthworks still survive.

Professor Hoskins traces the last stages of true castles in England but ignores the sixteenth-century revolution in military technology which led to the replacement of castles by artillery forts. Amongst the earliest of these developments are simple gun platforms, as at the so-called castles at Deal and Walmer in Kent, Calshot and Hurst Castles in Hampshire, West Cowes on the Isle of Wight and St Mawes and St Denis in Cornwall. Later in the century true bastioned defences were created around Berwick upon Tweed and later still, towards the end of the seventeenth century, complex bastioned forts were built as at Tilbury on the Thames and the Citadel at Plymouth.

PLATE 43. *As can be seen from their characteristic shape, these stone-walled fields at Castleton, Derbyshire, were created by enclosing individual open-field strips. The ridge-and-furrow of these strips is still visible within the fields. Whether they were enclosed for sheep is more doubtful.*

4

THE BLACK DEATH AND AFTER

The Abandonment of Villages

Despite the great colonisation movement of the twelfth and thirteenth centuries, England still contained many wild and secret places when the bubonic plague smote the country for the first time in the late summer of 1348, an event which had profound consequences in many ways, including the bringing about of considerable changes in the landscape. Successive outbreaks of the plague reduced the population of the country by somewhere between one third and one half. This put an end to the 'land hunger' of the thirteenth century, which had led pioneers higher into the moorlands and farther into the woods and heaths. The pressure of population eased off, and there followed a retreat from the marginal lands. The infertile farms were abandoned in favour of the more rewarding farms elsewhere. Instead of peasants seeking land, landlords now sought for tenants.

> As noted in the Introduction the onset of the Black Death only hastened a decline which had already begun.

The retreat from the marginal lands was most evident in the sandy Breckland of southwestern Norfolk and north-western Suffolk, and on the thinner soils of the Lincolnshire heaths and wolds. The Breckland had been only sparsely peopled at the end of the eleventh century. Domesday Book indicates that it provided a livelihood for only twenty to twenty-five people to the square mile as against seventy to eighty elsewhere in East Anglia. The region stands out noticeably as one carrying a considerable sheep population. Probably some of the Domesday sheep pastures were colonised and settled as arable

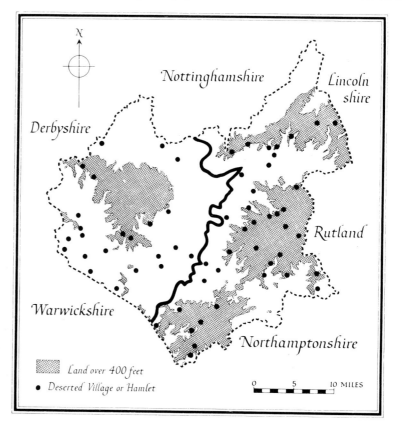

FIG. 10. THE DESERTED VILLAGES OF LEICESTERSHIRE
Several of the sites in the west of the country are the result of early conversion into monastic granges. In the eastern half of the county, the concentration of sites on the liassic clay uplands is very noticeable. The western edge of the liassic clays is indicated on the map by the thick black line. Most of the sites on these clays were deserted in the period 1450-1600.

PLATE 44. *Deserted village of Holworth, Chaldon Herring, Dorset. Though it was deserted in the fifteenth century, and is thus a good example of what happened to many villages at that time, its main interest lies in its former shape now preserved as banks and scarps in the grass. Holworth has a remarkably regular form with neat house and yard sites close to the main street and equal sized garden plots behind. Such a pattern can only be the result of planning in the tenth and eleventh centuries, in this case almost certainly by Milton Abbey to whom it was granted in 933.*

villages in subsequent generations, as we know happened at Aunby on the west Lincolnshire heaths. An abstract of a title deed dated 10 September 1626 says that 'the village of Aunby was first constituted from the ancient use of Pasture for sheep, Beasts, and a warren of Coneys [rabbits], with a shepherd's and a warrener's lodge only thereon, to be broken up for corne, and used in tillage and building of houses fitt for husbandry and other necessaries there convenient'. It appears that the neighbouring village of Holywell originated in the same way, for we are told that the inhabitants of the two places 'were first planters, tenants, and occupiers thereof'. Probably the original 'planters' of the two villages came from the ancient mother-village of Castle Bytham some time in the latter part of the twelfth century. We hear of Holywell for the first time in 1190, and of Aunby in 1219. Aunby is a pure Scandinavian name: it is 'Outhen's *by* or farm'. The history of Aunby's origin tells us incidentally that not all villages with Scandinavian names go back to the days of the Danish Conquest in the ninth and tenth centuries. Danish personal names were in common use throughout the twelfth century in Lincolnshire and other parts of the Danelaw, so that Outhen or Authun could well have given his name to a village founded during the reign of Henry II or a little later. Aunby had only a short life: it seems to have been abandoned during the fifteenth century and is now only a solitary farm beside a stream. Two miles away over the heath is the deserted village of Pickworth, where a single arch remains of the medieval church. Pickworth, too, is last heard of as a village in the fifteenth century.

There are more than thirteen hundred deserted villages in England. The sites of most of them are to be found in the Midlands, and the eastern half of England – the Lowland Zone. In the East Riding of Yorkshire about a hundred sites are known, in Lincolnshire nearly a hundred and fifty, in Norfolk a hundred and thirty. Back in the Midlands, there are about two hundred and fifty deserted village sites in the three counties of Warwickshire,

Some 2,000 deserted villages have now been recorded, mostly in the Midlands and the eastern parts of England. Many of those noted elsewhere are abandoned hamlets rather than true villages. The final abandonment often only took place after many years of decline. Enough evidence exists to indicate that settlements were being abandoned all through medieval and earlier times, even in periods of great prosperity. The Black Death seriously weakened many places and this either led to more rapid decline or allowed them to be forced into extinction by later generations of pastoral farmers or emparkers.

Leicestershire and Northamptonshire. The number of sites falls appreciably as we go north and west into the upland regions of England, but that is probably because villages are much fewer in these regions, and here we have the harder task of locating abandoned hamlets and single farmsteads. For example, Crowndale Farm, the reputed birthplace of Sir Francis Drake just outside the Devonshire market town of Tavistock, had been a hamlet with seven farmsteads in 1336. Sixty years later it had been reduced to one holding and its corn-mill lay derelict; and it has survived as one farm down to the present day.

The Black Death, though it wiped out possibly as many as one and a half million people altogether within thirty years, was not the immediate cause of this large-scale extermination of villages and hamlets. Some villages, it is true, were completely depopulated and never re-settled, such as Tilgarsley in Oxfordshire, Middle Carlton in west Lincolnshire, and Ambion in west Leicestershire, over the empty site of which in 1485 the battle of Bosworth Field was fought. Occasionally a village was emptied by plague and re-settled on a new site some little way off. This happened at Combe in Oxfordshire and possibly at Steeple Barton, a few miles away. In both instances the survivors returned, not to the original village, but to one of its hamlets, leaving the old site forlorn and rat-ridden.

The making of the New Forest in the eleventh century, and of many of the Cistercian granges in the twelfth, had already caused a number of villages to be deserted. In addition to these deliberate erasures of villages, it seems that some villages, settled late in difficult, unrewarding country, were decaying and on the point of collapse even before the Black Death. Asterleigh, a twelfth-century clearing on the edge of Wychwood Forest in Oxfordshire, acquired a parish church and parochial rights by the early thirteenth century; but by 1316 it was united with the neighbouring parish of Kiddington for reasons of poverty. England is full of sizeable villages, founded back in Saxon and Scandinavian times, which have survived to this day; but there were also many hundreds of villages like Asterleigh, or like Maidenwell on the Lincolnshire Wolds, which struggled along on marginal lands, blessed with a parish church but unable to keep it going, and to such places as this the plague dealt a further and ultimately fatal blow.

It was the vast mortality of the successive epidemics that led to the piecemeal abandonment of these villages and hamlets on marginal land. On and around the edges of the Breckland there are no fewer than twenty-eight deserted villages. Most of them were small and poor, and the desertions were gradual, extending over two, three or four generations, so that most instances of final abandonment occur during the fifteenth century. There are four ruined churches within four miles of Colkirk, in the north Norfolk country, small chapels built by the pioneers of the High Middle Ages and abandoned to the weather before the Middle Ages ended.* Ruined churches abound on the Wolds of Lincolnshire, as at Calceby. The one-inch map of Lincolnshire reveals over and over again where these lost villages are to be sought for. It abounds in examples of united parishes such as Lenton, Keisby and Osgodby or Careby, Aunby and Holywell (both on Sheet 123). In such instances it will generally be found that one place survives as an ecclesiastical centre and the other two are each represented by a solitary farmstead.

If one visits such a site, the evidences of the former village may generally be found in a field adjoining the farmstead which perpetuates the old name. Often the fragments of a small medieval church meet the eye and identify the site at once, but more often even these have entirely disappeared and the only visible signs are the grassy banks which cover the rubble foundations of the peasant farmsteads, and the shallow depressions between them that mark the line of the former streets and lanes. It is best to visit these sites in the six months between autumn and spring, before the new grass and the nettles have half obliterated the markings on the ground.

PLATE 45. *The deserted village of Wharram Percy, Yorkshire. Though the area was intensively occupied throughout later prehistoric, Roman and Saxon times, the medieval village here was not planned and laid out until the twelfth century. It was deserted in the fourteenth century after a life of little more than two hundred years.*

* J. Saltmarsh, 'Plague and Economic Decline', *Cambridge Historical Journal*, 1941.

As Professor Hoskins says, the first hedged fields created from the 'enclosure' of the open fields were very large indeed. They were only later sub-divided into smaller units when sheep farming became more intensive and more developed. For example, when the village of Papley, Northamptonshire, was finally deserted in 1499 and its fields turned over to sheep, the former township only consisted of thirteen fields of up to seventy acres each. Later these were sub-divided into forty fields of between five and twenty acres. It is these that now exist.

The final stages of the abandonment were very often hastened by landlords, whether laymen or monastic houses. The dwindling population was insufficient to maintain the traditional arable husbandry of the demesne, and since pastoral farming required only a fraction of the labour needed by arable, where a landlord had absolute ownership of most of the soil he evicted the remnants of the village population in order to convert the open arable fields into large enclosures of pasture for cattle and sheep. The village houses were demolished – an easy business, for above their rubble foundations they mostly had mud walls – and men, women and children departed in tears to find a new livelihood elsewhere. The landscape in such parishes and districts changed completely. The strips disappeared under the grass (though they are perpetuated all over the Midlands in the rolling ridges), the vast and hedgeless open fields gave way to hedged enclosures – usually still very large by modern standards – and more than a thousand villages and hamlets were wiped off the scene, their site marked only by a solitary farmstead or a shepherd's cottage.

New Colonisation

But the century and a half that followed the first outbreak of the Black Death was not entirely a picture of retreat, decay and melancholy. There is some reason to suppose that the profound economic decline that marked these generations was at its worst in the Midlands, where equally the prosperity of the thirteenth century had been at its highest. In the west and north, where life was harder and more primitive, settlement more scattered among the hills, and estates perhaps generally smaller, life seems to have gone on much the same as before, once the worst of the epidemics was over. Indeed, in south-western England we see plenty of evidence of moderate growth rather than decline, and of modest prosperity among some social classes at least.

In some parts of England new land was still being brought into cultivation from the wilderness, though on nothing like the scale of thirteenth-century colonisation. In the thick woods of Buckinghamshire and Hertfordshire, and perhaps in the Sussex Weald also, new fields were being added to existing farmsteads; and the priors of Canterbury were still engaged in making reclamations in the marshlands of eastern and south-western Kent. Prior Thomas Goldston (1449-68) spent £1,200 during his rule – some £80,000 in modern values – on the 'inning' of Appledore Marsh, and Prior William Petham (1471-2) spent a further £300 on reclaiming six hundred acres of marsh. At Monkton, in the Isle of Thanet, there were also considerable reclamations of marsh by the priory.

A few new settlements came into existence in the fifteenth century – the fishing villages. We first hear of Staithes (Plate 46), the fishing-village on the north Yorkshire coast, in 1415. The name means 'landing-place'. It was the landing-place for the older villages of Seaton or Hinderwell, a mere cleft in a mighty cliff-wall, of no interest until the fishing industry developed along the coast. Similarly, we first hear of the south Cornish village of Mevagissey in the year 1410, and on the north coast both Newquay and Bude are first recorded in the fifteenth century. There may have been a few cottages at any of these places before this time, but not enough to attract a separate name. It is when they suddenly begin to grow that we hear of them by name; and they probably owe their growth to some marked development in the offshore fishing industry which enabled whole villages to gain a livelihood by it. The industry may have become organised on a more or less capitalistic basis instead of the casual fishing for individual needs which had gone on from time immemorial. At any rate it paid someone to build quays and breakwaters at suitable points in order to create artificial harbours on otherwise dangerous coasts.

The best example of this type of village comes from the late sixteenth century when the north Devon village of Clovelly was given a breakwater or quay by the squire, George Cary. Clovelly had been an obscure agricultural parish until this time, turning its back on the sea in which it had no interest. But all was changed by the building of the massive stone pier, which created the only safe harbour on this merciless coast between Appledore in Devon and Boscastle in Cornwall. In his will dated 9 August 1601, George Cary says:

I have of late erected a pier or key in the sea and river of Severne upon the sea-shore, near low water of the said seas, within or near about one half mile of my said capital messuage of Clovelly, and also divers houses, cellars, warehouses, and other edifices, as well under as in the cliff and on the salt shores of Clovelly aforesaid, and also near above the cliff there, which standeth and hath cost me about £2,000 and which place was of none or very small benefit before my said exertions and buildings.

It is rarely that we get such an authentic picture of the creation of a new village. Until this date Clovelly had merely been a parish of scattered farms and cottages on the plateau. The squire built cottages up the narrow valley on either side of a tumbling stream – the only practicable way down to the seashore – and fish-cellars and warehouses below the cliffs.

PLATE 46. *Jammed into a very awkward space, Staithes on the North Yorkshire coast cannot be anything but a deliberate creation, set up as a fishing village in the late fourteenth century.*

The watercourse was later diverted into a cascade to fall into the sea elsewhere, and its dry bed converted into a series of terraces or broad steps paved with cobbles. The village scene as we know it was then complete.

New Buildings

The years between 1350 and 1500 saw a great number of new buildings added to the landscape. Hundreds of parish churches were rebuilt or enlarged, more so in some parts of England than others. Hundreds of little private oratories or chapels appeared during the fifteenth century, most of them attached to remote houses, but some built at a lonely crossroads to serve an area far from a parish church. More castles were built, and finally more bridges were built or rebuilt of stone in these generations.

There is very little evidence of new church-building in the Midlands, where the agricultural depression was most general and acute, except in special cases like Fotheringhay which was magnificently conceived by the royal dukes of York between about 1400 and 1440, and added something superlative and civilising to the peasant landscape (Plate 48).

In south-western England a great number of churches were entirely rebuilt or enlarged, so that Perpendicular Gothic is the characteristic and almost monotonous style of the region. Most of them were given beautiful gilded and coloured roodscreens running the entire width of the church. Torbryan in Devon is an outstanding example of early fifteenth-century craftsmanship in wood and stone, but there were scores of others until the Low Church vandals got to work in the eighteenth century and the Victorian 'restorers' in the nineteenth.

It is perhaps incorrect to say that there is little evidence of new church building in the Midlands in the fifteenth century. Certainly there were not the vast numbers of completely new churches as in, say, Norfolk or Somerset but new fifteenth-century churches do exist. For example, in Northamptonshire, as well as Fotheringhay, the churches at Apethorpe and Lowick were almost completely rebuilt in the fifteenth century and those at Aldwincle All Saints, Ashby St Ledgers, Brampton Ash, Chipping Warden, Collyweston, Islip, Kettering and Luddington were largely so. In addition most others had some fifteenth-century additions or alterations. The amount of fifteenth-century work in most counties if not always noteworthy is staggering in its bulk.

Not all parishes had the funds to rebuild or even enlarge their churches. The little building at Honeychurch in Devon (Plate 49) was given a plain tower and three new bells in the fifteenth century, the chancel arch and roofs were renewed and some new windows put in, but substantially the twelfth-century church was left untouched. There was no need to enlarge the fabric in this sequestered hamlet. Some simple carved oak benches were provided, probably the first seating the little church had ever had, and everything settled down again for the next five hundred years.

Even Honeychurch, remote and small as it was, managed in adding a tower to its church, to follow the prevailing fashion. Towers sprang up everywhere in the countryside and in the towns, some of them magnificent. The towers of Somerset, Suffolk and Yorkshire are especially notable and numerous. Those of Devon and Cornwall are very numerous – there are hardly a dozen medieval spires in the two counties – but with rare exceptions that are usually copied from elsewhere, they are not beautiful or striking. Most are plain and dull. It was partly the lack of suitable building stone, though not entirely, for even granite could be made to produce grand towers like those at Widecombe-in-the-Moor and Moretonhampstead. Some of the finest towers among the parish churches are the product of local industrial prosperity in the years down to 1550. Widecombe tower is traditionally said (and probably rightly) to have been built at the cost of the tinners of the parish; Lavenham tower in Suffolk was built at the cost of two generations of the Spring family, the wealthiest clothiers of their age. Indeed, the clothiers and wool merchants often paid for the complete rebuilding of their parish churches, as witness the fine church at Steeple Ashton in Wiltshire, built at the cost of two local clothiers, Walter Lucas and Robert Long, between 1480 and 1500. And the Cotswold 'wool churches' are too well known to require any further comment.

In some parts of England, where parishes were large and houses scattered, private

PLATE 47. *Polperro, Cornwall, is one of the late Cornish fishing villages, established perhaps in the thirteenth century. This settlement was never the centre of a parish but merely one of a number of hamlets and farmsteads in Llansallas parish. The village of Llansallas is two and a half miles to the west, well away from the sea.*

◁◁
PLATE 48. *Fotheringhay church, Northamptonshire, built by the royal Dukes of York. The lantern-tower, nave and aisles are the work of William Horwode, who contracted to build them in 1434. The splendid choir, completed by 1415, was unroofed and destroyed in the sixteenth century, so giving the church its present unbalanced appearance. Fotheringhay was built at a time when practically all other church-building in the Midlands had ceased.*

◁
PLATE 49. *The church at Honeychurch, Devon, is virtually as it was rebuilt in the early twelfth century. Yet like most other churches it was updated in the fifteenth century. The chancel arch and the large windows show this.*

oratories or chapels began to appear in considerable numbers in the fourteenth and fifteenth centuries. Landowners, large and small, applied to the bishop for licence to have such chapels, mainly on the ground that their houses were too far from the parish church to make access possible during the winter months. These private chapels were particularly numerous in the south-western counties, where at least two or three hundred existed in pre-Reformation days. Sometimes the chapel or oratory was a room in the squire's or franklin's house, but often it stood as a separate building such as the still-perfect medieval chapel of Trecarrel, four miles south of Launceston. Trecarrel, the ancient home of a family who took their name from their dwelling, lay about a mile and a half from the parish church of Lezant, quite far enough in the deep mud of a Cornish winter. Robert Trecarrel and his wife and mother therefore petitioned the bishop to have a chapel within their 'mansion' and on 8 May 1405 the necessary licence was granted. The present structure, which stands detached from the surviving medieval hall and other buildings, represents a rebuilding in granite of about a hundred years later, probably by the Sir Henry Trecarrel who rebuilt Launceston church between 1511 and 1524.

Some of these chapels stood by the roadside in lonely places, like No Man's Chapel which in the fifteenth century stood at a cross-roads where three parishes met, to the north of Exeter. Mostly, however, they lay inside the house or in the yard outside, as they were not intended for public worship. Licences were usually granted only for the land-owner and his own household, and even then were subject to further conditions such as attendance at the mother-church upon all the great feasts.

Most of the houses for which these private chapels were licensed have become farm-houses with the passage of time, and have been rebuilt since the Reformation so that all trace of the chapel has been lost. But in scores of instances in south-western England one may yet find considerable traces of the medieval chapel in one of the out-buildings, in a hay-loft or a small barn. At Bury Barton, in the Devonshire parish of Lapford, the chapel of St James, licensed by Bishop Lacy in 1434, still stands by the roadside, very largely intact

▷

PLATE 50. *Tarr Steps, Exmoor, Somerset. A remarkable clapper bridge of seventeen spans on an ancient routeway across the moor. It cannot be dated but is most likely to be medieval.*

▷▷

PLATE 51. *Julian's Bridge, Wimborne Minster, Dorset. The main road west from the late Saxon town of Wimborne must have crossed the broad River Stour on a bridge here from an early date. The present structure was built in 1636 and was widened and enlarged in 1844, probably as part of the construction of the Wimborne-Dorchester turnpike road improvements.*

and in use as a barn. In other houses which have been rescued from the exigencies of day-to-day farming – such as Fardel and Bradley, also in Devon – the fifteenth-century chapels are quite complete and are occasionally used for their proper purpose. Where, however, they have fallen into ruin or been desecrated, traceried windows, or buttressed walls, or a dimly seen cradle roof, reveal their original purpose.

Such private chapels or oratories are not to be confused with the parochial chapels which sprang up in the vast parishes of northern England. These were designed for public worship in some village or hamlet far from the mother-church, as in the enormous parishes of Halifax and Whalley, and they were parish churches in all but name. Sometimes certain rights, such as that of baptism or burial, were carefully reserved to the mother-church, but in the great moorland parishes even these rights generally had to be conceded to distant chapelries. Very often, the relationship of mother- and daughter-churches gives us a valuable clue to the nature of early colonisation of which we have no other record.

The mother-church stands in the parental village, from which pioneers went out to colonise in the woods, moors and marshes, and to found new villages and hamlets that ultimately got a dependent chapelry of their own. This is not so obviously true in the northern moorland parishes where this simple relationship is obscured by the sheer size of the parish, but it is generally true to the south of the Trent. Mother-churches indicate the primary settlements of a district and by mapping them we can get some sort of picture of settlement before the Norman Conquest, at a period when records are few and scattered.

These so-called mother-churches cannot be so easily equated with early colonisation as is suggested here. Many are early to mid-Saxon minster churches. They were built where they are because at the time they were founded they were either the centres of large estates, or at the place where most people lived, or both. But neither they, nor their daughter churches, tell us about the origins of the outlying settlements. Some of these settlements were very old indeed, others were the result of later colonisation. The churches tell us more about the hopes and aspirations of lords and the conservative institutional power of the church than they do of the origins of settlement.

The late fourteenth and the fifteenth centuries also saw the building or rebuilding of a great number of bridges in stone. Some of our most handsome bridges date from this time. Although most of the important English bridges originated in the twelfth and thirteenth centuries, with the great growth of road traffic these early bridges proved too narrow or too unsafe, and were replaced by stone structures. The bridges over the Ouse at Huntingdon and St

PLATE 52. *Medieval bridge at Wadebridge, Cornwall, built about 1468-70 and widened in 1847. Wadebridge started as a ford over the Camel estuary, and was simply called 'Wade' from the Old English word for a ford. This medieval bridge is still, in the words of Carew (1602), 'the longest, strongest, and fairest that the Shire can muster'.*

Ives are particularly notable examples of this period of rebuilding, and East Farleigh bridge over the Medway is another very fine medieval stone bridge. In the north of England, the splendid Devil's Bridge over the Lune at Kirkby Lonsdale probably dates from the fifteenth century, and the remarkable bridge over the Till at Twizel (Northumberland) certainly existed by the early sixteenth. Leland saw it about 1540 and describes it, just as it is today, as 'of stone one bow, but greate and stronge'.

Some beautiful medieval bridges survive in Devon, especially over the Tamar. Grey-stone Bridge (built about 1439) is perfectly preserved. A little downstream is Horse Bridge, built in 1437, and below that again is New Bridge, a noble bridge of white granite, built by Sir Piers Edgcumbe, a neighbouring landowner, about 1530. In north Devon, the famous Bideford bridge – twenty-four pointed arches in stone – replaced a timber bridge some time after 1460, and is still one of the most striking medieval bridges left in England.

Cornwall contains a number of interesting medieval bridges, though some of the best – such as Looe bridge (1411-36) – were destroyed in the nineteenth century. At Wadebridge in north Cornwall there had been for centuries a ford over the Camel, here widening towards the sea; but about 1468-70 a stone bridge was built (Plate 52), much like that at Bideford with which it is contemporary. Abingdon bridge, over the Thames, replaced an old ford in 1416, and considerably enhanced the importance of the town.

Not all the medieval bridges were on important roads or across noble rivers. One can find little medieval bridges tucked away in the upper reaches of English rivers, especially in the remoter counties like Cornwall. Such are Panters Bridge at Warleggan, which carried the old road from Bodmin to Liskeard, or Treverbyn bridge over the Fowey at St Neot, both perfect fifteenth-century bridges. But in the more sophisticated and busier parts of England these ancient little bridges, so full of charm if not of beauty, have been replaced by brick, iron, or concrete and one passes by with averted eyes.

New churches, new chapels, new bridges, new quays: the fifteenth century saw the sparkle or the golden warmth of new-cut stone almost everywhere up and down the

PLATE 53. *Tattershall Castle, Lincolnshire. Hardly a real castle this. It was built by Lord Ralph Cromwell, Treasurer of England between 1434-47, though only the great red brick keep and the moats survive. The numerous doors and windows indicate that defence, particularly in the new age of the cannon, was not its prime function. It was surely intended to be a comfortably appointed domestic dwelling for one of the most powerful men in England, yet impressive and dominating enough to demonstrate that power.*

country though less in the Midlands than elsewhere. And rich and powerful men were still building themselves castles. In Yorkshire, the lordly Scropes erected Bolton Castle in the last quarter of the fourteenth century, with its four massive angle-towers looking southwards across Wensleydale. Raby, in County Durham, is of the same period, the most perfect of the northern castles. The great castle of Berkeley, in Gloucestershire, was also remodelled in the fourteenth century.

> *Berk'ley's towers appear in martial pride,*
> *Menacing all round the champaign wide.*

With the revival of anarchy and private warfare in the fifteenth century, great men built themselves new castles, or, more strictly, fortified houses, of which the keep at Ashby de la Zouch in Leicestershire, built by William, Lord Hastings, about 1475-80, is one of the most remarkable. Not far way he built himself a fortified house of brick, within a moat, at Kirby Muxloe.

Many castles were built of brick in the fifteenth century. Tattershall in Lincolnshire (begun about 1434), and Herstmonceux in Sussex (about 1460) are perhaps the finest of these, and did much to spread the use of brick in English building. It was not indeed an entirely new material, for examples of thirteenth-century brickwork can be found in East Anglia, that of Little Wenham Hall in Suffolk (*c* 1260-80) being the best known. The building of Eton College called for two and a half million bricks between 1442 and 1452. Most of the early bricks were imported from Flanders, but those for Kirby Muxloe Castle (1480-84) were made on the spot and pointed the way to the builders of country houses in the succeeding generations. Brick was only employed where suitable building stone was difficult to obtain, and its use was restricted to large houses for a good while to come. Not until the end of the seventeenth century did it become a common building material for the houses of ordinary people.

Chapter 5
TUDOR TO GEORGIAN ENGLAND

Introduction

The period 1500-1800 was undoubtedly Professor Hoskins' favourite. In it he saw, probably correctly, the development of all that is aesthetically most pleasing in the English landscape. In particular the appearance of much of the best vernacular architecture, country houses and parks, which together make up so much of England's countryside, led him to regard these centuries as more civilised and more productive of pleasurable landscapes than any other. In essence he saw these years as a wonderful respite between the harsh realities of death, disease and a constant struggle with nature during medieval times, and the appearance of the dark satanic mills of the nineteenth-century industrialisation, and as a period when people had time to produce fine landscapes.

While one sympathises with Hoskins' feelings, this picture is not entirely a true one. For certain people, notably those towards the top of the social ladder, some times in these years were undoubtedly peaceful and conducive to developing the arts and civilised life in all its forms. There were certainly notable increases in the standard of living for many other people. Yet life also remained brutally harsh and often short for the great majority of the population. Infant mortality was still at a level of perhaps more than one in ten; and plagues, albeit on a lesser scale than the fourteenth century, still occurred. Disease of all kinds was endemic, for example malaria in the fenlands of Eastern England. The poor were probably worse treated at this time than earlier and repressive laws greatly restricted religious, political and even social freedom at all levels of society. In addition a violent civil war took place in the middle of the seventeenth century.

Even the making of much of the best of the English landscape took its toll of both earlier achievements and contemporary livelihoods. The great wealth that enabled so much to be carried out in the late sixteenth and seventeenth centuries was, at least in part, founded on the dissolution of the monasteries and the break-up of their estates. Not until the twentieth century was there ever such an orgy of destruction of exquisitely fine buildings as occurred in the mid-sixteenth century. Likewise, the evidence submitted to the 1607 Commission on Enclosures is but one indicator of the destruction of homes and livings perpetuated by ruthless landlords in their drive for wealth, while the creation of many of the glorious parks of this country in the eighteenth century was only achieved by the removal, usually without redress, of numerous villages, hamlets and farmsteads, or at least the annulment of the extensive rights of people living in the area. Such actions certainly produced much that still gives us pleasure and is perhaps of a much higher standard than anything our present 'democratic' society has produced, but it was largely carried out by an exercise of power which would be totally rejected by most people living today, and on a population which had little or no say in any matters.

At a more specific level, many architectural historians would perhaps now take issue with Professor Hoskins over the 'remarkable surge of rebuilding and new building' which he claimed took place in all but the northern counties between 1560 and 1640. Recent work is making it clear that the process was not as simple or as restricted in time as Hoskins believed. What we have, from the late fifteenth century onwards, is the physical evidence for the first time of a cyclical pattern of rebuilding that has continued unabated until the present day. Certainly the new prosperity of the sixteenth century helped to initiate the movement as new and enlarged classes of gentry and yeomen appeared and strove to show off their wealth and status in a permanent way. But the actual process was very complicated and took place at different times and in different areas as a result of regional economic and environmental factors and even local ownership and social conditions. The first identifiable rebuilding, for example, in Lin-

PLATE 54. *Warden Abbey, Bedfordshire, was a Cistercian house, founded in 1135 and dissolved in 1537. Nothing remains of the abbey buildings, though extensive fishponds and the dam of a great lake survive. This delightful building is a fragment of a house built about 1540 by the Goswick family who had taken over the abbey's estate. It is surrounded by the terraces and banks of a mid-sixteenth-century garden.*

colnshire seems to be rather later than that in Leicestershire. The apparent beginnings of the rebuilding may be seen to be in the late sixteenth century in one village and fifty years later in an adjacent one. The reasons for this are still not fully understood and in any case once the rebuilding was started, it was then not only repeated at various times as fashion changed and wealth varied, but it passed down the social scale to the owners of smaller buildings. Evidence of earlier building and rebuilding may be obscured or even totally destroyed by a later phase. Much more work is needed in this field before we can fully understand the development of smaller houses in England.

Professor Hoskins may also have underestimated the amount of agricultural change, especially enclosure, which seems to have taken place in the late sixteenth and seventeenth century. It is true that most of the Midland counties remained open-field country; but elsewhere, as noted in the text below, forests, parks, fens, moors, heaths and commons were all subjected to enclosure and there was, in certain areas, large-scale enclosure of the open fields. The actual amount of land enclosed is still difficult to quantify but certainly involved very large areas.

At the beginning of this chapter Professor Hoskins rightly emphasised the number of sheep in England in the sixteenth century. Because they were so important to the country's economy then, but thereafter relatively less so, it is often forgotten that the numbers of sheep continued to rise. Many still grazed in the traditional areas of East Anglia, on the new enclosure in the Midlands as well as on the upland moors. But there was a particularly remarkable increase in the number of sheep on the downs of Wessex from the early seventeenth century onwards. This was achieved by a little known or appreciated agricultural invention, floodable water-meadows. The system involved the diversion of water from rivers along high-level leats into small channels set into the tops of parallel ridges. The water flooded over the ridges, flowed along the intervening furrows and then either back to the river or, more usually, over many more ridges set lower downstream. This idea of 'floating' meadows was probably invented in Herefordshire in the late sixteenth century. It spread rapidly and was taken up particularly in Wessex. By the late eighteenth century almost

every major river valley in Hampshire, Dorset and Wiltshire was crammed with channels, dams, sluices and ridges. By running water over these meadows in the late winter, just at the time when downland growth was non-existent and winter fodder was in short supply, an early growth of grass was produced. This enabled far more sheep to be kept than would have been possible without water-meadows. Thus ironically the very large-scale downland sheep farming in southern England in the eighteenth and nineteenth centuries was only achieved by the winter flooding of the river valleys. Most of the water-meadows still survive, although almost all have now been abandoned. We can no longer see them as Thomas Hardy did in Dorset, as 'watered . . . like silver gridirons'.

TUDOR TO GEORGIAN ENGLAND

The Landscape in 1500

The most striking single aspect of the English landscape at the beginning of the sixteenth century was that there were about three sheep to every human being. There were only two and a half to three million people in the whole country, and possibly eight million sheep. After a thousand years of settlement and hard labour, England was still a colonial economy with too few people to civilise the whole landscape (or even that part of it capable of improvement), too few to develop the rich mineral resources, which were as yet hardly scratched, too few to develop any large-scale industry. 'The population of this island,' wrote an Italian visitor about the year 1500, 'does not appear to me to bear any proportion to her fertility and riches.' England was a green and quiet agricultural country in which miles of deep forest alternated with thousand-acre 'fields' of barley, beans, or wheat, or with variegated heaths and bleak moors, and little pasture closes.

At the end of the seventeenth century, Gregory King estimated that about a half of England and Wales was under cultivation as arable, pasture or meadow. He thought that there were three million acres of woods and coppices, and another three million acres of 'forests, parks and commons'. The woods and coppices were worth on an average nearly as much as the arable (5s. an acre as against 5s. 6d.), and the forests, parks and commons he valued at an average rent of 3s. 8d. an acre. Then there were, he reckoned, no fewer than ten million acres of 'heaths, moors, mountains and barren land', worth on an average one shilling an acre for sheep feed. Pasture and meadow were the most valuable, being worth generally 8s. 8d. an acre. These are all averages: there were wide variations between the good and bad lands of each type. But the figures serve to show in a rough and ready way the relationship between the different uses to which land was put in the 1680s, and the approximate extent of each category. It is possible that King over-estimated the amount of waste land; but we have no better figures than his either for the seventeenth century or the sixteenth.

At the beginning of the sixteenth century the extent of the woodlands was considerably greater than in Gregory King's day, for there had been immense destruction of timber in

PLATE 55. *The village of Wormleighton, Warwickshire, was cleared away for sheep by William Cope in 1498. In this remarkable photograph the former main street, now a grassy hollow-way, is visible, lined with the embanked and ditched closes of the peasant holdings. Top left is the site of the medieval moated manor house which was replaced by the Spencers' new house in the early sixteenth century. On the right is the ridge-and-furrow which marks the medieval open fields.*

As always, a landscape like this was not static. The large embanked former fishpond bottom left cuts through the village street and was thus presumably constructed after its desertion. The broad plough ridges within the pond result from a fish/arable rotational system of farming, whereby the pond was periodically drained, cultivated for a few years and then restocked with fish. This perhaps took place in the sixteenth or seventeenth centuries. At the top of the photograph the Oxford Canal, built in the 1770s, also cuts through the village remains.

the intervening period. Timber alone served the purposes of coal, steel and concrete today – as a fuel, as material for ship-building and house-building and for many other constructional purposes, and for an infinite variety of repair work. When we read that one Durham man alone was said in 1629 to have felled more than thirty thousand oaks in his lifetime, and reflect that similar destruction was going on in all the iron-working districts of England – in the Weald, the Forest of Dean, round Birmingham and Sheffield, and in the Clee Hills – we can envisage something of the extent of woodland lost between 1500 and 1688.

Nor were the iron-workers the only destroyers of the woods. The revolutionary improvements in farming in the sixteenth and seventeenth centuries led to large tracts of woodland being grubbed up for corn and cattle. In 1553 William Cholmeley spoke of 'the unsatiable desyre of pasture for sheep and cattel' which had resulted in much permanent destruction of woodland during the preceding thirty years. Blith, in *The English Improver*, a hundred years later, spoke of woodlands all over the West Midlands, and also in Derbyshire and Yorkshire, 'which now enclosed are grown as gallant cornfields as be in England'. The historian of Nottinghamshire (1641) had seen 'numberless numbers of goodly oaks' replaced during his lifetime by sheep and oxen 'grazing upon a Carpet Green'.*

If Gregory King's estimate for 1688 is about right, there must have been at least four million acres of woodland in England at the beginning of the sixteenth century, and all hardwoods at that. The forests of Epping and Arden, Sherwood, Dean and Wychwood, and a score of others famous in their own countryside, were a living reality. Smaller woods abounded all over England, though they were fewer in the Midlands than elsewhere. Few boys lived beyond easy walking distance of thick woodland, or of wild and spacious heaths, where they could work off freely the animal energies that in the twentieth century lead too many of them in the foul and joyless towns into the juvenile courts. There was plenty of scope for poachers of fish and game, and plenty of fresh air and space for everybody, and silence if they wanted it. No industrial smoke, nothing faster on the roads than a horse, no incessant noises from the sky: only three million people all told, spread thinly about the country. The largest provincial town (Norwich) could be described as 'either a City in an Orchard, or an Orchard in a City, so equally are Houses and Trees blended in it' – how infinitely more pleasant a place England then was for the majority of her people!

People took their own wild places for granted. There are no contemporary descriptions of the woods, the heaths and the moors as scenery. The taste for 'scenery' had yet to develop, and the few travellers who mention the wild places do so only in terms of distaste, for such country produced nothing useful and was inclined to be dangerous for strangers. Chaucer, however, makes a casual and pleasant reference, most unexpected in a medieval writer:

> *His dwelling was full fair upon an heath*
> *With green trees shadowed was his place,*

a description that Clare would have appreciated.

The most usual attitude to wild places was that of Defoe in the eighteenth century. His description of the crossing of Blackstone Edge, the high moorland between Rochdale and Halifax, even in the middle of August, has almost the scale and feeling of a crossing of the Andes today. After running into a blinding snow-storm 'near the top of the mountain', losing sight of all the tracks, and finding themselves on the edge of a 'frightful precipice', they began to talk seriously of returning to Rochdale: 'but just then one of our men called out to us, and said, he was upon

Many of the deer-parks created in the medieval period were abandoned or 'disparked' in the early seventeenth century and returned or turned over to arable land or used for grazing. They were often sub-divided into small fields and some have ridge-and-furrow within them which may be of this period. An example is the great royal park at Gillingham, Dorset, probably created in the early twelfth century as a hunting park for King John and covering some 760 acres. It was finally disparked in 1628 and broken up into fields.

The destruction of woodland in the early seventeenth century was extremely widespread and by no means confined to the Midlands and Yorkshire. For example vast areas were cleared in north Dorset and west Wiltshire at this time.

In addition to these 'wastes' there were also thousands of acres of fenland in eastern England which were even more hostile. Much of this country was only accessible by water.

* H. C. Darby, 'The Clearing of the English Woodlands', *Geography*, XXXVI, 1951.

the top of the hill, and could see over into Yorkshire. . .' There are, however, two more solid pages about mountains, precipices, wind and snow, and apprehensions of all kinds, before they struggle into Halifax.

As for the heaths, here is his description of Bagshot Heath in Surrey:

Here is a vast tract of land, some of it within seventeen or eighteen miles of the capital city; which is not only poor, but even quite steril, given up to barrenness, horrid and frightful to look on, not only good for little, but good for nothing; much of it is a sandy desert, and one may frequently be put in mind here of Arabia Deserta, where the winds raise the sands, so as to overwhelm whole caravans of travellers, cattle and people together; for in passing this heath in a windy day, I was so far in danger of smothering with the clouds of sand, which were raised by the storm, that I cou'd neither keep it out of my mouth, nose or eyes: and when the wind was over, the sand appear'd spread over the adjacent fields of the forest some miles distant, so as that it ruins the very soil. This sand indeed is check'd by the heath, or heather, which grows in it, and which is the common product of barren land, even in the very Highlands of Scotland; but the ground is otherwise so poor and barren, that the product of it feeds no creatures, but some very small sheep, who feed chiefly on the said heather, and but very few of these, nor are there any villages, worth mentioning, and but few houses or people for many miles far and wide; this desert lyes extended so much, that some say, there is not less than a hundred thousand acres of this barren land that lyes all together, reaching out every way in the three counties of Surrey, Hampshire and Berkshire; besides a great quantity of land, almost as bad as that between Godalming and Petersfield, on the road to Portsmouth, including some hills, call'd the Hind Head and others.

The heaths and commons often extended for a dozen miles or more, with hardly a habitation upon them, and only rough and narrow tracks crossing them, so that travellers feared the sudden onset of bad weather or the premature falling of darkness. There were more than a hundred thousand acres of wastes in Hampshire even at the end of the eighteenth century (excluding the Downs), and sixty thousand in Berkshire. As for the moors, three quarters of Westmorland was still uncultivated in 1793, and in Devon there were more than three hundred thousand acres wild and untamed.

On the other hand, some parts of England were highly cultivated and fruitful at the beginning of the sixteenth century. Leland observed how the aspect of the country changed for the better as soon as one crossed the Trent, coming away from the northern parts. All over the lowlands of central England the ancient and hedgeless open fields stretched to the horizon, but in the regions towards the west, and towards the east and south-east, the typical landscape was one of small, hedged fields, as we know them today, of scattered farmsteads, and winding lanes and paths joining farm to farm. In the south-east of England, Kent and Essex were probably wholly enclosed; so, too, were the eastern halves of Suffolk and Surrey. In the south-west, the open fields of Cornwall, Devon and Somerset were mere remnants of what they had once been. In Henry VIII's time, Leland observed that 'most part of all Somersetshire is in hedgerows enclosed'. What little open field remained was largely enclosed, as in Devon and Cornwall, during the sixteenth century. The counties along the Welsh border, too, were nearly all enclosed by Leland's time, extending well up into Lancashire; and considerable areas of the North Riding and of Northumberland were similarly devoid of open field.

In all these peripheral regions, a great deal of land had been enclosed into small hedged fields direct from the original woodland. There never had been open fields in these districts. But in all these counties, too, there had been open fields in some parts, around the Old English villages, and these also had been transformed into smaller, hedged fields like those reclaimed direct from the waste in later times. Why were counties like Kent, Essex and Devon enclosed so early? One reason may be that the existence of so much farmland cultivated in separate small enclosures, with all the evident advantages this had over the

Though usually termed 'wastes', these moors, downlands, fens, heaths and commons were very productive and important to the local economies. Most had common grazing rights and were extensively rather than intensively used as such. Almost as important were the rights, on the heaths and moorlands, to cut bracken for fodder and bedding, and in the fens to cut peat for fuel and rushes for roofing; and the abundant fish and wild fowl available for food. Almost everywhere there were rights to cut wood and scrub for fuel and building material. Many industrial processes, particularly mining, also took place on these wastes. For example, coal was dug on the Clee Hills in Shropshire, tin was 'streamed' on Dartmoor and lead was mined in Derbyshire.

communal management of the open arable fields, led the open-field farmers, persuaded by the evidence of their own eyes, to agree to the enclosure and rearrangement of their strips at a very early date – some centuries before the open-field farmers of central England were so persuaded. Another reason undoubtedly was the abundance of pasture in these counties. A shortage of pasture made a wholesale enclosure more difficult, if not impossible, because common rights and the right to pasture animals on the open-field stubbles were jealously safeguarded and preserved. No change in the *status quo* was likely to be agreed by the multitude of peasant-farmers in these circumstances. Where pasture was abundant, as in the *denes* of the Weald of Kent and Sussex, or in the woodlands of Essex and East Suffolk, or near the Devon and Cornish moors, there was no such obstacle to change, and the great change to small fields held in severalty was duly accomplished.

It is doubtful whether the counties of Kent, Essex and Devon, as well as elsewhere in parts of Suffolk, Surrey and the Welsh Marches, ever had many large open fields. Certainly, even by the thirteenth century, most land in such areas was already enclosed fields and probably always had been. Where strip or open fields did exist they were usually small and only part of an agricultural system which mainly comprised enclosed fields. The reasons for this preponderance of enclosure in these areas is still not clear. It may in part relate to the extensive areas of land which were always available for colonisation, especially in the Weald and in Devon, which enabled farmers to reclaim land on an individual basis. The fact that the early medieval pattern of dispersed settlement never developed into one of nucleated villages must also have had a considerable influence. More important, it is likely that many of these fields, especially in Devon and Cornwall, are prehistoric in origin and have never been abandoned.

Such open fields as had existed in these areas were at least partly enclosed in the fifteenth to seventeenth centuries, often as a result of increasing specialisation. This certainly seems to be true of Kent.

We do not know precisely how this important change in the landscape was accomplished, nor even when; though if the Devonshire evidence is typical it seems to have begun in the thirteenth century, and to have continued into the fourteenth and fifteenth.[*] By Elizabethan times there was very little open field left anywhere in Devon.

Sometimes it appears that single strips or perhaps pairs of strips were enclosed, by a hedge-bank, so giving a pattern as it were of 'fossilised open field' which is still preserved in some parishes. Sometimes, however, it is clear that a whole furlong or block of land was enclosed in a single piece of perhaps thirty or forty acres. Probably such comparatively large enclosures were separate parcels of the lord's demesne land, either always of that size and separateness or built up by purchases and exchange of other men's strips.

We can see the creation of this new kind of landscape clearly on the Tavistock Abbey estates in Devon:

It begins with a consolidation of holdings, brought about by purchase and exchange. Then a trench is dug to mark the limits of the holder's land, and the soil removed from it is thrown up into a mound on the inner side of the ditch. (A lease of Furze Close at Woodovis in 1465 specifies that the ditch shall be four feet wide and four feet deep; and the same dimensions are given at Leigh in 1398.) The mound is planted with a quickset hedge, and grows in course of time by the addition of soil thrown up whenever the ditch is cleared. No feature of the Devon landscape is more characteristic than these vast banks, crowned with oak, ash, hazel, or other coppice wood growing to a height of twenty feet or more and forming an impenetrable screen. Wasteful as they are of space and soil, they have the merit of permanence and they provide cattle with the shelter that is badly needed in so boisterous a climate. Marshall suggests that coppice fences may have been designed at first to make good the loss of fuel attendant upon forest clearance. He adds: 'Many farms have no other woodland, nor supply of fuel, than what their fences furnish; yet are amply supplied with this; besides, perhaps, an overplus of poles, cord wood, faggots, and the bark of oak, for sale.'[†]

Each of these enclosures was called locally a *park*, but the process of change did not end there. Areas of twenty to forty acres were generally found to be too large for good farming, especially in a pastoral region like Devon. They did not give the best control of grazing, and in upland and windy country they did not give adequate shelter for livestock. They were therefore reduced in size by making more hedge-banks. Two fields at Bowrish, near Tavistock, of twelve and twenty acres respectively, were each divided into three at some date after 1491, and remain as six fields to this day. Another enclosure of about thirty-two acres was divided into three after 1416; and it seems likely that subdivision may have been carried much farther than that until the original enclosures were reduced again to something hardly bigger than open-field parcels, difficult to distinguish on the map from the piecemeal enclosures taken in direct from the waste. The significant difference was probably

[*] See W. G. Hoskins and H. P. R. Finberg, *Devonshire Studies* (Jonathan Cape, 1952), especially pp. 277-8.

[†] H. P. R. Finberg, *Tavistock Abbey* (Cambridge University Press, 1951), p.50.

that the direct enclosures from woodland and moorland were irregular in shape, while those that resulted from the later subdivision of enclosed 'parks' usually had more or less straight hedges.

The creation of tiny fields could also result from the division of an estate among co-heirs. When Lord Dynham died in 1501, for example, the small manor of Wreyland near Lustleigh (Devon) was divided, like the rest of his lands, between his four sisters, and each farm on the manor was cut up into four parts. Later, one of these quarter shares was halved, so producing two eighth parts. 'Whenever a tenement was divided, each fraction had to be equipped with a fair share of every sort of land – garden, orchard, meadow, arable, pasture, wood and heath – so that it generally was formed of several patches of ground at some distance from each other.'* The result was a fantastically small set of fields – many of them only an acre or so in size, some as little as half an acre. All these hidden factors, so to speak, have gone to the making of the landscape in different parts of England. The facts of topography, soils and climate explain much, but beyond them lie purely historical facts like the laws of property and inheritance. The peculiar field patterns and other features of the Kent and Norfolk landscapes can probably only be explained in the last resort by the social and legal history that lie behind them; and they still await their interpreter. Here, as in Devon, we have, for the greater part, landscapes of dispersed farmsteads and hamlets, enclosed fields, winding lanes and large hedge-banks.

At the beginning of the sixteenth century, the towns were still relatively unimportant as features in the landscape. They were small, neat and contained. Even where suburbs extended outside the medieval walls, they were not large; and within the walls there was a great deal of open well-tree'd ground, large gardens and orchards. The city of Exeter, capital city of a large province, contained within its walls only ninety-three acres of ground, and of this fully one quarter, possibly as much as a third, was not built upon. Considerable suburbs lay outside the East Gate and the West Gate: possibly a fifth of the total population lived outside the walls. But one could have walked around the entire circuit of the city walls in half an hour, or could have reached the open country from the centre of the city in any direction in fifteen minutes. And this was equally true of such cities as Norwich, Bristol, York, Salisbury and Coventry, the largest in the provinces. Even London, with its sixty or seventy thousand people, was soon left behind if one had a mind to see green fields and natural heaths.

In Norfolk the open fields had been subjected to piecemeal enclosure throughout the medieval period and this process of enclosure increased markedly in the sixteenth and seventeenth centuries. It was largely due to the development of specialised agriculture in the area as a result first of the wool trade and industry, and then of the demand for corn and meat for the rising and relatively wealthy population that the wool trade encouraged. As a result enclosed farming developed here much more rapidly than in the Midland counties.

The Enclosure of the Midland Fields

The open-field system took its classic form, and had its deepest roots, in the Midlands. Here the great majority of villagers lived and worked within the frame of a two-field or a three-field system, though in a few places a somewhat greater number of fields were making their appearance by subdivision. But even in the Midlands the ancient landscape was not everywhere left untouched. We have already observed the creation of large arable or pastoral granges by the Cistercian houses in the twelfth and thirteenth centuries; and the decay and abandonment of villages, in the two subsequent centuries, to be replaced by large enclosed pastures for cattle and sheep. The earlier stages of this second movement were mainly the result of a passive decay of village life and arable husbandry, following a prolonged decline of population; but in the later stages it was actively assisted by the more progressive landlords who could not wait for Nature to complete her leisurely work.

At Wormleighton, in the deep country where Warwickshire and Northamptonshire

* Cecil Torr (ed.), *Wreyland Documents* (Cambridge University Press, 1910), XXV, p. 155.

meet, William Cope, Cofferer of the Household to Henry VII, evicted the occupiers of twelve farms and three cottages in the October of 1498. He enclosed 240 acres of arable with hedges and ditches, and converted the new fields to sheep and cattle pastures, displacing sixty persons all told. Sir Edward Raleigh, another landowner in the same parish, destroyed six other farms in the same way. Eight years later, Squire Cope sold the manor to John Spencer, a neighbouring squire, who soon afterwards began the building of 'a fair Manor House'. The house was completed and there he was keeping up a good estate 'with sixty Persons of his Family', when in 1517 he was arraigned before Wolsey's commission of inquiry into depopulating enclosures. Despite the fact that Cope had enclosed the manor several years before Spencer bought it, the latter was ordered to pull down the new hedges and restore the lands to tillage.

His petition against this order is an interesting document for the light it throws upon the changes in the local landscape consequent upon enclosure. He described what he had done for his adopted parish since he came:

First in building and maintaining of the church and bought all ornaments, as cross, books, cope, vestments, chalice, and censers, for all the church gear that was within the church at the time when husbandmen were there inhabited was not worth £6, for they had never service by note. For they were so poor and lived so poorly that they had no books to sing services on in the church. And where they never had but one priest, I have had and intend to have two or three. And also he hath builded and inhabited four houses. And men, women, and children dwelling in them. And so, what with his own house, and the other four houses, there is within twenty persons as much people as was in the town [village or township] before.

And where there is no wood nor timber growing within twelve or fourteen miles of the same lordship, the said John Spencer hath there set trees and sown acorns for timber and wood, and double ditched and set with all manner of wood both in the hedgerows, and also betwixt the hedges adjoining to the old hedges that William Cope made before in the said lordship, whereupon now groweth much wood which is already grown to the profit of all them that should dwell in the said lordship, as also in the country adjoining thereunto. For in those parts there is no wood, so that the poor men of the country are fain to burn the straw that their cattle should live by. Therefore it were a great loss to destroy these hedges, for it is a greater commodity than either corn or grass in these parts . . .

He hath no other pasture left him now in his country [i.e., his own part of Warwickshire] but the same. Which if [it] now should be put in tillage . . . it should be to his utter undoing, for his living is and hath been by the breed of cattle in his pastures, for he is neither buyer nor seller in common markets as other graziers be, but liveth by his own breed of the same pastures, and sold it when it was fat to the City of London, and other places yearly, as good cheap in all this five or six years past as he did in other years. . . He hath bred and fed within the said lordship, which was never good for corn, as the country will testify, more cattle this six years than was bred in the lordship when the town was inhabited in twenty years before, or shall be in twenty years after it shall be inhabited.

The petition was apparently of no avail, for three years later (1522) he was peremptorily ordered to restore all his lands at Wormleighton to tillage by Candlemas next (2 February), to destroy his hedges and ditches by the same date, and apparently to rebuild all the houses that had been destroyed by William Cope. An agitated second petition went up from Wormleighton to London, begging for more time, at least, in which to restore the *status quo*, with what result we do not know. Whatever happened the Spencers were not ruined by this ill-fortune; they acquired more land in the pastoral uplands of Northamptonshire and installed themselves at Althorp, whence they founded two noble families – the Earls Spencer of Althorp and the Spencer-Churchills, Dukes of Marlborough.

John Spencer's defence – apart from the fact that he himself had not committed the crime of depopulation – was a very reasonable one. The destruction of timber had gone on so recklessly for centuries in the Midlands, and there was so little room for replacing it in the open-field landscape, that he was performing a valuable service to the entire neighbourhood in planting so vigorously in the new hedgerows. And further, the replacement of tillage by grass was, in these heavy liassic claylands, a step forward in the long process of finding out what each type and quality of land was best suited for, of looking beyond the ancient pattern of mixed open-field husbandry to more profitable and varied ways of using land. By the end of the sixteenth century there was, if not a continuous belt of grassland on the liassic uplands of Northamptonshire and Leicestershire, at least something very near it, and tens of thousands of cattle and sheep grazed over what had been the arable lands of the medieval peasantry. And instead of a hundred peasants, the typical figure was that of John Isham. 'The astute merchant turned squire, perambulating his newly made enclosures at Lamport in 1586, lovingly counted his sheep and jotted down the totals in his account book. Piously he added, "God Bless them all".'

Where such landlords, lay or monastic, owned the whole or greater part of the manorial soil, the eviction of the open-field farmers was easy enough. At the end of the farming year, immediately after the corn-harvest, they were ordered to go; their farmsteads were demolished; and the multitudinous strips of the open fields were laid down to grass. The two or three arable fields were replaced by a number of large pastures, enclosed by a hawthorn hedge and a ditch.

It seems likely that the enclosed pastures so created were of great size. Indeed for all we know no new hedge may have been made at first; each of the original open fields may have been converted to pasture just as it lay. Thus the one thousand acres of pasture in the south Leicestershire manor of Pulteney were contained in 1547 in two great closes – Middle Field and High Field. The Middle Field in the depopulated parish of Knaptoft, not many miles away, contained no less than six hundred acres of pasture in 1525. At Whatborough, in east Leicestershire, the original enclosure made by Launde Priory in 1494 covered rather more than four hundred acres, but when the lordship was surveyed and mapped in 1586 this ranch-like pasture had been broken up by hedgerows into a number of smaller fields, though they were still large by modern standards. At Galby, in Leicestershire, a lease of 1640 shows two yeoman-graziers renting a pasture covering one hundred and twenty acres. One could find similar examples of vast pasture closes in all the Midland counties where the Tudor encloser had been at work. Defoe, in the reign of Anne, saw a single enclosed field of pasture in the Vale of Aylesbury that was let to a grazier for a rent of £1,400 a year. He does not state the acreage, but it must have been enormous.

These great pastures, undulating away almost to the horizon, were possibly the first exuberant experiment in large-scale sheep and cattle farming by men with little practical experience of a new kind of farming, and it was not long before the disadvantages of these enormous fields were revealed – lack of shelter in the Midland winters, especially on the uplands, and the impossibility of achieving close grazing over such a large unfenced area. As time went on, new hedges were made inside the original fences, and smaller fields created; but even then some of them were still large and betray themselves today by their size. In Knaptoft, for example, the Great Close still covers nearly eighty-eight acres. Many of these large fields were reduced during the late eighteenth century when graziers like Bakewell found by experience that enclosures as small as ten to twelve acres were the right size for the most economical grazing of pastures, but some hundred-acre fields remain to this day in the green uplands of central England.

Probably the largest enclosures were to be found where the landlord owned the entire parish and could do as he liked. But in many parishes there were other freeholders besides the squire, and however small they were their agreement was necessary before this kind of enclosure could be carried through. Their lands lay intermixed with the squire's in the open fields, and he could not move far without coming up against them; and they also possessed rights of common pasture over the entire open fields after harvest which he could not arbitrarily take away or in any way diminish. In such parishes, therefore, the squire was obliged to obtain their consent to enclosure and to offer them a tempting bargain. So we have, from Elizabethan times onwards, hundreds of examples of parishes being

The 'green uplands' of central England no longer exist. Most of the land is permanent arable as a result of the agricultural policies of the last twenty years. Nor do the small grazing fields remain. Modern cereal farmers require large prairie-type fields, similar to those of the earlier graziers. The wheel has turned full circle.

enclosed by agreement, and where the lesser freeholders had not been bought out before the change they received two or three enclosed fields as their share in lieu of the hundreds of strips they may have thrown into the pool for redistribution. Hence many fields of Tudor or Stuart origin are not of great size, for they represent the allotment to small freeholders. There is no mark that one knows of whereby hedges of this period can be distinguished on the ground. They are probably less massive than hedge-banks of medieval origin and possibly carry less great timber, and they are certainly more substantial than the rather flimsy hawthorn hedgerows that were planted as a result of the parliamentary enclosure movement of the eighteenth century. But our best evidence for their date lies in this instance in the written documents.

The enclosing activities of the Tudor squires generally diminished during the middle decades of the sixteenth century but the spread of enclosure by agreement among all the freeholders led to a renewed wave of change from the last quarter of the century, continuing down to the outbreak of the Civil War. After 1660 the government ceased to oppose enclosure by private landlords, as it had done ever since the early years of Henry VIII's reign. Its efforts had, it is true, been largely ineffectual, but down to 1640 they had acted as a brake on wholesale agrarian change. The new government of landlords at the Restoration was of a different mind, and all over open-field England parishes were transformed from a medieval to a modern landscape. In Durham, for instance, 'the common fields of townships were for the most part enclosed soon after the Restoration', according to Joseph Granger, who reported on the county to the Board of Agriculture in 1794. North-west Wiltshire – the great dairying country – was being enclosed about the same time, and in Leicestershire the movement was particularly active in the 1660s and succeeding decades. We hear more in contemporary sources about the iniquities of the Tudor enclosers, but it is likely that there are more miles of seventeenth-century hedges in the Midlands than sixteenth. It may be surprising to some who look upon the Midland landscape as the undoubted product of the parliamentary enclosure movement to know that even in Northamptonshire one half of the county had been enclosed and transformed to a modern landscape before the first private enclosure act; and in the adjacent county of Leicestershire three in every five fields had been created before the parliamentary period. English hedges are of all dates – Celtic, Saxon and Danish, medieval, Tudor, Stuart, Georgian, even Victorian in places. It is a complex pattern with a complicated history, and generalisations do not do it justice. All the pleasure and the truth lie in the details, as Stendhal remarked in another connexion.*

Total enclosure of the former large open fields in the seventeenth century was not confined to the Midland counties, Durham or Wiltshire. In Lincolnshire, for example, numerous parishes were enclosed in the early seventeenth century as new families, whose wealth was based on the acquisition of former monastic land, exploited their new and extensive estates.

Much 'waste' land was also enclosed in this period. Parts of the heaths of Dorset and Hampshire were reclaimed on a massive scale, as well as the lower slopes of the Pennine Hills. There was also a massive attack on the fenlands of eastern England and in the Somerset Levels. In 1602 Sir John Peyton embanked and drained 1,400 acres of fen at Littleport, Cambridgeshire. More impressive was the work of the Adventurers in the fenlands. Between 1631 and 1653 almost 100,000 acres of land were drained, although not entirely successfully. The fields resulting from this work still exist, often known as Adventurers' Land or Adventurers' Fen.

* Quoted by H. P. R. Finberg, *The Local Historian and his Theme* (University of Leicester, Department of English Local History, Occasional Paper no. 1, 1952), p. 5.

The specific instance of Collyweston well illustrates the complications of the alleged early seventeenth-century rebuilding in England. The village has now been studied in detail. Very few houses can be dated to the early seventeenth century and many more belong to the later seventeenth century. The majority, however, are of the eighteenth century, built in a traditional style that gives them an apparently early date.

The Flowering of Rural England

The total effect of the depopulating enclosures of the fifteenth and sixteenth centuries, devastating though they were in certain small districts, where three or four adjoining villages and hamlets might be wiped off the face of the landscape, must not be exaggerated. Thus in the small county of Leicestershire some sixty villages and hamlets disappeared, mainly between about 1450 and 1600 (earlier rather than later). This represents about one settlement in every six of the medieval total. A number of other villages and hamlets shrank considerably in size, like Cold Newton and Illston-on-the-Hill, and one finds them today as a little huddle of houses at the head of a 'main street' which passes through a field-gate and becomes a grassy track between the mounds of the lost farmsteads and cottages. What happened in Leicestershire is typical of nearly all the counties in the Lowland Zone of England. Many places vanished; others shrivelled in the economic blizzard; but most survived into the warm and expansive age of Elizabeth I and flowered forth as never before. All over England, except in the four most northerly counties, we find abundant visual evidence of a great age of rebuilding in the two generations between about 1570 and 1640. The wave of country house building, from Henry VIII's time onwards, is well enough known (and is touched upon later in this chapter); but what is less well known, though it is very evident when one's attention is drawn to it, is the remarkable surge of rebuilding and new building among all social classes except the poorest, in town and country alike.

In some parts of England the squires and franklins had been rebuilding their houses throughout the fifteenth century. Devon still contains some scores of houses of this type and period, now often disguised by the improvements of a later age; and one can find examples of fifteenth-century manor houses and farmsteads in other counties. But in 1550 most English people were still living in the rather dark, squalid and cramped dwellings of their medieval forefathers. These were generally two-roomed houses – a hall and bower – built of a timber frame with walls of reinforced mud, the whole raised upon a rubble foundation. There were no glazed windows, and only one fireplace. The two rooms were not

125

ceiled over, but were open to the rafters and the thatch of the roof. Few houses were built of stone, even in stone country.

By the 1560s and 1570s, the wealthier yeomen had begun to build themselves larger and better houses. Sometimes they added to and reconstructed the ancestral dwelling; often they made a clean sweep of the older house and rebuilt in free-stone where it was available. Before the end of the century the fashion for rebuilding had spread down to the lesser farmers – the husbandmen – and in some instances perhaps to the more prosperous cottagers. Cottages were generally built, however, by landlords and probably cheaply built, at any rate not a single sixteenth-century cottage appears to survive in England. What the estate agent calls 'an olde worlde cottage' – even if it is genuinely a sixteenth-century house – was originally a husbandman's farmhouse. There seem to be no true cottages left in England of an earlier date than the latter part of the seventeenth century; most are probably eighteenth-century in date.

The wave of rebuilding or enlargement of farmhouses, large and small, in the country-side grew in force down to the 1620s. It was so general that whole villages on and near the great Stone Belt, that crosses England diagonally from the Dorset to the Yorkshire coasts, seem to have been rebuilt about the same time. Collyweston in Northamptonshire is a good instance of this (Plate 56), but there are innumerable villages of which one could say the same.

Nor was the rebuilding confined to the villages: the yeoman-farmer in his isolated dwelling was similarly moved to acquire a better house. In the upland parishes of Lancashire and in the dales of Yorkshire we find sturdy, stone-built farmsteads with their mullioned windows, and frequently a date-stone over the lintel of the front door, standing four-square to the moorland blasts.

These northern farmsteads are often sheltered by sycamore trees, which were introduced into England towards the end of the sixteenth century. Gerard, in his *Herball* (1597), says that the sycamore is 'a stranger to England'. The common maple, which it closely resembles, is indigenous to Great Britain, and was well known to the Anglo-Saxons. A number of place-names from Yorkshire down to Dorset (for example, Mappleton and Mappowder) are derived from the presence of this tree. The sycamore, or great maple, is a bigger tree altogether, of quick growth, and with large leaves that afford a grateful shade. It withstands sea and mountain winds better than most timber trees, and was therefore widely planted in the upland and exposed parts of England as a windbreak for farmhouses. Its abundant shade in summer was a blessing to cattle in otherwise rather treeless landscapes. And so we get a very characteristic northern scene: the low-browed farmstead of moorland stone and stone-slated roof, with a clump of burnished sycamores on the windward side:

> *A stately sycamore,*
> *That spreads, in gentle pomp, its honied shade.*

One finds the same composition in the windy uplands of west Devon. Many people profess not to like the sycamore – it seeds itself too prolifically in the garden – but some of the poets have had an affection for it, as witness both Wordsworth and Matthew Arnold.

The villages of the Midlands, whether on the Stone Belt or the claylands, show thousands of houses built in these two generations. Here the elm and the ash are the characteristic trees, planted to give shade and to add beauty to the stone or brick walls. The 'black-and-white' timbered houses of the west Midland counties are almost all of this period between 1570 and 1640. Eastwards, in Leicestershire and Northamptonshire, much has been destroyed or swamped in the Victorian red brick of the industrial villages, but there is still plenty to see away from the hosiery and boot-and-shoe districts.

There is no need to elaborate the examples of this great rebuilding, which one finds all the way from Kent to Cornwall in the south, and over a good deal of the eastern counties.

PLATE 57. *St John's Hospital, Lichfield, Staffordshire, was probably founded about 1140 by Bishop Roger de Clinton who was also responsible for the creation of the planned town of Lichfield at about the same time. The hospital was refounded and rebuilt by Bishop Smyth in 1495 and most of the surviving buildings are of this date.*

PLATE 58. *The old grammar school at Market Harborough, founded in 1614 and endowed with £22 8s. a year, is a fine example of a local grammar school of the Elizabethan and Jacobean period, standing characteristically in the market place and beside the church.*

PLATE 59. *The school at Ewelme, Oxfordshire, founded in 1437, together with the contemporary almshouses and magnificent church, were all the gift of Alice, Countess of Suffolk, grand-daughter of Geoffrey Chaucer, and her husband William de la Pole.*

In these two generations or so, the rich variety of regional styles of building – the vernacular of the English countryside – established itself everywhere, based upon the abundant local materials that a peasant economy, a peasant culture indeed, knew how to use well and beautifully. If we are to study and record the variety of minor English building before it is too late, in both country and town, it is in these generations that we shall find our richest evidence, and to a lesser degree in the second rebuilding that flourished in the late seventeenth century and the early eighteenth.

This flowering of English peasant building in the countryside, and of minor buildings in the towns, was the product of two causes – money, and a desire for privacy and comfort. England was filling up with people, recovering vigorously from the long decline of late medieval times; the towns were growing quickly, London above all, and constituted a large food-market; industries were growing and needed in ever-increasing quantities such country products as leather and wool. Farmers had an assured market at prices that were rising rapidly from the 1540s onwards. Those who enjoyed security of tenure and relatively fixed rents and fines, whose labour was often supplied by the family, enjoyed more or less fixed costs and ever-rising selling prices. It was an age of profit-inflation for farmers as well as merchants and industrialists. There was far more money about – several contemporary writers like Harrison and Carew commented on this – and, as they do today in similar circumstances, farmers set about improving their houses.

The desire for some personal privacy, too, had percolated down from the lordly ones to the merchant and the yeoman and husbandman. This entailed more rooms devoted to particular purposes, and it led among other things to the introduction of a second floor in ordinary houses, reached by a staircase. Many a medieval house with its large, draughty hall, and other rooms open to the roof, was 'modernised' in the closing decades of the sixteenth century and the early years of the seventeenth. The old rooms were ceiled over about halfway up, so creating another floor above. More fireplaces were put in (Harrison speaks in 1577 of 'the multitude of chimneys lately erected'), and partitions inserted on each floor, producing possibly half a dozen or more smaller and warmer rooms in place of the two or three barn-like rooms that had served until then. More windows were inserted, and most of them were glazed for the first time. The glass industry had found a means of producing cheap glass, which was now made available to the middle class in town and country, and this meant that houses could be built with far more windows than before. Many old houses were modernised along these lines. In Devon it is common to find, upon internal inspection, a fifteenth-century house modernised and effectively disguised in this way about 1600. But far more houses were completely rebuilt, and these are a conspicuous feature of the oolitic limestone belt – the so-called 'Cotswold Stone', though it extends right down to Dorset and up into north Yorkshire. The two generations between about 1570 and 1640 gave to the English landscape some of its most photographed buildings. Many yeomen signalised their ascent in the social scale by building themselves new and beautiful houses, such as Richard Cooper, the successful yeoman who bought the manor of Warmington, on the borders of Warwickshire and Oxfordshire, in the year 1572, and rebuilt the manor house in the brown ironstone from Edge Hill. We find his son Henry described as 'gentleman': it was a common story in these prosperous generations.

The four northern counties underwent their great rebuilding during the eighteenth century. Possibly money was harder to come by in the wilder parts, or not so lightly spent. One notices in the Lake District how many of the old farmsteads were rebuilt from the 1690s onwards, about a hundred years later than in southern England. At the same time, a good deal of the rest of England underwent a second rebuilding or wave of new building. In the Midlands, for example, and perhaps in East Anglia too, the graziers were prosperous in the days of William and Mary and Anne, and built themselves many seemly houses in hand-made brick. Much of the very attractive village of Rockingham, in Northamptonshire, appears to have been rebuilt between 1660 and 1720.

PLATE 60. *The manor house at Warmington, Warwickshire, the home of a successful Elizabethan yeoman who bought the manor in 1572 and built this handsome house shortly afterwards. It is built of the warm brown ironstone found in the adjacent hills and roofed with the stone slates of the oolitic limestone akin to those of Collyweston, Northamptonshire.*

It was in this latter period of prosperity in the English countryside, when the philanthropic impulse perhaps reached its height also, that we get so many attractive schools and almshouses in villages and country towns. One thinks of Peter Blundell's noble benefaction at Tiverton as an example of educational philanthropy in the earlier period: the original school of 1604 still stands on the edge of the town. At Market Harborough stands the original little grammar school founded by Robert Smyth in 1614: the same Robert Smyth who made a fortune in Elizabethan London and left money in his will to the poor of all the parishes round about his native town in whose fields he had gleaned as a boy. In the later period, one thinks of the grammar school in the remote Northamptonshire village of Clipston, built in 1667 and externally still unchanged, or of the grammar school at Guilsborough, an impressive building of ironstone with a Collyweston slated roof (1688). At Blewbury, in Berkshire, a handsome brick-built school stands on the edge of the churchyard. It was built and founded as a charity school in 1709 by a merchant named William Malthus, and children have been taught there for over two hundred and sixty years.

It may not be entirely true that the philanthropic impulse reached its height in this period. There was much philanthropy in medieval times, even if it took different forms – the founding of monasteries, medieval guilds and schools – and little survives to be seen. Similarly there was much more later on in the nineteenth century with almshouses, more schools, hospitals and even housing, although most of the standing structures are not so aesthetically pleasing as the instances quoted by Hoskins.

The English village, in so far as it still remains untouched by the acid fingers of the twentieth century, with its farmsteads, cottages, school, almshouse, and perhaps a decent early chapel, is essentially the product of these two centuries between about 1570 and 1770. Before that time life had been hard and comfortless, with little or no margin to spare beyond the necessities of living: what little there was went to the adornment and beautification of the parish church. After that time we witness the break-up of the village community, the degradation of most of the rural population, and the flight into the towns. But for those two hundred years – seven human generations – rural England flowered. The exhausting labour of colonisation was over, except in small patches here and there. There were now enough people for an agricultural country at least, and there was time to rest and play. The narrow margin between a hard life and death from starvation, which had haunted so many generations from the dim Saxon times onwards, had widened with the bringing into cultivation of millions more acres of land. There was no longer the need to go out at the end of a hard day's farming to hack down more trees and clear more ground: it was all done, all that was worth doing: now there was time to contemplate, and to think beyond the mere utilities of life. The Stuart or the Georgian yeoman reached for a book in the evenings, rather than for the axe or mattock of his forebears.

PLATE 61. *Compton Wynyates, Warwickshire, has been described by Sir Nicholas Pevsner as the most perfect house of the early Tudor period in England. It was built by Sir William Compton and completed about 1520. Set around a courtyard with a great hall and originally enclosed by a moat, it is entirely medieval in layout. Yet it is a country house, not a castle. On the other hand it was largely unaffected by any Renaissance ideas which were to so dominate the appearance of later sixteenth-century houses.*

Country Houses and Parks

The country house, built for the pleasure of living, originates in the early sixteenth century. Before that time magnates had lived in castles, or fortified houses, or within a moat. Defence against enemies occupied much of a rich man's thought. Now, with a strong central government and judiciary, such men could relax from continual self-protection and build defenceless houses. Thornbury (Gloucestershire) was the last house to call itself a castle, built (but never finished) between 1511 and 1521; but 'the building was purely domestic and the castellated details were unaffectedly ornamental'.

Many country houses were built during Henry VIII's reign. Compton Wynyates (Plate 61), in a fold below the marlstone escarpment, was built on the site of the deserted village of Compton Superior. In 1510 Sir William Compton had licence to enclose two thousand acres of land, and two years later he began to make a park here. The house, one of the most attractive Tudor houses in England, was actually built of bricks brought from another deserted village – Fullbrook – where the Duke of Bedford, brother of Henry V, had created a park and destroyed the village and the church a hundred years earlier. It was the brick from his castle that was used at Compton Wynyates.

East Barsham in Norfolk was built between about 1500 and 1515, and Hengrave Hall in Suffolk about 1538. In Somerset, the medieval manor house of Lytes Cary was enlarged about 1530-33. It is impossible to catalogue all the substantial country houses built in these years: one finds them in every county of England, often disguised today by eighteenth-century enlargements and reconstructions.

Most of the country houses built before 1550 followed the traditional medieval plan, with its emphasis on the great hall, and were haphazard in disposition; but Hengrave Hall foreshadows the new Renaissance style. It is 'a stepping-stone from the medieval to the Elizabethan type'. It was in the second half of the century, and particularly in the last

PLATE 62. *Burghley House and Park, Northamptonshire. Burghley is an entirely Elizabethan house, built by one of the great officers of state – William Cecil, Lord High Treasurer. He began the reconstruction of a small house in 1556 and completed this palace – for such it is – in 1587. Most of the work falls into the period 1577-87. The park was landscaped, and the lake made by Capability Brown in the late eighteenth century.*

generation, that the country house made its fullest impact on the landscape. This was pre-eminently the age of great houses; some of them indeed were palaces, and the largest of them were built by the high officers of state under Elizabeth. Both Lord Burghley, the Lord High Treasurer, and Sir Christopher Hatton, the Lord Chancellor, said that they were building on this extravagant scale in order to accommodate the queen and her vast retinue; but there was a good deal of plain rivalry in these monstrous and really rather vulgar houses built by the new rich, often out of monastic spoils.

In the west, Longleat was completed by the Thynnes after a generation of building (1550-80) and Montacute (1580-1601) by Sir Edward Phelips, Queen's Serjeant and afterwards Master of the Rolls. In Northamptonshire, Cecil completed his palace of Burghley (Plate 62) in ten years of concentrated building (1577-87), and Hatton built on a still more tremendous scale at Holdenby. Holdenby, as a house, was even larger than the eighteenth-century palaces of Blenheim and Castle Howard: its fronts were 360 ft and 224 ft long, as against 320 ft and 220 ft at Blenheim, for example. Hardly anything remains of this vast house today – only two gateways in a field and part of one side of one quadrangle. Not far away, Hatton was also building at Kirby Hall, a house begun in 1570 and not completed until 1640, and now the most appealing ruin perhaps in all England. And in the same county Sir Thomas Tresham was building at Rushton and Lyveden. In Derbyshire, Elizabeth, Countess of Shrewsbury ('Bess of Hardwick'), began the building of Hardwick in 1576 and was still supervising the work when she died in 1607: and so it remains, a splendid example of the prosperity and vigour of the Elizabethan Age. Other great houses went up in the early years of the seventeenth century – Knole in Kent, Burton Agnes in Yorkshire, Audley End in Essex. Of the last house, completed in 1616, James I remarked, upon seeing

With few exceptions the country houses built after 1555 and before 1640 were largely planned in the medieval tradition. They still had great halls, with living quarters at one end and kitchen or service rooms at the other. It is true that the influence of the Renaissance was considerable but only in a limited way. There was an emphasis on decoration, often highly elaborate in style, and houses became more regular in appearance and symmetrical in elevation, but underneath the symmetry and highly fashionable detail, the traditional way of living remained. All the sixteenth- and seventeenth-century houses mentioned here are entirely medieval in arrangement despite their superficial appearance. Only Hardwick, with its use of second-floor state rooms, double pile plan and the hall reduced almost to a vestibule in function – all features not fully developed until a century later – is a radically new type of house.

Although little remains of Hatton's house at Holdenby, much of its contemporary setting still exists. This includes the greater part of the magnificent formal gardens, remarkably still preserved in later parkland. Ponds, terraces, a mount and even flower-beds are recognisable. The tiny village of Holdenby too was a creation of Hatton. He destroyed the existing village and rebuilt it to a new and very regular plan. Its rectangular green was intended to form part of the total garden and double courtyard layout around his house. It is perhaps the earliest 'estate' village in England.

it, that 'it was too much for a King, though it might do very well for a Lord Treasurer'. A good deal of this vast house was pulled down in the eighteenth century in order to make it more habitable.

A great number of smaller country houses were built between the sixteenth century and the nineteenth, and since this is not a study of architectural history but of the impact of the country house upon the landscape one need say little more about them. Palaces were built in the eighteenth century, such as Castle Howard and Blenheim, but the most characteristic scene in the countryside is the smaller Georgian mansion set in a park of modest proportions – a warmth of red brick, a flash of stucco, among luxuriant trees. In the eighteenth century 'the sites of new country houses were chosen for aesthetic, not merely for practical reasons. They were often placed on rising ground to "command the prospect". This was rendered possible by the increasing control of the wealthy over artificial supplies of water',* but Cowper complained that people were induced to build on exposed hill-tops and were swept by all the winds of heaven until trees had grown up to shelter them.

The building of country houses continued steadily down to the last quarter of the nineteenth century. Monstrous Gothic Revival piles arose, many of them the houses of successful industrialists and merchants. Many landowners, too, rebuilt their ancestral houses on the last wave of Victorian prosperity in farming. The very last country house to be built in

The house at Lyveden was never built. Hoskins is referring here to the curious lodge or New Bield. This was intended to be a banqueting hall or pavilion-summer-house at the far end of an immense formal garden, at the other end of which Tresham planned to erect a new house. The hall was incomplete and the gardens, whose canals and mounds still remain, were unfinished when Tresham died in 1602.

▷
PLATE 63. *Harlaxton Manor, Grantham, Lincolnshire. In 1830 George de Ligne Gregory, a Lincolnshire gentleman, employed Anthony Salvin to help him design and build the biggest country house in the county. The result is one of the most remarkable and best nineteenth-century houses in England.*

▷▷
PLATE 64. *Blenheim Palace, Oxfordshire, was designed and built by Sir John Vanbrugh for the Duke of Marlborough between 1705-25. No hint here of changes of mind or alterations. It was presented to the Duke by Queen Anne as a token of the nation's gratitude for his victory at Blenheim. It is thus a national monument and a symbol of power. It dominates the landscape, as its first owner dominated the armies of Europe. Not many English buildings do this.*

* G. M. Trevelyan, *English Social History* (Longmans, 1966), p. 403.

England – the last that will doubtless ever be built – was Castle Drogo, built by Lutyens in Devon between 1911 and 1930 for a wealthy grocer. It is a dramatic composition in granite rising sheer from the moorland, and it makes a fitting end to the four hundred years of country-house building in England.

More important than the houses themselves, so far as the landscape was concerned, were the parks with which their owners surrounded them. The word *park* originally meant no more than a tract of ground, usually woodland, enclosed for the protection of beasts of the chase. Many of the well-known parks around country houses today originated in this way. Overstone Park in Northamptonshire was originally enclosed in 1255, and we hear of Exton Park (then a wood) as far back as 1185. Ashridge, Hatfield and Knowsley parks are all first heard of in the thirteenth century. Woodstock Park (now Blenheim) is even more ancient: it was fenced around and separated from the surrounding forest of Wychwood, as a game preserve for the Anglo-Saxon kings, before the year 1000. Plot says it was created by King Alfred. The dense woodland within the enclosing fence or wall gave way to a more open scene, as grazing animals thinned out the trees and prevented their natural regeneration by consuming the seedlings. Many early parks were kept for deer; but in general, castles and other large houses were surrounded by a rather formless and uncouth landscape.

Parks have come and gone, commemorated only by a small name on a

Entirely new sites for country houses were rare. More often the smaller Georgian country houses were either on the sites of medieval manor houses and thus set within villages which had to be removed to create the fashionable parkland, or they were the development of similar earlier manor houses which were the only survivors of villages which had been removed centuries earlier by the late medieval sheep farmers. Hoskins gives examples of the former on page 134. The latter include Easton Neston in Northamptonshire and Castle Howard in Yorkshire.

From 1800 numerous architectural styles emerged for country houses. Not all were Gothic Revival and by no means all were monstrous. The early Gothic Revival style was relatively simple, admirably suited to the then fashionable romantic ideas. As the century advanced Elizabethan, Jacobean, Italian, French and even classical and oriental forms were entangled in house design, resulting in buildings which often only superficially resembled the source of their inspiration. Knebworth, Hertfordshire (1843-70), is a fine instance of medieval extravaganza, exactly as no medieval house ever was!

Just as interesting is the increase in size of the nineteenth-century country houses, as they were adapted to a new way of life for their owners which usually involved the provision of accommodation for armies of servants.

map. Flitteris Park, on the borders of Rutland and Leicestershire, was enclosed from the forest of Leighfield by Richard, Earl of Cornwall, in the year 1250. It is marked on Saxton's map (1577) but has long since been disparked and the name survives only in a lonely farm. Not many Northamptonshire parks are older than the time of Elizabeth I. Burghley, the largest park in the county, was created as a deer park by the Lord Treasurer after he succeeded to the estate, on his father's death, in 1552. By 1562 it was apparently completed, as we read in the state papers of that year of 'the deer brought to Burghley Park'.

Not a few parks in England today run to a thousand or fifteen hundred acres: Woburn in Bedfordshire is twelve miles around and contains 2,400 acres. Knowsley, the largest park in the north of England, covers 2,500 acres. In the middle of Nottinghamshire lie, or lay, a famous group of great parks – Welbeck (nearly 2,300 acres), Clumber, Thoresby and Rufford.

Such great parks are usually the result of a series of expansions from comparatively small beginnings. Apethorpe Park in Northamptonshire was enlarged in the time of James I after the king had been the guest there of Francis, Earl of Westmorland, and had found the deer-park neither large enough nor sufficiently stored with covert. James directed the earl to take in and impale another 314 acres. At Althorp and Deene, in the same county, the Spencers and Brudenells were constantly adding to their deer parks by purchases and exchanges of land in the late sixteenth and early seventeenth centuries. Many expanding parks began swallowing up good cornland in this period; there are frequent complaints about this development.

Parks grew yet more extensive during the eighteenth century, in the age of the territorial aristocracy. Building themselves magnificent houses, they needed (or thought they needed) more square miles of conspicuous waste to set them off. Not only village cornlands vanished inside the park walls: whole villages were destroyed and rebuilt elsewhere when they were found to stand in the way of a 'prospect' or some grand scheme of landscape design. Sir Gilbert Heathcote, who created the park at Normanton in Rutland about 1764, demolished the medieval church and village to do so. The village was rebuilt elsewhere, the church rebuilt in the park. At Burton Constable in Yorkshire the enlargement of the park involved the permanent destruction of the village. At Wimpole in Cambridgeshire the old village stood in the way of eighteenth-century improvements and was rebuilt as a model village outside the gates of the park. The first Earl Manvers built a model village of Gothic cottages at Budby near Thoresby Park in 1807, to replace the ancient village. Perhaps the best known example is that of Milton Abbas, the little Dorset market town which nestled for many centuries at the gates of the Benedictine monastery of Milton. The first Earl of Dorchester bought the entire site in 1752 and decided to build a great family mansion where the abbey ruins stood. The little town, now somewhat decayed, stood in the way and was demolished. In 1786-7 a model village was built on a new site nearly a mile away. Thatched cottages were built in pairs, each pair separated by a plot of ground on which stands a chestnut tree. The church and the almshouse were also rebuilt in the new village, but the grammar school was removed to Blandford.

Three names remain to be noticed as having influenced the form of the English landscape through the great landowners. The unremitting destruction of the woodlands ever since Saxon times had produced by the seventeenth century a timber famine. Large tracts of countryside, especially in the Midlands, had been denuded of timber as early as Henry VIII's time, as we have seen in John Spencer's petitions of 1519 and 1522. In 1664 John Evelyn, a Surrey landowner, published his *Sylva*, a plea for afforestation, in which he was able to assert that he had induced landowners to plant many millions of trees. In the eighteenth century, especially, landowners followed his principles of arboriculture; and it is to this

The story of Wimpole is now known to have been much more complicated than is suggested here. The original medieval village comprised five separate parts, spread out over a distance of a mile. In the early seventeenth century two parts were removed when the original medieval manor house near the church was rebuilt as a country house and a formal garden laid out around it. Two other groups of houses went in the early eighteenth century when the development of the great landscaped park was begun. The last part of the village disappeared during the eighteenth century as a result of estate re-organisation. The model village, called New Wimpole, was not in fact laid out until 1849, when the parkland finally reached its greatest extent.

PLATE 65. *New Houghton, Norfolk, stands at the gates to Houghton Hall. Old Houghton was removed in the early eighteenth century when the house and its park were being constructed. The new village not only housed estate workers but also provided a suitably impressive approach to the park.*

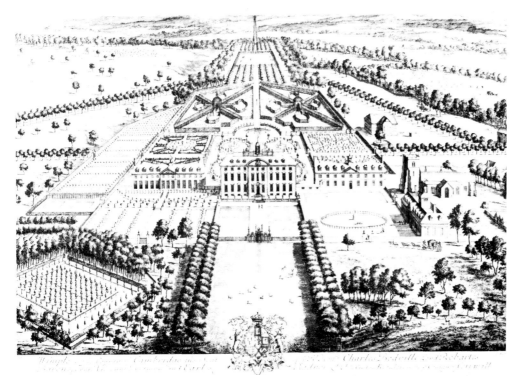

◁◁
PLATE 66. *Here at Wendons Ambo, in north-west Essex, the white plastered timber-framed houses seem superficially typical of the seventeenth-century great rebuilding. In fact these houses are of very different dates. The left-hand thatched cottage is indeed mid-seventeenth-century, the next is eighteenth-century, the tall jettied house is of the late sixteenth century and the right-hand cottage eighteenth-century again. They reflect continuous rebuilding and alteration rather than a single revolution in living.*

◁
PLATE 67. *Wimpole, in Cambridgeshire, as it was about 1709. Kip's drawing shows the house built by Sir Thomas Chicheley around 1640. The pavilions on either side of the house as well as the elaborately formal gardens probably date from the late seventeenth century and were commissioned by the then owner, the second Earl of Radnor.*

period that we owe a number of foreign trees that are now conspicuous in some favoured parts of the country. Many of the oaks planted under Evelyn's inspiration in the late seventeenth century came to maturity just in time for the great naval struggle with France a hundred or so years later and went to the building of the enlarged navy.

William Kent (1685-1748) is important as the real founder of landscape gardening, though his successor Lancelot Brown (1715-83) – generally known as Capability Brown – exerted a wider influence. Indeed, it is the pervasive influence of Kent, Brown and such later men as Repton upon the laying-out of parks for the country houses, that has helped to give rise to the wholly inadequate view that the English landscape is 'the man-made creation of the seventeenth and eighteenth centuries'.

Kent's view of landscape gardening was a reaction against the excessively formal gardens that had surrounded the seventeenth-century houses, a formality which was further emphasised through the introduction by William III from Holland of straight vistas of water, regular avenues of trees, and trim-clipped box edges, a style exemplified in the palace gardens of Kensington. Kent's gardens were irregular and romantic, 'with sudden changes of scene to ravish and surprise the beholders of temples, cascades, groves, and statues in unexpected corners'. One of the most perfect examples of the new style was the park at Stowe in Buckinghamshire, which Pitt helped to create. Rousham (in Oxfordshire) remains the only untouched example of Kent's handiwork in the country.

Capability Brown worked on a grand scale at Kew and at Blenheim. In 1764 he created at Blenheim (Plate 64) the most magnificent private lake in the country by damming the little river Glyme: 'there is nothing finer in Europe,' says Sacheverell Sitwell.

The establishment of these great landscape parks also led to the destruction of the often elaborate formal gardens laid out in the sixteenth and seventeenth centuries (Plate 67) which by the mid-eighteenth century were regarded as old-fashioned. The new parks were swept up to the very walls of the houses. Traces of the earlier gardens are sometimes visible within the park. The most remarkable are those created in a French style between 1686 and 1709 at Boughton, Northamptonshire by Ralph, First Duke of Montagu, former ambassador to the Court of Versailles. Great canals, basins, terraces and a huge 'mount' all still survive.

*The boundaries of parks have been
taken from the first edition of the
Ordnance Survey map (1833). The
principal changes since that date
have been the creation of Barton
Abbey park (which has been inserted
on the map), the enlargement of
Ditchley park (indicated by a broken
line), and the disparking of more
than a half of Heythrop (all to the
north-west of the line on the map).
Most of this district lies upon the oolitic limestone and has always been
favoured for large houses and estates.
To illustrate this point, the known
sites of Roman villas – most of which
were equivalent to our country
houses – have been added to the map
and are marked thus: + One uncertain villa site is marked with a query.
(For an even fuller picture of the
Romano-British concentration in
this district see Fig. 2). The parks
shown here cover a wide range of
date. Blenheim originated in the
tenth century (perhaps a little
earlier), Ditchley in 1605, Barton
Abbey about 1870.*

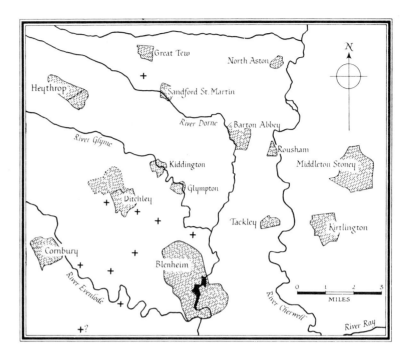

PLATE 68. *Levens Hall, Cumbria, is
typical of many English country
houses. It has been rebuilt and
altered many times. Basically it is a
medieval, semi-defensive manor
house, extensively remodelled
towards the end of the reign of
Elizabeth I. It was altered again a
century later and added to around
1800. The garden topiary dates from
about 1700.*

He manipulated square miles of landscape in the park, planting trees on a scale consonant
with the massive Vanbrugh house.

Brown also made the lake at Burghley about 1775, wiped out the formal gardens of the
earlier age, and 'landscaped' the park beyond them on a grand scale. A guide to Burghley
House, published in 1797, says:

*It was the genius of the late Launcelot Brown, which, brooding over the shapeless mass, educed
out of a seeming wilderness, all the order and delicious harmony which now prevail. Like the great
Captain of the Israelites, he led forth his troop of sturdy plants into a seemingly barren land; where
he displayed strange magic, and surprised them with miracle after miracle. Though the beauties,
with which we are here struck, are more peculiarly the rural beauties of Mr Brown, than those of
Dame Nature, she seems to wear them with so simple and unaffected a grace, that it is not even the
man of taste who can, at a superficial glance, discover the difference.*

Besides creating a lake nearly a mile long, Brown moved trees of the most enormous bulk
from place to place, to suit the prospect and landscape, set up a Gothic temple, made
shrubberies and new walks. There are no 'follies' at Burghley – none of the extravagances
that led William Kent to plant dead trees in Kensington Gardens for verisimilitude, or to
erect 'ruined' cottages for Earl Fortescue at Castle Hill in Devon, a folly which a more economically minded descendant reconditioned and made habitable for some of his tenants.
Sham ruins dating from this period give point to not a few hill-tops in England.

Parks continued to be made throughout the greater part of the nineteenth century, until
landowners began to feel the draught of the great agricultural depression of the 1880s.
One gets some idea of the number of parks of nineteenth-century origin by comparing the
first edition of the Ordnance Survey map with the contemporary map. It would be interesting to know when the last private park was made in England; the last grand gesture,
so to speak, of the landed aristocracy before the bell began to toll.

Chapter 6
PARLIAMENTARY ENCLOSURE AND THE LANDSCAPE

Introduction

Professor Hoskins, perhaps because of the years he lived and taught in the Midland counties, dwells at considerable length on the impact of parliamentary enclosure on the English landscape. Though he rightly acknowledges that large parts of the country were unaffected by this enclosure movement, his concentration on it gives us a somewhat unbalanced picture. This has had an unfortunate result. Because of the success of *The Making of the English Landscape* people who had no interest in the countryside have read the book and been inspired by it. But others have used the book and particularly this chapter as an authoritative statement that most hedges are modern and thus do not constitute a serious loss if they are removed to accommodate modern agricultural techniques. This totally misguided view which, of course, Professor Hoskins certainly did not put forward, has to be corrected and, at the same time, the somewhat unbalanced concentration on late enclosure rectified.

First, the enclosure movement, as Professor Hoskins describes, was indeed limited to a broad zone between Yorkshire and Dorset, and was primarily concerned with the removal of the traditional open or common fields and their replacement by the enclosed fields which cover almost the entire area today. Second, though before the enclosures of the eighteenth and nineteenth centuries the pattern of agriculture in this zone was basically a medieval one, it is also true to say that that in most of the rest of England was also medieval or even earlier in appearance. The enclosed fields which covered and still cover much of say Kent, Norfolk, Shropshire, Devon and Cornwall were equally medieval in origin and function or, as we have already seen, had their beginnings in perhaps prehistoric or Roman times. In such areas the landscape was as much medieval as in the open-field lands but it was very different and had a different pattern of settlement within it.

Third, and perhaps most important, both within the open-field lands and far beyond them, parliamentary enclosure and other forms of enclosure as well were involved with the final removal of much of the existing forests, heathland, moors, marshes and fens. It was in this period that they too were cleared, drained and divided into fields and new patterns of occupation were established within them. It is the totality of these new enclosures, beginning perhaps in the seven-

teenth century and increasing rapidly through the eighteenth and nineteenth centuries that, together with the industrial and urban development discussed in the following chapters, mark the last 250 years out as the latest revolution in the English landscape.

Yet, even so, these new enclosures need to be put in perspective. Over great parts of England enclosed fields had always existed, perhaps from prehistoric times. Elsewhere enclosed fields have been created by Saxons, and produced by medieval forest clearance, moorland reclamation and marshland drainage. The open fields themselves had always been subject to piecemeal enclosure, even as early as the fourteenth century. Individual peasants and lords could and did remove strips or groups of strips from the rotation sequence of their neighbours and fence them around. This was often done on a temporary basis at first, but usually the fences became permanent hedges or walls. Such early enclosed fields still remain, their characteristic feature being their elongated form and curved or reversed-S long sides, showing their origin as open-field strips.

In the fifteenth and sixteenth centuries enclosure of open fields was widespread in the Midland counties with the change to pastoral farming and the consequent desertion of settlements. In the seventeenth century there were considerable improvements in livestock management, land drainage techniques, crop rotation and, most important of all, convertible husbandry. Under the latter system arable land was put under grass for a long period after which it was returned to arable. Even where open fields remained, the methods of operation were radically changed to accommodate these new techniques, but the advantages of convertible husbandry were clearly greatest for those farmers with enclosed fields. As a result there was much new enclosure. In parts of Lincolnshire, for example, the early seventeenth century saw a massive attack on the former open fields.

Nevertheless, from the middle of the eighteenth century, the process of enclosure of the Midland open fields developed apace and in a relatively short time produced the landscape that Professor Hoskins describes so well. Equally important was the enclosure of the wastes by various methods. Professor Hoskins certainly mentions these, but perhaps fails to give them their true significance. What remained of woodland by the end of the medieval period was devoured at an ever increasing rate. The greatest demand on timber was for industry. The new or greatly expanded extractive industries needed pit props; iron smelting, at least until Abraham Darby discovered the use of coke in 1709, required charcoal; and other industries such as glass-making, tanning and salt-making all required timber for various reasons. The expansion of both the Royal Navy and the mercantile marine also entailed a heavy demand for timber. The result was a continuous attack on woodland that produced great concern and numerous investigations. Though much new woodland was planted, the overall result was a major reduction in the area under trees which continued into the nineteenth century. The landscape that this forest clearance created is often very similar to the better known areas of open-field enclosure with geometrically-shaped fields and new straight roads and lanes. Most of what remains of Needwood Forest in Staffordshire has such an appearance, as has Charnwood Forest in Leicestershire, the latter dating from 1829. In Oxfordshire much of the last blocks of Wychwood Forest were cleared and replaced by regular stone-walled fields in 1857-8. The bulk of this type of enclosure was carried out by formal acts of parliament, but there was much private enclosure, most of which is unrecorded and can only be dated by contemporary maps. At Glanvilles Wootton, in Dorset, there are nearly two hundred acres of neat rectangular fields in an area which was mapped as woodland in 1839 but as enclosed by 1847.

Even more extensive was the enclosure of the former common heaths and upland moors. In Yorkshire for example, the formal acts of parliament of the late eighteenth century were far more concerned with the enclosure of the upland pastures than with open-field land, most of which had been enclosed by agreement long before. As Dr Raistrick has pointed out, of 386 Enclosure Acts for the West Riding, less than twenty are for the enclosure of open fields only. Most are involved with large areas of moorland. Thus in the Dales, the Act for the Enclosure of Burnsall and Threshfield townships involved 1,690 acres of common pasture but only seventy acres of open-field land. At nearby Applewick only nine acres of open-field land remained to be enclosed by parliamentary act but 6,330 acres of upland moors were dealt with. In Shropshire too a similar picture has been revealed by Mr Rowley. Between 1845 and 1891 some twenty thousand acres of

upland commons of the old Clun Forest were enclosed by act of parliament. Former heathland too was broken up into fields on a huge scale, as Professor Hoskins rightly stresses. It is also true to say that most of the traditional chalk downlands were divided into fields in the century after 1750. In central Dorset, of the nearly fifty parishes with Acts of Enclosure, nine were for open-field arable alone, thirty include huge areas of downland and ten are solely concerned with downland.

It is worth noting that, though Professor Hoskins points to John Clare as almost the only rural poet to express his dislike at the destruction of his native heaths, William Barnes wrote in a very similar vein of Dorset. There he was concerned both with the removal of the grass-covered downlands and the break-up of the Dorset heaths:

> *Oh! no, Poll, no! Since they've a-took*
> *The Common in, our Lew wold nook*
> *Don't seem a-bit as used to look*
> *When we had runnen room;*
> *Girt banks do shut up ev'ry drong*
> *An' stratch wi' thorny backs along*
> *Where we did use to run among*
> *The vuzzen an' the broom.*

The marshlands too continued to be drained and enclosed. Chat Moss in south Lancashire was finally drained and divided into fields in 1833. In the Somerset Levels large areas of land were reclaimed and given straight-sided, drain-edged fields. Far more impressive was the reclamation of the eastern fenlands. Relatively little of the peat fens had been reclaimed in medieval times. Reclamation was begun on a large scale in the mid-seventeenth century by the so-called Adventurers who adventured their capital in an attempt to drain the fens. Over ninety-five thousand acres of land were improved by various methods, not always very successfully and the actual blocks of land involved are still recognisable by both their landscape and sometimes their name, Adventurers' Land. This early reclamation was followed by more extensive piecemeal reclamation and enclosure. From the late eighteenth century onwards, normal parliamentary Acts of Enclosure authorised the break-up of many thousands of acres of fenland. All the

141

PLATE 69. *Wicken Fen, Cambridgeshire. Almost the last surviving piece of 'natural' fenland. In fact it has been carefully managed for centuries and was indeed enclosed in the late seventeenth century. Left on its own it would quickly revert to a wilderness. The 'windmill' is a wind-driven machine for lifting water into high-level drains. It was built in 1907, though not on its present site.*

phases of reclamation are still visible today, together with traces of the complex methods of water removal which ranged from wind-driven scoop wheels, through steam engines and diesel pumps to the electric pumps of today. The present landscape of all the eastern fenlands, from Lincoln to Cambridge, is almost entirely the creation of the mid-seventeenth century and later.

These new enclosures also produced their new isolated farmsteads, set in the fields. All over England the enclosure of each area produced a local form of architecture and building materials for the farmhouses which date from this period. Professor Hoskins picked out the red-brick farmhouses of Leicestershire as perhaps his favourite. In Cambridgeshire, both on the former open-field areas and in the reclaimed fens almost identical farmhouses are made of a grey-white brick. In Yorkshire the houses of the period tend to be of stone rubble while in the former Wiltshire downlands they are more often than not made of cob, a mixture of chalk, straw and manure, or of flint rubble.

Although the enclosure movement in all these forms was the last great revolution in the English landscape, radically changing much of the countryside as it took place, it also gave us a landscape which is aesthetically much more pleasing to most people. Open-field farming, with few or no hedges must have produced a very bare landscape, totally lacking in visual interest which the great modern prairie farms of East Anglia have actually re-created in the last few decades. Much of the upland moors are given a scale and a softer appearance by the long fingers of eighteenth- and nineteenth-century stone walls which push up their valley sides. The enclosure movement gave us much of what is said to be the traditional English landscape.

PARLIAMENTARY ENCLOSURE
AND THE LANDSCAPE

Inclosure, thou'rt a curse upon the land,
And tasteless was the wretch who thy existence plann'd.
JOHN CLARE

At the beginning of the eighteenth century the rural landscape of England was still far from assuming its present likeness. Over large tracts of the country, especially in the west and the north, and to a considerable extent in the south-east also, the pattern of field and hedgerow, hamlet and farm, road and lane, had established itself pretty much as we know it. But over millions of acres between the Yorkshire and the Dorset coasts, the country scene was still largely medieval. Farming was carried on in open fields that had not changed basically since the thirteenth century, and beyond the arable fields and their meadows lay great tracts of common pasture, much of it covered with gorse and furze, rising in places to moorland and mountains.

Much of the detail contained in this chapter remains as true now as when it was written. The description of the landscape of parliamentary enclosure is perhaps one of the best that Professor Hoskins ever wrote.

The Extent of the Enclosure

It is impossible to say precisely how much of England still lay in open field in 1700 or thereabouts, but one can make a rough estimate. We know that enclosures by parliamentary act and award dealt with about 4,500,000 acres of open field, leaving aside for one moment the enclosure of the commons and other 'wastes'. Gregory King had estimated in 1688 that the arable land of England and Wales amounted to nine million acres in all. We shall not be far wrong then if we say that in 1700 about one half of the arable land was already enclosed in the kind of fields that we see today, and that about one half still lay in open field, a landscape which survives today only in patches of a few hundred acres at Braunton (north Devon), at Laxton (Nottinghamshire) and at Hazey and Epworth in the Isle of Axholme.

Gregory King also estimated that no fewer than ten million acres of England and Wales were still 'heaths, moors, mountains, and barren land', rather more than one quarter of the total area of the country as he reckoned it. In 1795 the newly formed Board of Agriculture put the 'wastes' at a little under eight million acres. It seems likely that both figures are too high. There are today some five million acres of common, waste and wild land in England and Wales. About two million acres of waste have been enclosed by act since 1700, so that we may reasonably assume that at the beginning of the eighteenth century there were about seven million acres of 'waste' all told rather than the ten million estimated by Gregory King.

The enclosure of open fields into the smaller fields that form our familiar world today, and the reclamation of the wild lands, had been going on intermittently and at a varying pace in every century. But after the Restoration the government ceased to interfere with the enclosure of open field by private landlords, and the pace of change quickened sharply. Up to about 1730 most of this enclosure was carried through by private agreements between the owners of the land in question. Very few enclosures were dealt with by act of

parliament. But under George II, and above all from the 1750s onwards, enclosure by private act of parliament, working through special commissioners in each of the affected parishes, was the great instrument of change. From then onwards the transformation of the English landscape, or of a considerable part of it, went on at a revolutionary pace.

This revolution affected nearly three thousand English parishes, as near as we can tell. In many, the enclosure award of Georgian days was only the final clearing-up of remnants of open field that survived after piecemeal enclosure had been going on for generations or even centuries. Here the revolution in the landscape was a mild one. But in the great majority of the parishes it was a complete transformation, from the immemorial landscape of the open fields, with their complex pattern of narrow strips, their winding green balks or cart-roads, their headlands and grassy footpaths, into the modern chequer-board pattern of small, squarish fields, enclosed by hedgerows of hawthorn, with new roads running more or less straight and wide across the parish in all directions. It was a triumph of planning in so short a time for so complicated a matter, most of it carried through in most places within a year or two years of the passing of the act. One cannot help reflecting what would happen nowadays in a problem of similar magnitude.

PLATE 70. *The landscape of parliamentary enclosure at Brauston, Leicestershire. The pattern of hedged fields, trees and copses produces a varied and deeply satisfying countryside. It was not so before enclosure when most of this land was open-field strips.*

145

It is true that the paper plans, as set out in the award made by the commissioners, did not produce all the physical changes at once, as we shall see in due course; but the transformation of the landscape was, all the same, remarkably swift. A villager who had played in the open fields as a boy, or watched the sheep in the common pastures, would have lived to see the modern landscape of his parish completed and matured, the roads all made, the hedgerow trees full grown, and new farmhouses built out in the fields where none had ever been before. Everything was different: hardly a landmark of the old parish would have remained. Perhaps here and there the old man would have found some evidences of the former world: the windmill of his younger days still standing in the corner of a new field, though now derelict and forlorn, or the traces of the former strips in the ridge-and-furrow of the new pastures, but not much else. This transformation of an ancient landscape into a modern one did not, however, affect the whole of England. In some regions the transformation had taken place much earlier, as in Kent, or Essex, or Devon, where it had taken a different form altogether, and most of the fields had been reclaimed direct from forest and moorland without passing through the open-field stage at all, or had been enclosed from open field at an early date.

We can indeed be fairly precise about the extent to which this parliamentary enclosure movement altered the English landscape. It affected the Midland counties most of all, and it is here more than anywhere that we find the planned landscape of Georgian times. Yet even here the actual extent to which the rural landscape was altered is considerably less than we might suppose. Of all counties the one most affected by the transformation of the open arable fields was Northamptonshire. Here just about half the total area was dealt with by parliamentary act and award. A block of counties adjoining it – Rutland to the north,

PLATE 71. *The landscape of parliamentary enclosure at Oare, on Exmoor, Somerset. Once part of the common grazing of the parish, this land was only finally enclosed in 1863.*

PLATE 72. *The Welland Valley, south Leicestershire. On the far side of the meadows of the River Welland are the regular fields of parliamentary enclosure. These date from the late eighteenth century.*

147

Huntingdonshire and Bedfordshire to the east, and Oxfordshire to the south, showed nearly as great a transformation. We ought to include also the northern half of Buckinghamshire in this belt of planned country, for though parliamentary enclosure affected only one acre in three in the county as a whole it was largely concentrated in the plain to the north of the Chilterns. On the eastern side of the county, indeed, where it lay along the Bedfordshire border, one acre in every two was dealt with by the Georgian planners. Roughly speaking, the parts of England most affected by this type of planning form a great belt which sweeps round from Flamborough Head on the Yorkshire coast, down through the Midlands as far as the Dorset coast, and thence north-eastwards along the chalk uplands to the Norfolk coast. Within this stretch of country, some two hundred miles at its greatest from north to south, and 120 miles or so at its widest from west to east, an average of three acres in every ten was dealt with by parliamentary enclosure. The large counties of Warwickshire, Gloucestershire and Wiltshire, which form a solid block to the west of this 'concentrated' area, show about one acre in four dealt with by the enclosure commissioners, rising on parts of the Wiltshire chalk to one in two. Berkshire is very similar in this respect to Wiltshire: on an average about one acre in four enclosed by private act, but rising on the chalk downs to more than one in two. There is, too, a marked contrast in landscape history between the west of the county and the east.

Outside this great tract of central England, the influence of parliamentary enclosure on the landscape dwindled rapidly in every direction. In the six northern counties of England, it had very little effect on the landscape, except in the East Riding of Yorkshire. Over large stretches of northern England not one acre in a hundred had been shaped by the Georgian planners. It is the same all down the Welsh border, from Cheshire down to the Severn, and thence across the Severn to the three south-western counties of Somerset, Devon and Cornwall. The landscapes of the Welsh border counties and of south-western England

△
PLATE 73. *The landscape of parliamentary enclosure on King's Sedgemoor, Somerset Levels. The large drain was cut following an Act of Enclosure in 1791. It created a twelve-mile long new course for the River Cary which then allowed the reclamation of the land alongside it.*

◁◁
PLATE 74. *The landscape of parliamentary enclosure at Exning, Suffolk. The overall pattern of the fields is the result of planning by the late eighteenth-century enclosure surveyors. The broad tree belts along the former hedges are late nineteenth-century additions to protect valuable race horses. Newmarket, the home of British racing, is only three miles away.*

have an entirely different history from those of the Midland Plain. In the south of England, Dorset, Hampshire and Surrey were affected to some extent – again much more in some parts than others – but the south-eastern corner of England owes little or nothing to the enclosure commissioners. Large tracts of country in this part of England, especially in Sussex, Kent and Essex, had anciently been thickly wooded and never brought within the open-field system. When the forest was cleared, mostly from the twelfth century onwards, the small fields were enclosed directly from the wild state. Both Essex and Kent are noted by John Hales in his *Discourse of the Common Weal* (1549) as mostly enclosed even in the middle of the sixteenth century.

East Anglia has a peculiar history also, so far as its landscape is concerned. In both Norfolk and Suffolk the eastern and western halves of the county are noticeably different. One sees this not only on the ground, travelling through these parts, but it is also brought out clearly on the Ordnance map. Even if one had never visited this part of England, the map would suggest that there are fundamental differences in the way in which the landscapes of the two halves of the counties have evolved. This is particularly striking in Norfolk. In the east and centre of the county we find a close network of narrow, winding lanes, wandering from hamlet to hamlet and farm to farm, churches standing alone, isolated houses dotted all over the map, many of them called Hall or Old Hall – significant names. It is a closely-packed map with hardly a straight line or an empty space in it. The west of the county is entirely different, even to the casual glance of a motorist: far fewer lanes and by-ways, more villages, the whole landscape or map more 'open' altogether. To put it broadly – ignoring all the smaller points of detail – one landscape has grown up piecemeal over centuries, the other is almost entirely planned on a large scale.

As a result of recent work by Dr T. Williamson, it now seems likely that much of the existing field pattern in central Norfolk is Roman or earlier. Large areas of basically rectangular fields around which the narrow lanes wind are cut obliquely by Roman roads.

Much of the south-western part of Norfolk is covered by sandy soils, the Breckland. Most of this was heathland until the eighteenth and nineteenth centuries when it was largely enclosed.

William Marshall, the best of the agricultural writers of his time, describes the landscape of east Norfolk as it was in 1787 in his *Rural Economy of Norfolk*.

The roads, notwithstanding King Charles was pleased to say the county of Norfolk was only fit to be cut into roads for the rest of his kingdom, are unpardonably bad; narrow, shaded, and never mended; they are numerous, however, especially the bridle-roads; so that a traveller, on horseback, has generally the choice of two or three ways, of nearly equal length, to the same place. . . The inclosures are, in general, small, and the hedges high, and full of trees. This has a singular effect in travelling through the country: the eye seems ever on the verge of a forest, which is, as it were by enchantment, continually changing into inclosures and hedgerows.

This is a typical landscape of ancient enclosure, as Marshall rightly observes, of fields taken in direct from woodland and waste in medieval times, such as we find in Devon, Sussex and the other peripheral counties of England.

The Date of Parliamentary Enclosure

Before we see how the enclosure commissioners replanned the landscape of central England, and how we can identify their work today, it is necessary to say something briefly about the dating of the parliamentary enclosure movement as a whole. Practically the whole of this vast transformation was effected between 1750 and 1850, and, so far as the open fields alone were concerned, in the sixty years of George III's reign. There were only eight private acts for enclosure in the whole of England before 1714, eighteen under George I (1714-27), and 229 under George II (1727-60), most of these in the latter part of his reign.* The total area dealt with before 1760 could hardly have exceeded 400,000 acres, a negligible amount when one thinks of England as a whole – only just over one per cent. In the next forty years no fewer than 1,479 enclosure acts were passed, dealing with nearly 2½ million acres. Altogether, between 1761 and 1844, there were more than 2,500 acts, dealing with rather more than four million acres of open fields. After the General Inclosure Act of 1845, there were another 164 awards which cleared up nearly 200,000 more of the remaining open field.

Besides the open arable fields, there were the extensive 'wastes' of various kinds. These were mostly dealt with from 1800 onwards as the high prices of the war years brought more and more marginal land into cultivation. More than five hundred acts had already enclosed three quarters of a million acres of 'waste' between 1760 and 1801. During the nineteenth century, another thirteen hundred acts and awards brought, or attempted to bring, another one and a quarter million acres of heath and moor and commons under cultivation. Some at least of this reclamation of the 'waste' by enclosure was a failure, for it was applied indiscriminately to good land and bad. Much of the extensive heath country of Lincolnshire was successfully enclosed and converted into good arable land, but between Sleaford and Lincoln, Arthur Young saw, in the 1790s, 'hundreds of acres in the veriest state of waste I ever saw land, whether appropriated or unappropriated, in this kingdom. Half a dozen wild rabbits were all the stock I observed upon them with scarcely a blade or leaf of herbage to keep even these alive; doubtless through the folly or madness of the first occupiers (after appropriation) in converting them to arable farms instead of sheep walks and rabbit warrens'.†

The New Landscape

The parliamentary enclosure movement had its most pronounced effects in the Midlands and in eastern England, in a solid block of sixteen counties. The Record Offices of these counties possess a considerable number of awards made by the commissioners, often accompanied by a map showing the new lay-out of the parish, with the fields and roads marked out pretty much as we know them today.§ Here and there minor changes in field boundaries may have been made during the past 150 or 200 years, but on the whole the enclosure map lays down the present-day pattern exactly. In the same Record Offices there may exist – but in much smaller numbers – even more interesting maps which show the lay-out of the village and its open fields, with every strip separately shown, and all the other features of the fields, as they were on the eve of the enclosure. It is a completely medieval picture. Superimposed on this map of things as they were, one sometimes finds the lines drawn in by the commissioners showing where they propose to create the new fields and hedges, and the new roads, public and private. One sees on such maps the new landscape actually in course of being planned, and can see how completely it was drawn afresh, regardless of almost everything that had gone before. Such maps are rare. The Leicestershire Record Office possesses only two, for the parishes of Stathern (1792) and South Croxton and Barsby (1798). The Lincoln Record Office does not possess a single map of this kind, in an otherwise rich and varied collection of records.

Sadly it is no longer true that the present day pattern of fields is much the same as that shown on enclosure maps. Thousands of miles of Midland and East Anglian hedges have been ripped out in the last thirty years or so to accommodate the new agricultural demands and techniques. In many cases enclosure maps, later Ordnance Survey maps and air photographs taken before 1950, are now the only record of a relatively short-lived type of the English landscape.

* W. E. Tate, *Handlist of Sussex Inclosure Acts and Awards* (Lewes: Chichester, 1950), p. 8. The earliest acts were for the parish of Radipole in Dorset in 1602, and for Marden in Herefordshire in 1606.
p.151
† Quoted in W. H. R. Curtler, *The Enclosure and Redistribution of our Land* (Oxford: Clarendon Press, 1920). pp. 188-9.
§ A map always accompanied the award originally, but in a considerable number of instances it has since been lost. Thus, the Leicestershire County Record Office possesses official copies of 102 awards, but only twenty maps, a fairly typical state of affairs.

By far the most conspicuous element in the new landscape were the small, hedged fields – small, that is, by comparison with the vast open fields that had preceded them, which usually ran to several hundred acres unbroken by a single hedge. As far as possible the enclosure commissioners formed square or squarish fields. Where we find long narrow fields they are nearly always adjacent to the village, lying behind or beside the 'ancient homesteads', as they are called in the awards. These represent in most instances the crofts or separate paddocks of half an acre to an acre in size which have been hedged around since medieval times.

The new enclosures varied in size according to the size of the farms. On small farms, of which there were great numbers in the Midlands and East Anglia – the holdings of the free peasantry, as we have seen – the new fields were usually five to ten acres in size. On large farms they ran up to fifty or sixty acres.* But in grazing country these larger fields were soon reduced to a number of smaller fields of round about ten acres apiece. Robert Bakewell (1725-95), experimenting with sheep and cattle-breeding on his farm in north Leicestershire, was convinced that 'fifty acres of pasture ground divided into five enclosures will go as far in grazing cattle as sixty acres all in one piece' and his opinion was shared by other big graziers. Each ten-acre field in turn was grazed bare – 'till you could whip a mouse across it' – and the cattle moved round from one field to another so that they were always eating fresh, springing grass.†

Not only were the new enclosures reduced to smaller fields for grazing purposes, but so were some, at least, of the older enclosures made generations or centuries earlier. Thus we find a much more uniform field-pattern, uniform as regards both size and shape, than we might have expected in the grazing counties of central England. Wherever the enclosure of the open arable fields resulted in conversion to pasture we find this regular field-pattern of straight hedges and squarish fields of roughly the same size. We must not overstress this uniformity, for even in the Midlands there are considerable variations, but compared with the variety of landscape elsewhere in England, the Midland pattern is markedly monotonous.

Perhaps 'monotonous' is unfair. The rolling Midland landscape, even despite the amount of modern hedge-row removal, still has much to offer in visual terms. The most important aspect of it are the trees that still line the hedgerows even after the depredations of Dutch elm disease. The profusion of trees in the field-sides of Midland England, especially when viewed from afar and from a vantage point, gives it a well-wooded appearance far in excess of what is actually there.

The conversion of the former arable fields to small enclosed fields of pasture had therefore two visible effects on the landscape. It tended to produce this monotonous field pattern, and it also produced 'a continuous sheet of greensward', as William Marshall observed of Leicestershire in 1790, instead of the multi-coloured patchwork of the old arable strips. These changes were particularly noticeable in the contiguous counties of Leicestershire, Northamptonshire, Warwickshire, Bedfordshire and Buckinghamshire, and to a lesser extent in the counties that marched with them. They were most marked on the heavy clays that overlie most of the Midlands, which produced good pastures. Where the clays gave way to the lighter soils of the Stone Belt, considerable areas of mixed farming remained. Parts of Northamptonshire did not, for this reason, go as uniformly green as Leicestershire after enclosure.

Elsewhere in England, enclosure – especially of the heaths and common pastures – had the opposite effect. This was particularly true of the vast heathlands of western Norfolk and of Lincolnshire. According to Arthur Young 'half the county of Norfolk within the memory of man yielded nothing but sheep feed', but by the end of the century was covered with fine barley, rye and wheat. Even in east Norfolk there were localised patches of sandy heaths and commons, as at Felbrigg, a little inland from Cromer. Here, in 1781, there were eight hundred acres of heath and common out of 1,467 acres in the parish as a whole. The squire owned the entire parish, except one small farm, which he proceeded to buy on liberal terms from the yeoman who owned it. Having obtained this, he set to work

PLATE 75. *These high moorland stone-walled fields near Malham, West Yorkshire, were laid out in the eighteenth century. They are not all of the same date. Initially very large fields appeared and these were later often subdivided into smaller paddocks.*

* Curtler, op. cit., p. 64, citing the *Board of Agriculture Report*, 1808, p. 81.
† C. D. B. Ellis, *Leicestershire and the Quorn Hunt* (Leicester: Edgar Backus, 1951), p. 26.

to enclose the parish and to rearrange its landscape. The least fertile part of the heath was left as a common for the poor to collect firing from. The remainder, together with the open arable field, he divided into small squarish fields of eight to twelve acres each (sometimes more or less according to the convenience of the farmers) and parcelled out as farms among his tenants. He then laid out public roads for the convenience of the parish, and private roads and driftways for the individual occupiers, and so completed the transformation of the entire parish except his own park. Marshall, who gives these facts in his *Rural Economy of Norfolk*, supposes that three hundred acres of heathland were divided into thirty fields of ten acres each. Each field, he reckons, would require about seven hundred yards of quickset hedges, so giving a total of some twelve miles of hedgerow even on this comparatively small area of land. This was the visual transformation that enclosure brought about. In place of a sandy, open heath, supporting a rough pasture, there would be a dozen miles of flowering hawthorn in time, enclosing small fields that were being assiduously marled to produce corn crops.

The greatest transformation of heathland into corn fields was to be found on the estates of the famous Coke of Holkham, in the north of Norfolk. In the course of a long lifetime (1752-1842) he changed the entire face of this part of the country, through his own efforts and those of his imitators. When he began farming on his own account in 1778 he found an open and almost barren country, much of it worth only five shillings an acre. Chiefly by digging the underlying marl and spreading it over the sandy top-soil he converted it into rich cornlands and raised the value of his Holkham estate from £5,000 to £20,000 a year within fifteen years.* 'Half a century ago', wrote Arthur Young in 1804, 'Norfolk might be termed a rabbit and rye country. In its northern part wheat was almost unknown, in the whole tract lying between Holkham and Lynn not an ear was to be seen, and it was scarcely believed that an ear could be made to grow. Now the most abundant crops of wheat and barley cover the entire district.' But even at the end of the eighteenth century there were still in Norfolk about eighty thousand acres of unimproved common, and some sixty thousand acres of warrens and sheep walks, most of which had been enclosed and converted to arable fields or woodlands by the middle of the nineteenth.

Hardly a county in England did not possess extensive heathlands. Much of them are unreclaimed to this day, as in Dorset, Hampshire and Surrey. But more than two million acres of 'waste' were successfully enclosed, divided into fields, and brought under cultivation by act of parliament, mostly during the course of the nineteenth century. All this is a matter of statistics and arid generalities: but what the transformation of these local heaths meant to those who had grown up near them and upon them, what the change meant in *detail*, is revealed to us in the poetry of John Clare, who was born in 1793 on the edge of the heath country of northern Northamptonshire.

Clare was set to watch sheep and geese on Helpston heath as a child of seven, and spent years of his childhood, and of his later life, wandering over the heath and through the

---

* Kent, *General View of the Agriculture of Norfolk*, 1794, says that the Holkham rental was 'upwards of £20,000 a year. . . and is still increasing like a snowball'.

PLATE 76. *Though the massive reclamation of the eastern Fenlands began in the seventeenth century it was not entirely successful. The land, particularly where it was peat-covered, sank as the water was removed and thus drainage involved lifting water out of the fields into high-level drains and rivers. This was first achieved by crude wind-driven scoop wheels, similar to windmills. From the 1820s huge steam engines were built which did the work much more effectively. This engine house at Stretham, near Ely, Cambridgeshire, was built in 1830 and is typical of nineteenth-century pumping complexes. The low right-hand block held the boilers, the tall central structure the beam engine and the narrow left-hand building a gigantic wheel with slats that scooped the water into the river. The tiny shed to the left again houses a diesel engine, the more efficient successor to steam.*

patches of woodland that survived in the parish. It was a small world of heath and wood, a few hundred acres at the most, but it was a separate world as Clare describes it, for example, in *The Village Minstrel*:

> *Swamps of wild rush-beds and sloughs' squashy traces,*
> *Grounds of rough fallows with thistle and weed,*
> *Flats and low vallies of kingcups and daisies,*
> *Sweetest of subjects are ye for my reed:*
> *Ye commons left free in the rude rags of nature,*
> *Ye brown heaths beclothed in furze as ye be,*
> *My wild eye in rapture adores every feature,*
> *Ye are dear as this heart in my bosom to me.*
>
> *O native endearments! I would not forsake ye,*
> *I would not forsake you for sweetest of scenes:*
> *For sweetest of gardens that nature could make me*
> *I would not forsake ye, dear valleys and greens:*
> *Tho' Nature ne'er dropped ye a cloud-resting mountain,*
> *Nor waterfalls tumble their music so free,*
> *Had Nature denied ye a bush, tree, or fountain,*
> *Ye still had been loved as an Eden by me.*

In Clare's brief *Journal*, too, are entries that reveal the detail of the heath landscape. On Wednesday 29 September 1824 he

> *Took a walk in the fields saw an old wood stile taken away from a favourite spot which it had occupied all my life the posts were overgrown with Ivy & it seemed so akin to nature & the spot where it stood as tho it had taken it on lease for an undisturbed existance it hurt me to see it was gone for my affections claims a friendship with such things but nothing is lasting in this world last year Langley Bush was destroyd an old whitethorn that had stood for more than a century full of fame the gipsies shepherds & Herdmen all had their tales of its history & it will be long ere its memory is forgotten.*

Crabbe, in *The Village*, describes the heathland also, in a few savage lines. Doubtless they describe the hard life of the villager and the poverty of his surroundings as Crabbe saw them: but he was not a peasant, as Clare was, and he saw them from the outside as harsh, ugly and wretched. Clare's view of the heathland is the truer one, for it is the peasant's view from the inside, born in it and part of it. Though he never idealised it or pretended it was anything but 'the rude rags of nature', he saw things in it to which Crabbe was completely blind or hostile, and he felt their loss when change and 'improvement' came:

> *Ye injur'd fields, ye once were gay,*
> *When Nature's hand displayed*
> *Long waving rows of willows grey*
> *And clumps of hawthorn shade;*
> *But now, alas! your hawthorn bowers*
> *All desolate we see!*
>
> *The spoiler's axe their shade devours,*
> *And cuts down every tree.*
> *Not trees alone have owned their force,*
> *Whole woods beneath them bowed,*
> *They turned the winding rivulet's course,*
> *And all thy pastures plough'd.*

Clare is the only poet to describe the ragged, solitary heaths of England, though there is also Hardy's famous prose description of Egdon heath in Dorset. But what is even more remarkable is the entire absence of any poetry associated with the open fields, any lament in literature for their passing. There is indeed plenty in print about them, but it is economic, argumentative stuff, mostly condemnatory and lacking in any understanding of what this old world meant to the peasant, and of what he lost by its passing. Perhaps it is not remarkable, after all, that no poet should have described this world to us before it expired, described it in language that would bring home to us what kind of world it actually was and how its inhabitants looked upon it, for it was above all a peasant world and the peasant was inarticulate. Clare was the great exception, an articulate peasant, and he might have described that world for us in all its natural beauty and its deep associations for the human race – twelve or thirteen centuries of unbroken continuity – but he came almost too late for this kind of England. By the time he began writing, about the time of Waterloo, the open fields had nearly disappeared. In his own parish the changes had been begun immediately after the passing of the act in 1809,* while Clare was still a mooning youth. It is true that there were still considerable patches of open field left in some parts of the country: at Castor, which adjoined Helpston on the south, the fields remained open until 1898: but the Helpston fields had all been enclosed by 1820. One must have been born and have worked all one's life in such a landscape to understand its secret life, to be able to feel its poetry, and to express it. The English peasantry threw up only one John Clare, and he was born too late to experience this ancient world to the full. He saw only its remnants in the unenclosed heaths. The result is that we know nothing about it except its external face, how its economy worked, and that has mostly been described by unsympathetic observers. Of what it felt like to live in such a world we are, and must for ever remain, entirely ignorant.

One should not be too overwhelmed by the possible beauties of the unenclosed heath and marshland. It was also the setting for a way of life harsh in all its details, and often uncomfortable and brutally short.

PLATE 77. *A Thomas Bewick engraving in the 1795 edition of Oliver Goldsmith's 'Deserted Village'.*

*J. W. and Anne Tibble, *John Clare* (Cobden & Sanderson, 1932), p. 63. *The Prose of John Clare* (Routledge & Kegan Paul, 1951), by the same authors, gives a sketch-map of this heath country between Stamford and Peterborough, as it was in 1779, before much of it was enclosed.

Hedgerows and Trees

The new fields were hedged around with quickset, whitethorn, or hawthorn, to give its alternative names, with a shallow ditch on one side or both sides of the fence. In the upland stone country, dry-walling took the place of hedges. At first the hedges were no more than double rows of seedlings protected by a rail on one side or both, but after twenty years the thorns had grown high enough to be cut and laid, a practice which William Marshall describes as the latest improvement in his *Rural Economy of the Midland Counties* in 1790. Throughout the east Midlands ash trees were planted along the hedges, less often the elm, usually spaced out at wide intervals. Possibly this comparative scarcity of trees in the east Midland hedgerows – in Northamptonshire and Leicestershire especially – arises from consideration for fox-hunting. In Leicestershire organised fox-hunting developed during the 1770s, in time to enjoy the exhilaration of galloping over miles of unfenced country. Enclosure made things more difficult, or perhaps we should say necessitated new and exciting skills, but at least there were no close ranks of trees to make the fences impossible. Indeed, the first effect of enclosure was to reduce the number of trees in thinly wooded country, for the new fences – hundreds of miles of them – required vast quantities of oak, elm, and ash saplings for posts and rails. Clare, once more, was in no doubt about the diminution of woodland after enclosure:

> *Ye fields, ye scenes so dear to Lubin's eye,*
> *Ye meadow-blooms, ye pasture-flowers, farewell!*
> *Ye banish'd trees, ye make me deeply sigh -*
> *Inclosure came, and all your glories fell:*
> *E'en the old oak that crown'd yon rifled dell,*
> *Whose age had made it sacred to the view,*
> *Not long was left his children's fate to tell;*
> *Where ignorance and wealth their course pursue,*
> *Each tree must tumble down – 'old Lea-Close Oak', adieu!*

Fox-hunting had another effect upon the Midland landscape, and that was the creation of artificial fox-covers. The enclosure of heaths and commons reduced the extent of natural gorse patches where a fox could hide. Good arable farmers grubbed them up. To get more foxes and to get them distributed more evenly over the country, gorse covers and spinneys were started by hunting landlords in well-chosen spots. These were not less than two acres in size, and rarely more than twenty acres. Some of these covers were actually odd pieces of common land, old cow-pastures that had been allowed to get out of hand, taken over by the fox-hunters for fencing and preservation, in return for a money payment to the holders of the common rights. Such were Ashby Pastures or Cossington Gorse in east Leicestershire, in the 'Quorn country'.* These 'gorses' filled up the odd corners of parishes, and may be quickly spotted on the Ordnance map. Other covers were planted with trees, and fenced around by large fox-hunting landlords like Aylesford or Sir Francis Burdett, the radical politician, who hunted in Leicestershire in the 1820s. Most of these covers were made in the late eighteenth century or the early nineteenth, and often give away their date in their names. The famous Botany Bay cover of east Leicestershire dates from the 1790s, when the convict settlement was in the news. The one-inch maps of the east Midland counties are splashed all over with these shreds of green, usually distinguishable from true, ancient woodland by their small size and their regular shape. In the landscape itself, they

---

PLATE 78. *A typical enclosure road at Duxford, Cambridgeshire, laid out in 1830 when the open fields of the parish were swept away. Its overall width is greater than the needs of the twentieth century but it was designed for moving herds of animals, not for the motor car.*

* Ellis, op. cit., pp. 60ff.

are a very noticeable feature for they are often the only clump of trees anywhere in sight over thousands of acres.

The fox-hunting country was perhaps a special case. Over most of enclosed England, the small fields were hedged around with hawthorn fences, more or less thickly interspersed with ash and elm – the great trees of the Midlands – which when they were full grown gave the appearance of an almost continuous wood, especially when seen from an eminence. This is perhaps the most characteristic feature of any large view in the Midland Plain. Ash and elm were planted in the hedgerows, and the flashing grey-green willow along the banks of the streams. These are the three trees that dominate any Midland view in the deep country.

The greater part of the hedges is, however, made of white hawthorn. Some of these hawthorns, with their gnarled, twisted and burnished trunks, probably date from the first enclosure of the fields five or six generations ago. The hawthorn is the oldest of the hedgerow trees, for it gets its name from the Old English word *haga*, 'a hedge' or 'an enclosure', and it was used from Saxon times onwards to make impenetrable fences – the hedge-thorn. In the Midlands it is the tree one sees most often: and for a brief spell in early sum-mer it is the most beautiful of all the Midland trees, with its continuous miles of white may blossom glimmering as far as the eye can see. W.H. Hudson says somewhere that 18 May is the crown of the English summer: in the Midland fields on that day these miles of snowy hedges reach perfection, so dense and far-reaching that the entire atmosphere is saturated with the bitter-sweet smell whichever way the summer wind is blowing. From the hedgerow trees near and far come the calls of countless cuckoos, and the lesser sounds of an infinite number of small birds.

This description of the hawthorn hedges of the Midlands is again, alas, no longer true in most places. The modern practice of flailing the remaining hedges with crude machinery has not only destroyed the possibility of such views, but has also led to a considerable reduction of bird and animal life. The landscape is much poorer both visually and in content than it was thirty years ago.

The thousands of miles of new hedgerows in the Midland countryside, when they came to full growth after a generation, added enormously to the bird population, especially with the extermination of the larger hawks and kites as pests, a process that is abundantly recorded in the church-wardens' accounts or the field-reeves' books of Midland villages. Millions of small birds now sing in the hedges and spinneys. But it was not all gain. The heathland birds have disappeared over large areas, and become rarer altogether. The whole balance of the bird population altered where these changes were going on in the landscape. There were more hedges but fewer heaths; in some parts less arable than ever before, in other parts more than ever before; and the coming of the canals about the same time also introduced new varieties of birds to districts where they had previously never been known.

There is only one other thing to be said about the hedgerows of parliamentary enclosure, and that is when precisely they were made. Most enclosure awards, if not all, expressly stipulated that those who received allotments of land under the award were to fence these allotments within twelve months. This gives us, if we know the date of the award (which is easy to discover), the exact date of all the external fences or hedges, but it does not tell us the date of the internal fences on the bigger allotments. Where a biggish landowner received an allotment of two, three or four hundred acres, he would put a ring-fence around the whole within the specified twelve months, but he might not divide up his allotment into smaller fields until some years later. It is a small point, perhaps, but not without some historical interest in the evolution of the English landscape. Henry Alken's hunting print *The Death*, dated 1824, appears to show such a landscape around Ab Kettleby, in the 'wold' country to the north-west of Melton Mowbray. The parish had been enclosed as far back as 1761 – two generations earlier – but Alken's view still gives a general impression of wide spaces and open views. There are indeed several hedges to be seen, but the hedged areas are mostly still very large and the landscape as a whole not unlike that of the Cotswolds in its feeling of great space and skies. But where a parish was mostly in the hands of a small peasantry, and this was true of a great many parishes in Midland and eastern England, the effect would have been entirely different. In such parishes as these the present field and hedge pattern was laid down in the year following the enclosure award, for the allotments would have been many and small. Not all parishes enclosed by parliamentary act immediately sprang fully-hedged into view. Indeed, the immediate effect of enclosure in most places must have been a feeling of nakedness and rawness in the landscape, until the hedgerow trees were well-grown:

O samely naked leas, so bleak, so strange! . . .
The storm beats chilly on its naked breast,
No shelter grows to shield, no home invites to rest,

says Clare about his native Helpston in the years after its enclosure, and that must have been true of most parishes that underwent the great transformation.

Roads

A great number of new by-roads came into existence as a result of the enclosure movement. They are immediately recognisable on the one-inch map by the manner in which they run from village to village practically straight across country, with perhaps an occasional sudden right-angled bend and then on again. More significantly still, these straight roads sometimes do not run to the nearest village but continue for some miles through open country, reaching the villages by means of side-roads. There is none of that apparently aimless wandering in short stretches, punctuated by frequent bends, going halfway round the compass to reach the next hamlet or village, which characterises the by-roads in country that has never been in open field or left it several centuries ago. On the six-inch and the twenty-five-inch maps, too, the parliamentary enclosure roads stand out conspicuously with their wide grass verges. The road runs like a grey ribbon between verges full of tall grasses, cow-parsley and dog-roses, as may be seen above all in the Lincolnshire Wolds. But they are to be found in any of the 'enclosure counties' and may be identified immediately as the work of the enclosure commissioners.

In the parish of Norton-by-Twycross, on the borders of Warwickshire and Leicestershire, the award of 1748 specifies that the road to London, which is here the main road between Burton-on-Trent and Atherstone, should be not less than thirty-three yards wide. The lesser main road from Twycross to the local market-town of Ashby de la Zouch was to have a minimum width of twenty-two yards; and the other roads of the parish were to be 'of a proper width'. The immense width of the two main roads, one with a minimum width of practically a hundred feet and the other of sixty-six feet, reflects the state of even the main roads before the days of the turnpikes and above all of the scientific roadmaking initiated by Metcalf and Macadam in the late eighteenth century. Roads that carried any considerable amount of through-traffic had to be wide enough, and could be wide enough in unenclosed country, to allow of detours around the impassable stretches that developed in unsurfaced roads by mid-winter. The main London to Exeter 'road' was said to have been a quarter of a mile wide by the end of the winter where it crossed – or rather plunged through – the sticky morass of the chalk on Salisbury Plain. It seems to have been a fairly general rule in the later enclosure awards that the minimum width for inter-village roads should be forty feet between the ditches, though local roads carrying more than the average traffic for the district were often laid down forty-five or fifty feet wide. In Somerset, public roads were usually forty feet wide, of which – in 1795 – twelve feet were stoned to a depth of a foot in the middle and nine inches at the sides.* This would leave verges of four-

* John Billingsley, *A General View of the Agriculture of the County of Somerset* (Board of Agriculture, 1797), p. 91.

teen feet width on each side, if the paved road were dead in the middle. Often it was not, and the grass verge was very much wider on one side than the other. On most local roads today this width has hardly varied. All over the Midlands and Lincolnshire one finds roads with an overall width of forty feet, having a surface about fourteen or fifteen feet wide and grass verges of twelve or thirteen feet on each side.

It seems likely that a forty-foot width was regarded as the minimum for an unsurfaced road, allowing for detours as the winter went on, but when scientific roadmaking began these great widths were no longer necessary. Only a relatively narrow width was surfaced with stone, and the remainder was left under grass as we see it today. It is kept within bounds by county councils, but on the less frequented roads the cow-parsley, the dog-rose and the blackberry bramble flourish by the wayside. Some of these by-roads have developed a heavier traffic since they were first laid out, and in these instances it has been an easy matter to take in more of the verges and to widen the road surface.

The established main roads that had been used for traffic between the medieval towns, and had made their own width with the usage of centuries, were generally left untouched by any parish awards. So the Fosse Way, which at one time had been the main road from medieval Coventry to Leicester, was ordered in the Sharnford award of 1765 to be 'of the same width as it hath heretofore usually been'. Even so, quick set hedges were planted on either side of these roads to fence them in, where formerly they had wandered at large.

It is sometimes said that the public roads laid out by the enclosure commissioners followed the lines of the medieval footpaths and bridle paths between the villages, paths that had been trodden out first in Anglo-Saxon times. But this is by no means always true. The strip map of Barsby and South Croxton, already referred to, shows the public roads of these two parishes to be laid out on almost entirely new lines. Here and there they pick up and make use of the old common balks in the former open fields, which must have been the usual way of proceeding from one village to another in open-field country, but for the most part they are drawn straight across the old furlongs and strips regardless of all considerations but that of directness. Since the furlongs, strips and balks were all to be swept away in the ensuing award and a new field system devised, it was only natural that the commissioners should do this. The Stathern map of 1792 shows the same planning of new roads in more or less straight lines and judging by what the Ordnance map shows in other parts of the Midlands and eastern England the same thing happened fairly generally.

Often, however, it is clear that the commissioners took over an existing track between two villages and straightened it a little, without going to the extreme length of drawing entirely new roads. Where a road which bears all the marks of having been laid out by the enclosure commissioners makes, at longish intervals, a sudden right-angled bend, sometimes two bends in quick succession, one can be pretty certain that though it was planned by the commissioners it follows an even older line from one village to the next, a line which had deviated in the same way around the heads of medieval furlongs. These right-angled bends in the road, whatever the date of the enclosure award may be, reflect some stage in the medieval colonisation of the parish when a new furlong, brought in from the waste perhaps in the twelfth or the thirteenth century, cut across the direct path to the next village and forced it to make a sudden turn for a few yards before resuming its onward course. Even a Roman road might be interfered with in this way and diverted from its ancient line; and in the course of time its exact line became lost and the subject of an archaeological problem today. One sees all these little points of landscape in walking round the parish of Helpston, but they can be found in many parishes in these parts of England.

A local variant of these wide lanes and roads is on the fenlands of eastern England. There too the Enclosure Commissioners laid down wide droves, in order to produce access to the new fields. Despite this, on the marshy peat fens, even limited traffic reduced them to an impassable morass for long periods of the year. Most had to be ploughed flat every spring to enable them to be used at all. Such conditions produced a very isolated way of life for fenland farmers. Indeed, it was not until 1940 that, under the demands of world conflict and with cost almost no object, the War Agricultural Committees laid down thousands of miles of concrete roads along the droveways throughout the fens. These roads not only allowed the fenlands to be exploited to the full for the first time, they also changed the way of life there, to an extent never seen before or since.

PLATE 79. *Gidding Grove Farm, Great Gidding, Huntingdonshire (Cambridgeshire), is a very typical east Midland enclosure farmstead. It was built in the early nineteenth century, soon after the enclosure of the medieval fields of the parish, and still remains surrounded by the regular hawthorn-hedged fields planned by the enclosure surveyor. It actually consists of a large farmhouse and farm buildings, together with two groups of farm cottages. Its total population in the mid-nineteenth century was probably in excess of many medieval hamlets or even small villages.*

Another reason for such sharp changes of alignment in otherwise straight enclosure roads is parish boundaries. It was rare for two adjacent parishes to be enclosed simultaneously and thus the Commissioners in one parish would draw their new roads to join existing tracks through the next parish. When the latter were re-aligned or made anew they often met the earlier roads at a sharp angle on the parish boundaries.

With the enclosure of the open fields and the redistribution of the land mostly in compact blocks* instead of strips scattered all over the parish, one would have expected the old open-field village to disintegrate as the village farmers built new farmsteads on their allotments. Often, it is true, the commissioners drew the new boundaries so as to come to a point in the village where the ancient homestead lay, so that the farmer need not be disturbed from his old home. They did this, for example, at Middle Barton in north Oxfordshire. But it was not always possible to do this· the mere facts of topography were against it: and a great number of farms had to be created well away from the village. In such cases it was to the obvious advantage of the farmer to build himself a new farmstead in the middle of his lands.

This, indeed, is what happened in due course, but the old village was far from disintegrated by such new building unless it was already very small and decaying. Often many years elapsed before the village farmers built their new houses, however inconvenient it may have been to live in the centre of the parish and to farm on the boundaries. Enclosure had been an exceedingly expensive business, not only the heavy legal costs which worked out on an average at about £1 an acre (but were sometimes much heavier), but also the costs of making hundreds of yards of fences, which were heavier still. Many of the smaller farmers continued to live therefore in the ancestral homestead on the village street, but carried out no repairs to it and gradually allowed it to decay. When the old house was practically uninhabitable, they or their sons built a new farmstead in the midst of their own fields and migrated from the village. That is why one sees so many Victorian farmhouses in red brick in the midst of the fields in these parts of England.

The dates of outlying farmsteads elucidate the uneven process of the development of enclosure landscapes. At Swaffham Bulbeck in Cambridgeshire the act of parliament which led to the removal of the open fields and the break-up of the chalk downlands beyond was passed in 1800. Yet of the associated farmsteads, one was built about 1802, another in 1812 and another in 1830 and a fourth in 1833. On the other hand in part of Wychwood Forest in Oxfordshire, the first trees were cut down in October 1856 following an act of parliament. Sixteen months later, in January 1858, the first tenants were already in their new farmhouses.

On the other hand, the larger graziers, for the most part prosperous men, built themselves new farmsteads almost at once. In the adjoining parishes of Sileby and Seagrave, in mid-Leicestershire, one finds on the map such farm names as Quebec, Belle Isle, Hanover and Bunkers Hill, and New York not so far away, pleasant Georgian red-brick houses with white doorways gleaming across the home meadow. It is easy enough to guess when these parishes were enclosed. At Wiseton, in the Nottinghamshire plain between the Idle and the Trent, one landlord – Jonathan Ackham – built seven new homesteads on central sites on his estate after enclosure.

Yet the total number of farmsteads built out in the fields between the villages is very small. One would guess not more than half a dozen in the average parish, often fewer than that. There was rarely any sign of the village breaking up physically as a result of enclosure, whatever happened to it spiritually and culturally.

There were good reasons why the nucleated village should survive more or less intact. In the first place, the ownership of land and the occupation of farms was concentrated into far fewer hands in the eighteenth century than they had been in the medieval village. There is no need to labour this point, for every parish in England shows evidence of this tendency to concentrate ownership and occupation in the course of several centuries. Rider Haggard, in *Rural England*, gives a striking example of this: when the manor of Feckenham, in east Worcestershire, was surveyed in 1591, sixty-three different owners held

PLATE 80. *Quebec Farm, Sileby, Leicestershire, was built out in the new fields, away from the village, in 1760. It was named after Wolfe's famous victory in Canada in the same year.*

* The new allotments were not invariably made in one block, as is usually said. In some parishes the lands of the new farms were still scattered about, though much less widely than hitherto.

some 2,900 acres. By 1900 there were only six owners, who held all this and another three thousand acres besides.* Whatever the actual figures in any particular parish, the number of Georgian farmers was generally only a fraction of the number there had been in the medieval or Tudor village. In other words, there remained at the time of the parliamentary enclosure only half a dozen farmers who wished to build in the new fields.

Then again, the population of the country as a whole was rising fairly quickly at the time of the enclosure movement, especially in the industrial villages of the Midlands, and there was a demand for houses. Old and roomy yeoman farmhouses, those that had not been suffered to decay too far, were cut up into two or three cottages for a new class of 'industrial poor'. So far from disintegrating, the open-field village often grew larger after enclosure: larger, but often more squalid, for there was generally more poverty than there had been before.

This is an important point and one now increasingly difficult to see. Despite massive emigration, both abroad and to the new industrial towns, most villages doubled in population between 1800 and 1850. The increased numbers of people were housed by splitting up existing houses so that even modest cottages had sometimes up to twenty people living in them. Conditions were perhaps better than in the new urban areas but a good deal worse than in earlier times. Today the cottages are being largely restored to what purports to be their former glory, occupied by middle-class commuters with the standard family size of 4.4 people.

Nevertheless, a new element had been introduced into the landscape in this part of England – the isolated farmstead. Nearly all the farmhouses we see between the compact villages of the country between the Yorkshire and the Dorset coasts date from the century 1750-1850. The few that are older may be either the result of Tudor or Stuart enclosure, or examples of monastic granges which have already been discussed. But probably four out of five of these farmsteads in the fields are the consequence of parliamentary enclosure.

On the vast tracts of Lincoln Heath, stretching north and south of the city for some seventy miles, Arthur Young found 'a large range which formerly was covered with heath, gorse, etc., yielding in fact little or no produce, converted by enclosure to profitable arable farms . . . and a very extensive country all studded with new farmhouses, offices, and every appearance of thriving industry . . .' On the map this Heath presents an absolutely typical picture of a planned landscape: dead straight by-roads, almost empty spaces between the villages, solitary farmsteads sparingly dotted about and reached by occupation roads running off the public roads, a vast landscape utterly bare of woodland except for neat little fox covers, square or rectangular patches of green for the most part.

There is, too, another marked feature of this piece of country which is characteristic of all country enclosed from open fields or common of any kind. It is the complete absence of any *lanes*. It is this, more than anything else, which makes the map of this sort of country look so empty when compared with the map of anciently enclosed country in say mid-Sussex, Essex or Devon. Lanes – true lanes that is, deep and winding – are characteristic of country fabricated piecemeal with small medieval implements. In recently enclosed country we have instead an open regular mesh of by-roads, and a few field-paths and bridle-roads to fill in the larger spaces between the villages. In Leicestershire, the man who wishes to forget income-tax, hydrogen bombs and the relentless onward march of science walks the field-paths, to which special maps and guides are provided; in Devon he takes to the deep lanes between the farms. It is a fundamental difference in landscape history.

Such was the landscape created by the enclosure commissioners. But we must never forget that every few miles, even in the middle of this orderly landscape, an older scene may make its appearance. In passing from one parish to another, in simply crossing a nameless brook or road, we may step back into fields that were created, not by the commissioners of Georgian times, but by the Tudor squire or perhaps even by his monastic predecessors in the fifteenth century.

Thus if we are walking in the pastoral, remote country on the borders of Leicestershire and Rutland, following the Eye brook as it makes its way south through undulating fields to the Welland, we pass in a walk of nine or ten miles through a landscape modelled in five different centuries, and this in a part of England that is generally accounted somewhat dull, the monotonous product of parliamentary enclosure. We leave the main Uppingham to Leicester road at Allexton, a parish which is recorded as fully enclosed by 1555. Two miles

* Rider Haggard, *Rural England* (Longmans, 1902), vol. 1, pp. 405-6.

PLATE 81. *The landscape of parliamentary enclosure in Wensleydale, North Yorkshire. Set amongst rectangular stone-walled fields, the farmstead is a typical example of the late enclosures of the upland wastes.*

This 'open' pattern of compact villages and few roads and lanes should be compared with Fig. 7, which shows the 'close' pattern of early medieval colonisation on the heavy London Clays of south-east Hertfordshire. Here, in north Hertfordshire and south Cambridgeshire, we are on the chalk land, cleared of its woodland cover in pre-Saxon times. It was settled by the Old English in compact villages such as Ashwell and Litlington, which were surrounded by large open fields. Many of these open fields survived into the nineteenth century, those of Bygrave and Ashwell into the twentieth century. Farmsteads are still rare outside the villages: the few that exist were mostly built after the parliamentary enclosure of the parishes. The landscape of straight roads, often unfenced, and of small geometrical plantations, is characteristic of this late period. Reproduced by permission from the 1-inch map of the Ordnance Survey.

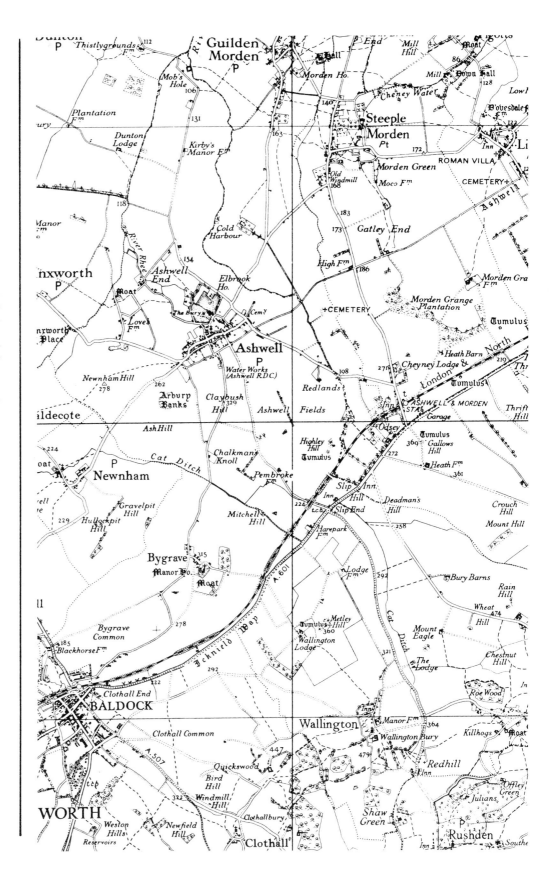

168

or so to the south lies the village of Stockerston, now shrunk almost to a hamlet, with its attractive Perpendicular church standing alone on the hillside – a sure sign of some interesting change in village history. Here we know that the enclosure of the open fields began in the 1570s, and had been completed by some date in the seventeenth century. The field-pattern we see is three to four hundred years old. Another half-hour's walk brings us to the site of a village which has disappeared altogether – the deserted village of Holyoak, now remembered by the solitary farmstead of Holyoaks Lodge. Here in the winter of 1496, Sir Robert Brudenell evicted thirty people from their small, open-field arable farms to make way for his cattle-pastures. The record tells us that 'they have departed thence, and are either idle or have perished'. Holyoak was only a hamlet. Only five or six farms were involved in this tragedy; but for a few minutes at least we traverse fields brought into being by the high-handed action of a fifteenth-century squire, and pass by the mounds where the hamlet of Holyoak once stood. Up in the hills to our right lies Nevill Holt, now only a church, a park and a great house. Here, too, the village has gone – probably deserted by Elizabethan times. Certainly all the fields were enclosed by the year 1572.

Then we emerge from these gentle hills into the broad levels of the Welland valley, and here, in the parishes of Great Easton and Bringhurst, we enter a landscape produced entirely (as far as we know) by the parliamentary enclosure of 1804-6. Another couple of miles up the valley and we are at Medbourne, the last bastion of the open fields in Leicestershire, enclosed in the year 1842. From Allexton to Medbourne is only five miles straight across the hills, yet we have passed through a period of some three hundred and fifty years in the history of the landscape. Perhaps even longer: for Thomas Palmer had a grant of free warren at Holt as far back as 1448 and this may be the beginning of the park of Nevill Holt. If so, this piece of Leicestershire landscape is the product of various forces over a space of four hundred years. So, behind every generalisation, there lies the infinite variety and beauty of the detail; and it is the detail that matters, that gives pleasure to the eye and to the mind, as we traverse, on foot and unhurried, the landscape of any part of England.

The landscape in this area of south-east Cambridgeshire and north-east Hertfordshire is certainly very different from that in Fig. 7 only a few miles to the south-east; until the nineteenth century it was a land of open fields. Whether all the villages were settled by the Old English is much more doubtful. Ashwell is certainly a planned village in its present form, perhaps of twelfth-century date as may be Steeple Morden and Wallington. Baldock is a 'new town' created by the Knights Templar on a formerly empty site soon after 1148. Its name is a corruption of Baghdad. It was apparently intended to be the north Hertfordshire commercial equivalent of Baghdad!

The numbers of 'tumuli' – burial mounds of the Bronze Age – as well as the site of Arbury Banks – are but a pale reflection of the dense prehistoric and later settlement in this area. Other more recent discoveries show that the area was already fully occupied and settled by at least 1000 BC.

Chapter 7
THE INDUSTRIAL REVOLUTION AND THE LANDSCAPE

Introduction

There is, surprisingly perhaps, very little that can be added to Professor Hoskins' account of industrial landscapes. This is in part a result of his excellent description and analysis which, despite his obvious dislike of the landscapes of industry, have stood the test of time. But it is also a consequence of the academic stagnation over the last few years of much that is called industrial archaeology in England. The study of industry by economic historians has progressed apace, but the understanding of industry in its landscape has not advanced very far. Much of the study of industrial remains is still at the level of recording 'nuts and bolts'. There is also a major preoccupation with 'firsts' and a consequent lack of appreciation of the difference between invention and commercial exploitation.

In two major respects the landscape of industry has changed since Professor Hoskins wrote. First, the pace of change and economic developments during the last twenty years or so have altered the landscapes he described very considerably. Not only have major industries virtually collapsed but their sites have often been totally cleared. In addition much of the associated housing has also been removed and replaced by dwellings which although sometimes materially better appointed are not always aesthetically or socially better.

As a result, almost nothing remains of, say, the pottery industry of Stoke on Trent and its neighbouring towns and most of the Lancashire and west Yorkshire textile mills have been abandoned, demolished or are under threat. Steel-making in the west Midlands has ceased and not only have many of the traditional coal-mining areas declined but the winding gear, pit-head buildings and tramways have gone and even tips have been levelled and landscaped. In essence, then, there is far less to see of the history of industrial landscapes than there was even a few years ago.

In the meantime new industrial landscapes have developed. Few are any more attractive than those they have replaced, despite the work of designers and landscape architects. Featureless sheds surrounded by the requisite area of unkempt grass and undersized dying trees as well as an extensive car park is the norm for most types of modern industry.

Nor are the worst of modern industrial landscapes in the traditional areas. One of the most depressing parts of England is the north side of the Thames Estuary around Thurrock, best viewed from the M25, travelling fast. Even nineteenth-century industrialists at their worst did not quite approach this.

With the demise of the traditional industrial landscapes nostalgia for them has grown. As a result various sites of former industrial activities have been taken over, cleaned up and displayed to the public in order to show what a real industrial area was never like. The great trans-shipment complex for the riches mined from the valleys at Morwellham, near Tavistock in Devon, is now a far cry from its original form, while Coalbrookdale, despite gallant work on it, is quite unlike it was in its heyday. The 'sanitisation' of industrial sites, and indeed much else in tourist England, produces a very unreal picture of the harsh realities of life in these places. Perhaps this is inevitable, but what we see today must not be taken as a true vision of the past.

It is also a curious fact that the older the remains of industry are the better they are regarded. The earliest industrial sites are now often looked after as carefully as those of abbeys and castles. Places where specific industrial processes were developed are tourist attractions, as at Coalbrookdale. The remains of eighteenth-century lead mines on the Pennines are preserved. Coal-pits of the sixteenth century, on the Clee Hills in Shropshire, are meticulously recorded by archaeologists while medieval quarries such as those at Barnack, Cambridgeshire, are protected. Perhaps the most remarkable of all, the Norfolk Broads, which are actually nothing more than the flooded workings of a huge medieval peat extraction industry, have recently been raised to the status of an Environmentally Sensitive Area and given their own Planning Authority.

Professor Hoskins disliked industrial towns, a fact which is obvious from his comments on them. While this was a reasonable attitude, it

PLATE 82. *Industrial redevelopment, Gateshead, Tyneside. The old industries of the north-east of England have now died. New ones are slowly appearing, producing a very different landscape.*

sometimes distorted his judgement. There is no doubt that conditions in these towns, particularly in the first half of the nineteenth century, were dreadful but Professor Hoskins seems more anxious to apportion blame for this than to explain why it happened, which is perhaps more important.

Moreover he omits, virtually without mention, the extraordinary improvements made in English industrial life, and elsewhere, in the second half of the nineteenth century and which made many of these towns what they are today. Water supply, which produced great reservoirs, gas supply and electricity, paved roads, urban transport, waste disposal and considerable numbers of public buildings and parks, all had a dramatic effect on the landscape and so their omission is serious.

THE INDUSTRIAL REVOLUTION AND THE LANDSCAPE

The Early Industrial Landscape

England was still a peaceful agricultural country at the beginning of the seventeenth century. Though she was passing through what has been called her first industrial revolution, there was as yet little to show for it in the landscape. Quarries and coal-pits were numerous in certain localities, salt-works and glassworks were flourishing, the cloth industry was growing; but so far as the visible signs upon the face of the country were concerned it was all a mere scratching on the surface. Neither Leland nor Camden has much to say about industry in England; and there was nothing that could be specifically called an industrial landscape. Perhaps the multitude of coal-pits near the Tyne were beginning to wear that look, and Camden observed in the 1580s that Sussex 'is full of iron mines, all over it; for the casting of which there are furnaces up and down the country, and abundance of wood is yearly spent; many streams are drawn into one channel, and a great deal of meadow ground is turned into ponds and pools for the driving mills by the flashes, which, beating with hammers upon the iron, fill the neighbourhood round about it, night and day with continual noise.' The iron industry, centred in the Wealden woods, was steadily changing the face of the landscape in this region from the middle of the sixteenth century onwards, and a good deal remains to be seen by the historically minded traveller.

By the end of the seventeenth century the industrial landscape was much more evident. Yarranton in 1677 thought there were more people within a radius of ten miles of Dudley, and 'more money returned in a year', than in the whole of four Midland farming counties. This was pretty certainly an exaggeration, but it shows unmistakably that the Black Country (though this name had yet to be invented) was in process of creation.

The early industrial landscapes differed essentially from those that developed with steam-power. They showed a thick scattering of settlement, of cottages and small farmhouses dotted about all over the place, and a corresponding splitting up of fields into small crofts and paddocks. It was a 'busy' landscape, full of detail and movement, like one of Breughel's paintings, not a massive conglomeration of factories and slums. The Black Country in its early days was still country, 'a countryside in course of becoming industrialised; more and more a strung-out web of iron-working villages, market towns next door to collieries, heaths and wastes gradually and very slowly being covered by the cottages of nailers and other persons carrying on industrial occupations in rural surroundings'.* The typical figure was that of the craftsman-farmer, combining, say, a smithy with a smallholding, living in his own small balanced economy; hence the minuteness of the detail in the picture. One still finds traces of this kind of landscape on the fringes of the Black Country, as for example in the hamlet of Lower Gornal, in the hills to the north-west of Dudley.

Defoe gives us a splendid picture of an industrial landscape in the time of Queen Anne or shortly after. It is the landscape of the cloth industry in the neighbourhood of Halifax before the revolutionary changes brought about by the invention of power-driven machinery:

> *The nearer we came to Hallifax, we found the houses thicker, and the villages greater in every bottom; and not only so, but the sides of the hills, which were very steep every way, were spread with houses, and that very thick; for the land being divided into small enclosures, that is to say, from two acres to six or seven acres each, seldom more; every three or four pieces of land had a house belonging to it.*
>
> *. . . This division of land into small pieces, and the scattering of the dwellings, was occasioned by, and done for the convenience of the business which the people were generally employ'd in . . .*

* W. H. B. Court, *The Rise of the Midland Industries*, 1600-1838 (Oxford University Press, 1938), p. 22.

PLATE 84. *Engine houses, Minions, Bodmin Moor, Cornwall. Here the landscape is still littered with the remains of the eighteenth- and nineteenth-century mining industry.*

This particular landscape had its origin in two sources – the outcropping of coal, and the presence of running water everywhere, even on the tops of the hills. Wherever Defoe passed a house he found a little rill of running water.

If the house was above the road, it came from it, and cross'd the way to run to another; if the house was below us, it cross'd us from some other distant house above it, and at every considerable house was a manufactory or work-house, and as they could not do their business without water, the little streams were so parted and guided by gutters and pipes, and by turning and dividing the streams, that none of those houses were without a river, if I may call it so, running into and through their work-houses.

The coal-pits near the tops of the hills were worked in preference to those lower down, for various reasons. The coal was easier to come at, water presented less of a drainage problem, and the pack-horses could go up light and come down laden. Every clothier kept a horse or two, to carry his coal from the pit, to fetch home his wood and his provisions from the market, to take his yarn to the weavers, his cloth to the fulling-mill and finally to the cloth market to be sold. He also kept two or three cows for the sustenance of the family, and so required two, three or four pieces of enclosed land around his house.

Having thus fire and water at every dwelling, there is no need to enquire why they dwell thus dispers'd upon the highest hills. . . Among the manufacturers houses are likewise scattered an infinite number of cottages or small dwellings, in which dwell the workmen which are employed, the women and children of whom are always busy carding, spinning, &c. so that no hands being unemploy'd , all can gain their bread, even from the youngest to the antient; hardly any thing above four years old, but its hands are sufficient to it self . . . After we had mounted the third hill, we found the country one continued village, tho' mountainous every way, as before; hardly a house standing out of a speaking distance from another, and . . . we could see that almost at every house there was a tenter, and almost on every tenter a piece of cloth, or kersie, or shalloon, for they are three articles of that country's labour; from which the sun glancing, and, as I may say, shining (the white reflecting its rays) to us, I thought it was the most agreeable sight that I ever saw, for the hills, as I say, rising and falling so thick, and the valleys opening sometimes one way, sometimes another, so that sometimes we could see two or three miles this way, sometimes as far another; sometimes like the streets near St Giles's, called the Seven Dials; we could see through the glades almost every way round us, yet look which way we would, high to the tops, and low to the bottoms, it was all the same; innumerable houses and tenters, and a white piece upon every tenter.

The steep-sided valley of Stroud-Water in Gloucestershire must have presented much the same kind of picture, but Defoe does not attempt any description of it beyond saying that 'the clothiers lye all along the banks of this river for near 20 miles'; and Celia Fiennes passed along the high road over the uplands from Gloucester to Bath and failed to notice it at all.

Water-Power and the Early Mills

Early inventions in most industries – except in those requiring large amounts of fixed capital, like the iron industry – benefited the small man, or at least kept him in business. Kay's flying shuttle (1733) and Hargreaves's spinning jenny (1767) multiplied the output of domestic workers in the textile industry without compelling them to enter mills or factories. Not until the application of water-power to machinery, and a consequent great increase in the size of machines, do we begin to see the large factory as an element in the landscape. Before that time the largest unit of production was what Defoe calls in Yorkshire the 'work-house'. But the great revolution was on its way.

The first true factory built in England was the silk mill built for John and Thomas Lombe

at Derby in 1718-22. It was five or six storeys high, employed three hundred men, and was driven by the water-power of the river Derwent. It was, as Mantoux says, in every respect a modern factory, with automatic tools, continuous and unlimited production, and specialised functions for the operatives. Within fifty years there were several silk factories employing four hundred to eight hundred persons, but the silk industry was of secondary importance and did not initiate the factory system. It was when power reached the cotton, woollen, and iron industries that the face of the country really began to change on a large scale, and that was not until the 1770s.

Matthew Boulton opened his great Soho factory, in the still unravished country outside Birmingham, in 1765, and shortly afterwards began the manufacture of steam engines. Wedgwood's new large factory at Etruria in the Potteries was opened in 1769. Richard Arkwright, the greatest of the new industrial capitalists, erected his first spinning mill, worked by horses, at Nottingham in 1768, but his second factory, built on a much larger scale at

PLATE 85. *Late eighteenth-century weavers' cottages at Littleborough, Lancashire. A relic of the domestic system of industry when spinning and weaving were done at home. The long window of the upper storey was designed to throw the maximum light on the loom.*

177

Cromford on the Derwent in 1771, was driven by water-power. In the 1760s, too, the Darbys enlarged their ironworks at Coalbrookdale in Shropshire to the largest works of any kind in the kingdom. With these four large-scale factories, the creation of the modern industrial landscape may be said to have begun.

The new mills, factories and works tended to be in more or less remote places, partly because of the need to be near a falling stream for the supply of power, and later to escape too close inspection and regulation of their uninhibited activities. One finds these early mills therefore, often windowless and deserted today, in the upper reaches of the moorland valleys on either side of the Pennines. Coalbrookdale, then a romantically beautiful valley, was chosen by the Darbys for their ironworks because here a rapid stream entered the broad navigable waterway of the Severn. Water was needed in the iron industry both for power and for the transport of heavy materials. It was not long before the ravishing of this scene attracted the lament of the poets. Anna Seward, 'The Swan of Lichfield', mourned over 'Colebrooke Dale' in a poem written about 1785:

> *Scene of superfluous grace, and wasted bloom,*
> *O, violated Colebrook! in an hour,*
> *To beauty unpropitious and to song,*
> *The Genius of thy shades, by Plutus brib'd,*
> *Amid thy grassy lanes, thy wildwood glens,*
> *Thy knolls and bubbling wells, thy rocks, and streams,*
> *Slumbers! – while tribes fuliginous invade*
> *The soft, romantic, consecrated scenes . . .*

Some ten years earlier, Arthur Young had already noted the discord between the natural beauty of the landscape and what man had done to it, but he saw, too – and painters also were on the verge of seeing it – that an unrestrained industrial landscape has a considerable element of sublimity about it. 'That variety of horrors art has spread at the bottom [of Coalbrookdale]; the noise of the forges, mills, etc., with all their vast machinery, the flames bursting from the furnaces with the burning of the coal and the smoak of the lime kilns, are altogether sublime.'

The scale of the new industries brought about a number of visual changes, some of them unexpected. The large sums of fixed capital sunk in the factory buildings and the machinery, and the fact that water-power, unlike human labour, needed no rest, demanded that the new buildings be used by night as well as by day. Shifts of labour were therefore organised, and these tall fortress-like structures were lit from top to bottom at night, and presented something new and dramatic to those who had the leisure to stay outside and contemplate it with detachment. So we get Joseph Wright of Derby as early as 1780 painting Arkwright's cotton mill by night – tiers of tiny yellow lights in the immemorial country

PLATE 86. *Tean Hall Mills, Upper Tean, Staffordshire. The timber-framed house of 1613, and its early eighteenth-century addition on the left, were occupied from 1747 by a loom manager. The looms were used in local cottages, and warehouses occupied much of this site. In the late eighteenth century the three-storey pedimented mill was built as the weaving became fully industrialised. In 1823 steam-power replaced water and in 1888 the mill was further extended along the street.*

darkness of the Derwent valley, the isolated forerunner of those tremendous galaxies of light that one now sees from the Pennine Moors after sundown.*

In the eighth book of *The Excursion*, Wordsworth sees the other side of this romantic scene:

> *When soothing darkness spreads*
> *O'er hill and vale, and the punctual stars,*
> *While all things else are gathering to their homes,*
> *Advance, and in the firmament of heaven*
> *Glitter – but undisturbing, undisturbed;*
> *As if their silent company were charged*
> *With peaceful admonitions for the heart*
> *Of all-beholding Man, earth's thoughtful lord;*
> *Then, in full many a region, once like this*
> *The assured domain of calm simplicity*
> *And pensive quiet, an unnatural light*
> *Prepared for never-resting labour's eyes*
> *Breaks from a many-windowed fabric huge;*
> *And at the appointed hour a bell is heard,*
> *Of harsher import than the curfew-knoll*
> *That spake the Norman Conqueror's stern behest ·*
> *A local summons to unceasing toil!*
> *Disgorged are now the Ministers of day;*
> *And, as they issue from the illumined pile,*
> *A fresh band meets them, at the crowded door ·*
> *And in the courts – and where the rumbling stream,*
> *That turns the multitude of dizzy wheels,*
> *Glares, like a troubled spirit, in its bed,*
> *Among the rock below. Men, maidens, youths,*
> *Mother and little children, boys and girls,*
> *Enter, and each the wonted task resumes*
> *Within his temple, where is offered up*
> *To Gain, the master idol of the realm,*
> *Perpetual sacrifice.*

Arkwright's son built 'a very elegant seat', after his father's death in 1792, commanding a view of his works, precisely as Josiah Wedgwood had built Etruria Hall within two hundred yards of his new pottery near Burslem. The early industrialists were proud of their achievements and liked to have them in full view. (Now they take good care to live well out of sight of them). Matthew Boulton lived close to his works at Soho; but his son bought the estate and country house of Great Tew in Oxfordshire and went to and fro by the coach which is still preserved in the stables there. It was not long before the new factories generated their full powers of ugliness, dirt and blight, and employers moved away. Etruria Hall still stands, in a landscape of demonic ugliness, backed not by tiers of green woods but by colliery tips higher than itself, and in front, not an ornamental sheet of water but a filthy 'flash', dark with coal-dust, arising from subsidence due to coal-mining below.

In the textile districts the new industrial landscape lay in the valley bottoms, which had been comparatively ignored in Defoe's day, when the thickest settlement was on the hillside. Now, down in the bottoms, arose the new many-storeyed mills, some of them handsome buildings not too unlike the plain country houses of the time. Around them grew up short streets of cottages for the workpeople, run up so quickly that they look as though they were planted flat on the surface, without any foundations; but still there was no congestion. The water-power age produced hamlets, at the most small villages, gathered around a new mill. Around Ashton-under-Lyne, for example, where it was reckoned there were nearly a hundred cotton mills within a ten-mile radius – all on the river Tame or its tributaries – we

PLATE 87. *Styal Mill, Cheshire, was begun in 1784 by Samuel Greg of Belfast as a silk mill. It was later much enlarged and here the 1810 additions lie against the stream which provided its power.*

The setting of Etruria Hall at Burslem, Stoke on Trent, has now been completely altered. The area has been redeveloped as part of the Stoke Garden Exhibition Centre and the 'squalor' has entirely disappeared.

* It was in 1792 that William Murdoch demonstrated the possibility of using coal gas lighting, and night-work spread rapidly from the early years of the new century. But Wright's painting, done in 1789, definitely shows the Cromford mill illuminated at night.

find hamlets in the 1790s with the significant names of Boston, Charlestown and Botany Bay.

Milford, in the Derwent valley just south of Belper, is a complete and almost untouched late eighteenth-century industrial village. Before 1781 it had consisted of only eight houses, but in that year the Strutts – who had gone into partnership for a time with the then-needy Arkwright – built the large cotton mill that still stands there. They built a great number of cottages for their workpeople; a Unitarian chapel for their spiritual welfare, a school for their children, and a mansion for themselves. It was what the Americans would call a 'company town', and is worth seeing as an example of what enlightened employers were doing at the time.

A mile or so north of Milford is the little town of Belper. Until 1776 this was a poor place inhabited chiefly by nailers. Then came Mr Jedidiah Strutt, who built a cotton mill on the Derwent and shortly afterwards three more. Here, too, the Strutts provided a chapel, and day schools and Sunday-schools, and another mansion. At the north end of the town stands one of their great eighteenth-century mills, now under the name of the English Sewing Cotton Company, which incorporated several new and striking features. By 1811 Belper was the second largest town in Derbyshire.

The Derwent valley, which exemplifies along its bottom so much industrial history of the water-power age, attracted large mills from the beginning by reason of its fast-flowing river; but not everyone admired the result as Wright of Derby did. Uvedale Price in his *Essays on the Picturesque* (1810) observed:

> *When I consider the striking natural beauties of such a river as that at Matlock, and the effect of the seven-storey buildings that have been raised there, and on other beautiful streams, for cotton manufactories, I am inclined to think that nothing can equal them for the purpose of dis-beautifying an enchanting piece of scenery; and that economy had produced, what the greatest ingenuity, if a prize were given for ugliness, could not surpass.*

Mills arose in the remote valleys below the moors, and hamlets and villages quickly clustered around them. But established towns too were advancing over the surrounding fields. Trees and hedges were torn up, red-brick or gritstone streets, short and straight, multiplied every year, even before the age of steam: Sheffield, Birmingham, Liverpool, Manchester, all were on the move. According to Langford, 'The traveller who visits [Birmingham] once in six months supposes himself well acquainted with her, but he may chance to find a street of houses in the autumn, where he saw his horse at grass in the spring.' The population of the town doubled in the last forty years of the eighteenth century (thirty-five thousand people in 1760; seventy-three thousand in 1801), but it was as yet far from being the dark and horrible landscape that it eventually became. Even in the early years of the nineteenth century the middle-class streets had 'prospects' of the country and the older working-class houses at least still had gardens. The dirt and overcrowding came with the steam age in the nineteenth century.

Sheffield, on the other hand, was 'very populous and large' in Queen Anne's time when Defoe traversed it, and its houses were already 'dark and black' from the smoke of the forges. Two generations later the population had trebled and the pall of industrial smoke had become permanent. As Anna Seward saw it:

> *Grim Wolverhampton lights her smouldering fires,*
> *And Sheffield, smoke-involv'd; dim where she stands*
> *Circled by lofty mountains, which condense*
> *Her dark and spiral wreaths to drizzling rains*
> *Frequent and sullied . . .*

In Lancashire and the Potteries the worst had still to come. Chorley was, when Aikin wrote (1795), 'a small, neat market town' with its river flowing through a pleasant valley, turning 'several mills, engines and machines'. It possessed the first water-driven factory to be erected in Lancashire (1777). Preston was 'a handsome well-built town, with broad regular streets, and many good houses. The earl of Derby has a large modern mansion in it. The place is rendered gay by assemblies and other places of amusement, suited to the genteel style of the inhabitants.' Aikin notes that the cotton industry had just come to the town. In the south of the county what was to be the most appalling town of all – St Helens – was just beginning to defile its surroundings. The British Plate Glass Manufactory had been erected at Ravenhead, near the village, in 1773, and other glassworks followed. And about the year 1780 'a most extensive copper-work' was erected to smelt and refine the ore from Paris mountain in Anglesey. The atmosphere was being poisoned, every green thing blighted, and every stream fouled with chemical fumes and waste. Here, and in the Potteries and the Black Country especially, the landscape of Hell was foreshadowed.

Steam-Power and Slums

Water-power in itself created no smoke or dirt. Only where industries used coal directly, like the forges of Sheffield, were towns yet blackened and the air poisoned; and only where they produced 'waste' in great quantities, such as in coal-mining, glassworks and chemicals, was the landscape beginning to acquire that sterile covering of 'tips', that were destined to go on piling up until they produced a mountain landscape in miniature; until the vast range of coal-tips around the old town of Wigan, for example, could be sardonically nicknamed the Wigan Alps and be illustrated in later years under that name on picture postcards. But until steam-power became generally used, these landscapes did not achieve their final horrific form.

Although Newcomen had produced the first practical steam-engine in the early years of the eighteenth century, it was capable only of a simple back-and-forth or up-and-down motion and therefore disappeared underground to be used for pumping water out of mines. Nor, when Boulton and Watt began producing steam-engines, from 1775 onwards, was there much perceptible change in industry for many years. Between 1775 and 1800, when their patent expired, 321 steam-engines were built. Of these, nearly one-third went into cotton mills, and the remainder were distributed between ironworks, collieries, copper-mines, canals (for pumping) and breweries. Even with all the Newcomen engines that still continued to be made, and the piracies of Watt's engine, the use of steam-power was neither general nor extensive in 1800. The steam age, with its dramatic impact upon the landscape, begins effectively in the early nineteenth century.

We are not concerned here with the general effects upon industry and the English economy of the use of steam-power, but with its visible effects upon the landscape, and these are now obvious enough. Steam-power meant a new and intense concentration of large-scale industry and of the labour force to man it. It meant that manufacturers no longer needed to seek their power where there was fast-running water, especially in the higher reaches of lonely dales, but found it near the canals which brought coal to them cheaply, or directly upon the coalfields themselves. So emerged what Wordsworth called 'social Industry'. No longer need they go out into the wilderness and create a village or a hamlet to house their labour. Manufacturers ran up their mills, factories and works on the edge of existing towns, and their workers were housed in streets of terrace-houses built rapidly on the vacant ground all around the factory.

The 'Wigan Alps' have now been transformed by landscape reclamation and tree planting.

The reference to Newcomen engines disappearing underground is puzzling and perhaps Professor Hoskins misunderstood their function. They were used for pumping but they were bulky machines and were never installed underground. Some of them had very long working lives and a few survive. The figure of 231 Boulton and Watt steam engines as having been built between 1775 and 1800 is now less certain. The number was probably greater than this.

Industry spread over the lower-lying parts of the towns, leaving the hills for the residences of the well-to-do, but this was not a conscious piece of 'zoning'. Large-scale industries in pre-railway days needed canal-side sites both for bringing in their coal and other raw materials and for taking away their heavy products. Thus they chose the flatter and lower ground where the canals lay. Moreover, it was the low-lying areas that were vacant when the industrialists appeared on the scene, for earlier generations had wisely avoided building on them wherever they could. The sites were there waiting. And again, it was easier and cheaper to build on a flat site than a hillside. As a consequence most of the new streets of working-class houses were built on land that presented difficult drainage problems (not that anyone except the victims gave much thought to this), and the sanitary conditions soon became appalling. The slums were born. The word *slum*, first used in the 1820s, has its origin in the old provincial word *slump*, meaning 'wet mire'. The word *slam* in Low German, Danish and Swedish, means 'mire': and that roughly described the dreadful state of the streets and courtyards on these undrained sites. It need hardly be said that the industrialist of the steam age did not build his own house near the works, as the country factory owners had done. He went to dwell on the 'residential heights' and walked down to the mill each day.

But there is more meaning in the word *slum* than simply a foul street or yard: it denotes also a certain quality of housing. In the early nineteenth century the quality of working-class houses, as structures, deteriorated rapidly. The industrialists of the water-power age, out in the open country, had put up houses for their workpeople – as at Cromford, Mellor and Styal, where many of them may still be seen – which were, in Professor Ashton's words, 'not wanting in amenity and comfort' and even possessed a certain quality of design and proportion.* These decent working-class houses were put up in the 1770s and 1780s, where land was cheap and when building materials were plentiful, wages in the building trades relatively low, and money relatively cheap.

* T. S. Ashton, *The Industrial Revolution, 1760-1830*, (Oxford University Press, 1948), p. 160.

With the outbreak of twenty years' war in 1793, the price of materials and wages in the building trades both began to rise steadily. Interest rates, too, increased and remained high for a generation. Since at least two thirds of the rent of a house consists of interest charges, the rise in interest rates alone was sufficient to bring about the drastic reduction in the size and quality of working-class houses in order to preserve an 'economic rent'. Further, land inside the older towns was acquiring a scarcity value, above all in the towns that were surrounded by open fields, so that they could not grow outwards (see Chapter 9), and a steady rise in the price of land for building was added to the rise in the price of borrowed money. Possibly, too, the building trade was invaded by a new class of speculator who made conditions even worse than they need have been by extracting high profits out of the unprecedented demand for cheap houses. No one has studied this particular class of parasite, how he worked, or what fortunes he made. One often wonders in what opulence his descendants live today, forgetful, or perhaps ignorant, of the origin of their wealth. Their forebears would make a fruitful study.

Bad materials and fewer of them, and bad workmanship, reduced the costs of building. Houses run up in the courts of Birmingham in the 1820s and 1830s cost £60 each to build. Birmingham specialised in close, dark and filthy courtyards: there were over two thousand of these in the town in the 1830s, and many of their houses were built back to back in order to get the maximum number on to each expensive acre. The local medical men did not object, but rather commended them for their cheapness. At first some of them had a deceptive brightness, but their abominable quality soon revealed itself and decay rapidly set in. Decent people moved out if they could, and the born-squalid moved in: the swamp of the slums spread a few years behind the speculative builder everywhere.

Open spaces inside the older towns vanished rapidly. The last remnant of Birmingham Heath was enclosed in 1799, and was built over forthwith with eight new streets. Precisely the same thing was happening around the Lancashire towns also, where the ancient com-

PLATE 90. *China clay working St Austell, Cornwall. The digging of kaolin, actually decomposed granite, on a vast scale for the pottery industry produces a tortured landscape unlike any other in England.*

mons were enclosed and grabbed by the private speculator for building, as at Oldham. Only Preston managed to save its commons from the vultures, and to transform some of them eventually into public parks.

Not only the commons but the large gardens of the eighteenth-century bourgeoisie disappeared under bricks and mortar. The house of Baskerville, the eminent Birmingham printer, was sold in 1788 and the seven acres of land that surrounded it were advertised as 'a very desirable spot to build upon'. In these older towns, too, the large houses of the middle class were divided into tenements to house the swarming population, and factories and warehouses went up on their gardens and orchards. Slowly the other features of the industrial towns were added: Anglican churches, Nonconformist chapels, schools and public houses. Public parks came in the 1840s, and public libraries a few years later; later still perhaps the grandiose Town Hall, by no means always to be despised as architecture.

Entirely new towns grew out of hamlets in the industrial north and Midlands. The germ of Middlesbrough was a single farmhouse near the banks of the unsullied Tees in 1830: by 1880 it was a town of more than fifty thousand people. Barrow-in-Furness, too, sprang from a single house, grew into a fishing village of about three hundred people by the 1840s, and by 1878 was a town of forty thousand. South Shields, St Helens and Birkenhead all shot up quickly during the first half of the nineteenth century. 'Meanwhile', said Wordsworth in *The Excursion* (1814):

> *Meanwhile, at social Industry's command,*
> *How quick, how vast an increase! From the germ*
> *Of some poor hamlet, rapidly produced*
> *Here a huge town, continuous and compact,*
> *Hiding the face of earth for leagues – and there,*
> *Where not a habitation stood before,*
> *Abodes of men irregularly massed*
> *Like trees in forests, – spread through spacious tracts,*
> *O'er which the smoke of unremitting fires*
> *Hangs permanent, and plentiful as wreaths*
> *Of vapour glittering in the morning sun.*
> *And, whereso'er the traveller turns his steps,*
> *He sees the barren wilderness erased,*
> *Or disappearing . . .*

Nor was the industrial landscape represented solely in the great towns, for between them stretched miles of torn and poisoned countryside – the mountains of waste from mining and other industries; the sheets of sullen water, known as 'flashes', which had their origin in subsidence of the surface as a result of mining below; the disused pit-shafts; the derelict and stagnant canals. The train journey between Leeds and Sheffield shows one this nineteenth-century landscape to perfection. In the Lancashire township of Ince there are today twenty-three pit-shafts covering 199 acres, one large industrial slag-heap covering six acres, nearly 250 acres of land under water or marsh due to mining subsidence, another 150 acres liable to flooding, and thirty-six disused pit-shafts. This is the landscape of coal-mining. As for the Black Country, one can hardly begin to describe it. Dickens has an horrific description of it in *The Old Curiosity Shop* (1841), when it had reached the rock bottom of filth and ugliness, and of human degradation. The early industrialists were not 'insensitive to the appeal of the country: the beauty of Cromford and Millers Dale suffered little by the enterprise of Arkwright, and stretches of the Goyt and the Bollin owe something to Oldknow and the Gregs'.* But the later industrialists, the heirs of the steam age, were completely and grotesquely insensitive. No scruples weakened their lust for money; they made their money and left their muck.

The industrial landscape is not confined to the north of England and the west Midlands. In Cornwall for instance one finds two distinct landscapes of industry, one dead, the other still active. Over central Cornwall, particularly to the north-west of St Austell, are the

* Ashton, op. cit., p. 157.

PLATE 91. *The view of the Black
Country in 1866. The full horror of
life in a Victorian industrial area is
obvious here. The combination of
coal mining and iron making
produced a world which fully
deserved its name.*

spoil-heaps of the china-clay industry, an almost lunar landscape that one sees gleaming on the horizon from almost any hill-top in the county (Plate 90). And there is the equally striking landscape of the vanished tin-mining industry: the windowless engine-houses, the monolithic chimney stacks against the skyline, the ruined cottages of an old mining hamlet, and the stony spoil-heaps – a purely nineteenth-century landscape, and perhaps because of its setting, the most appealing of all the industrial landscapes of England, in no way ugly but indeed possessing a profound melancholy beauty (Plate 92). Just across the Devonshire border is the old mining landscape of Blanchdown, west of Tavistock, where, in the middle decades of the nineteenth century, the Devon Great Consols was the richest copper mine in the world: now its miles of spoil-heaps have created a silent and desolate beauty of their own, and foxes and snakes haunt the broken buildings and the glades between.

There is a point, as Arthur Young saw, when industrial ugliness becomes sublime. And indeed the new landscape produced some fine dramatic compositions such as the railway viaduct over the smoking town of Stockport; or the sight of Bradford at night from the moorland hills to the north; or of the smoky silhouette of Nottingham on a winter evening as seen from the south-bound train on the Eastern Region line; or the city of Sheffield in full blast on a murky morning; even (one thinks sometimes) the sight of long gas-lit streets of red brick working-class houses in a Victorian town with not a tree or a bush in sight: only the lamps shining on pavements blanched by the autumn evening wind.

188

PLATE 92. *Abandoned tin mines at Botallack, Cornwall. A romantic landscape, yet one which in its heyday meant appalling conditions of work for those employed there and perhaps an even worse life when the mines were killed by cheaper metal from elsewhere.*

PLATE 93. *Delabole slate quarry, Cornwall. Traditionally the largest man-made hole in England, it is the result of the running together of a number of small quarries. Cornish slates were widely employed for roofing in the county by the fourteenth century and indeed by 1314 they were certainly in use on buildings in Winchester, Hampshire. Slate was being worked at Delabole in the sixteenth century and still is. Sometimes slate was also mined in caverns as at Carnglaze.*

Chapter 8

ROADS, CANALS AND RAILWAYS

Introduction

The landscape of communications has always fascinated historians and laymen alike. Generations of scholars and local historians have sought to understand the pattern of roads and tracks in England and in recent years the same enthusiasm has been shown for railways and canals. All these means of travel have their own intrinsically interesting features largely generated by the method of movement involved: bridges, turnpike cottages, milestones in the case of roads, and stations, cuttings, locks, warehouses, etc. in the cases of canals and railways. The actual line of communication is usually of little interest, an area of tarmac, a grassy lane, a sheet of water or two parallel rails. Thus the main interest in the methods of communication should lie in how they affect the wider landscape rather than in their specific details. Yet so many people fail to see these wider and far more important aspects in their search for minutiae such as the differences between the Midland Railway signal boxes and those of the Great Western. Even worse has been the invention of a whole pseudo-history of roads and tracks based on the tracing of communication across large areas of countryside and explaining the results in terms of prehistoric ways or medieval roads.

Apart from the major engineered Roman roads, limited lengths of eighteenth- or nineteenth-century turnpike roads, some nineteenth-century enclosure roads and modern by-passes and motorways, there is no way of dating a road. The Ridgeway in Wiltshire and Berkshire may well have been used in prehistoric times, but probably no more so than the line of the A4 across the same counties. Similarly the A11 between Thetford and Norwich is likely to be just as old as the nearby so-called Icknield Way, but we do not know, nor is there any way of finding out. More time and energy has been expended on the history of roads and tracks than on any other feature in the English landscape and most of it to little effect. Just because a road runs past a group of Bronze Age burial mounds does not mean that it is prehistoric. There are Bronze Age burial mounds in their thousands all over England and some road or track passes near most of them. Nor is the road between,

say, Salisbury and Winchester necessarily medieval just because it now links the two medieval towns. It may be older, it may possibly be later. Indeed one can safely say that almost all of our roads and tracks were used in medieval times and perhaps most were also used in the prehistoric period as well. But that said we have come to no great conclusion.

To understand roads we need to begin with the premise that all roads are very old indeed and that what we need to study is their changing importance through time as man adapted them to his requirements. Thus a minor lane between two Iron Age villages might have been improved and linked with others to become a road between a Roman estate centre and one of its dependent farms. It could then have been further extended and incorporated into a Saxon salt way stretching across three counties. Later it may have declined to a local field access path in the thirteenth century, been re-aligned by enclosure commissioners in the eighteenth century and turned into a dual-carriage trunk road in this century. It is still the same road, but has merely changed its function and thus its form. It is in the perception of these changes that we begin to understand the history of the landscape as a whole, the Iron Age village, the Roman estate, the Saxon trade, the medieval fields, the eighteenth-century agriculture and twentieth-century industrialisation.

Professor Hoskins was incorrect in suggesting that there is little new to say about roads. Basically there is everything to say, for most roads are not understood at all, at least in their wider context. Yet he was probably correct in attempting to explain some of the complexities of roads in England by using one sheet of the Ordnance Survey 1-inch map series. Much of what he says about the roads and tracks depicted there is perceptive and useful, but even Professor Hoskins is wrong in the attribution of many of them. Some of the alternative explanations and differences of interpretation are covered in the marginal notes to this chapter, but it is perhaps worth mentioning others at greater length here.

PLATE 94. *Wade's Causeway, Wheeldale Moor, North Yorkshire. This is the Roman road from Malton to Whitby and has been cleared of vegetation and exposed to show its structure. What is visible are merely the rough foundation stones. The smooth road surface has long since disappeared. It is thus a failed routeway.*

The Making of
THE ENGLISH LANDSCAPE

The area covered by the old Ordance Survey Sheet 145 is now included on parts of the new 1:50 000 scale series, Sheets 151, 152, 164 and 165. Within this region, as Professor Hoskins suggested, there are various names and alignments which raise questions in the mind of any landscape historian, questions which could be asked of any part of England.

Professor Hoskins was particularly interested in the Banbury Lane, largely because it had been identified as a prehistoric trackway by archaeologists in the 1950s, shortly before he wrote this book. It now seems unlikely that this was any more of a prehistoric trackway than other roads depicted on the map. The identification of the so-called Jurassic Way was always based on the very flimsy evidence that it linked some six or seven Iron Age sites. Now, hundreds of Iron Age sites are known from the area and the 'way' has no direct connection with any of them except by accident. The section west of Banbury is, in any case, by no means a continuous line, nor is the alleged early 'arc' via Byfield. The real importance of the Banbury Lane, regardless of exactly how old it is, is that it was the main medieval route from Northampton to Banbury. Northampton was founded in late-Saxon times, perhaps as a planned town. Banbury is certainly a planted town set up by the Bishop of Lincoln between 1123 and 1138. The important period of use of the Banbury Lane must have begun therefore in the late twelfth century. Yet by the late seventeenth century it is not one of the main roads described by John Ogilby in his atlas, *Britannia*, and had thus lost its former significance by that date. Nevertheless much of it is still an important road between the two towns.

Nor is the other alleged prehistoric routeway, the A432, any more convincing. It is indeed on a ridgeway in places, but the existence of long barrows near it is entirely fortuitous. It is no doubt an old road, though no older than most, whose importance developed in the medieval period as the main route between Oxford and Banbury. By 1676 it was part of the main Oxford to Coventry road and of course remains as a major trunk road today. That is, it had a similar status to the Banbury Lane in medieval times but it is one which it has kept and developed in response to changing circumstances, whereas the Banbury Lane has failed.

A similarly failed road, at least to the west of Bicester, is the Roman Akeman Street which is only used as a modern road in short sections. This is because it has been replaced by more suitable roads which have been adapted to the continually changing pattern of communications and settlement development. A much odder but more interesting Roman road is that running north-east from Bicester on its way to Towcester in Northamptonshire. As far as Finmere it is now the main road to Buckingham (A421). One might easily assume that it has always been an important road. Yet in the late seventeenth century the road to Buckingham ran roughly parallel to it, a mile or so to the south-east, through Stratton Audley. This is now merely a set of narrow winding lanes, cut at its north end by a second world war air field. Then it was part of the Oxford to Cambridge main road. It was not until the eighteenth century that the Roman road was re-used and became important as a through route.

In the late seventeenth century too the main road from London to Aberystwyth did not pass through Oxford but followed the present minor road (B4027) to the north, via Islip and Woodstock to Enstone and then via the modern A34 to Stratford-on-Avon. All these are examples of the changing importance of roads through time. They show well the difficulty of identifying 'old' roads. Even more interesting is the situation at King's Sutton, a village to the south-east of Banbury. Today no main road passes less than two miles from it. It is set at the junction of four minor lanes, none of which has any indications of antiquity. Yet recent research has shown that the village was the centre of a great late Saxon estate that once extended north-east to Towcester, south-east to Buckingham, north to Chipping Warden and west perhaps well into Oxfordshire, and was also the site of a great Saxon minster church. All the lanes must have once been extremely important, but nothing on the map nor indeed on the ground suggests this. The dangers of 'dating' roads from their former alignments are clear.

The canals of England had a much shorter life, though many are now gaining a new importance as recreational routeways. They were mainly constructed to link the new industrial areas to ports and markets, but were soon overtaken by the great railway construction. However, in the short time they flourished, they had an enormous impact, not so much on the towns they joined but on the countryside

192

PLATE 95. *Excavations for the cutting for the Park Village, Camden Town, 1836, on the London and Birmingham Railway. This splendid lithograph by Bourne gives one a vivid idea of the impact of the railway on urban landscapes. It is the scene of the 'earthquake' description in* Dombey and Son.

through which they passed. While the actual canals, together with their locks, bridges and wharfs, have their own intrinsic interest, far more significant is the fact that they allowed the easy and cheap movement of bulk cargoes over long distances. This, as Professor Hoskins rightly points out, was further developed by the railways, but the canals began the spread of standard bricks, tiles and slates which changed the visual appearance of much of England.

Railways have even more interest in terms of the resulting local alteration of the landscape with their cuttings, tunnels, bridges and embankments. But in the end their greatest impact was the way in which they helped to change most people's way of life and in so doing changed much of the landscape. Professor Hoskins gives some vivid contemporary descriptions of what happened and rightly stresses the effect of cheap standardised building materials. But in addition whole new settlements came into existence. Crewe, Wolverton and Eastleigh were all new railway towns, while Doncaster, Swindon and Ashford became major engineering centres. Other towns were changed out of all recognition because of their location at centres of major railway lines. Peterborough is perhaps the best known but March in Cambridgeshire and Gainsborough and Spalding in Lincolnshire are among many places where the railway transformed provincial towns. Perhaps the most greatly changed of all was York. The railways also produced or speeded up the development of some of the early resort towns such as Skegness, Mablethorpe, Bournemouth, Swanage and Weston-super-Mare, and certainly allowed minor villages such as Cromer to become lesser resorts and ports such as Grimsby to be developed into major exporting centres. Even sleepy rural villages were turned into minor railway settlements with the coming of the railways. An example of this was Woodford Halse, in Northamptonshire, which was transformed by the arrival of the Great Central Railway's locomotive depot in 1896.

Perhaps one of the most fascinating places is Melton Constable in north Norfolk. Up until 1880 it was a typical Norfolk village with no real centre but merely a dispersed pattern of cottages and farmsteads. Then, in 1882, the Lynn and Fakenham Railway Company extended their line from Fakenham to Norwich via Melton. In 1883 the company's successor, the Eastern and Midlands Railway, laid a further line

from Melton to North Walsham and also established Melton as their engineering headquarters. A year later another branch to Holt, ultimately Cromer, was completed and Melton stood at the centre of a minor railway junction. In 1889 the new Midland and Great Northern Joint Railway took over the lines and Melton was further developed as the new Committee's locomotive building and repair centre. For eighty years Melton was a railway 'town'. Then closure took place. Today all the rails have gone, as have most of the station buildings, but the cuttings, the locomotive works, the school and the 'Railway Institute', both dated 1896, and rows of neat terraced houses, clearly designed by a Great Northern architect, still survive. Visually Melton remains a railway centre even more than twenty years after the railway went. Its much longer history before the 1880s is hardly visible.

Elsewhere the overall impact of the railways on the English landscape is not as easy to assess as it at first appears. As Professor Simmonds has shown, it is by no means always clear what effect railways had. The arrival of a railway in a town did not always lead to expansion. For example, in 1851 just after the railway came, Macclesfield was larger than Coventry, Halifax or York, having had a 160 per cent increase in population in the previous forty years. Yet by 1911 its population had fallen by four thousand. Professor Simmonds is correct when he says that it is very hard to isolate the part played by railways in the growth of towns and the development of the countryside from all the other economic and social factors of the nineteenth century. The study of railways in the landscape has hardly begun.

ROADS, CANALS AND RAILWAYS

Roads

The roads of England have attracted a considerable literature, and it might seem difficult to say anything very new. It would be attempting the impossible to write about all the varieties of roads there are in England in the space of a few pages: such a wide-ranging discussion would be full of familiar generalisations and would make very dull reading. Let us take instead one comparatively small piece of country, which contains every variety of road from the prehistoric trackway to the modern by-pass, so that the detailed differences are brought out: for the interest of an inquiry such as this, and one cannot say it too often, lies in the detail of the subject. For this purpose I choose the country depicted on Sheet 145 of the Ordnance Survey (sixth edition), which runs from the edge of Oxford northwards to a few miles beyond Banbury, and from Chipping Norton on the west to beyond Brackley in Northamptonshire on the east. One could find as much to write about on almost any other sheet of the Ordnance Survey; and one could indeed write a whole chapter about a single sheet of the 2½-inch map, covering only some six miles each way.

A merely casual inspection of sheet 145 reveals a number of named roads suggestive of several different ages and uses. There are the Welsh Road, the Salt Way, the Port Way, Akeman Street, Traitor's Ford Lane and Banbury Lane; and besides these named roads a considerable number of roads, lanes and paths that excite our curiosity by their directness for miles across almost uninhabited country, or by their association with parish boundaries or ancient earthworks (like Aves Ditch), or some other suspicious circumstance.

Banbury Lane, now in part a main motor road, is the oldest of the roads on the map, though there is little about it today to indicate its great antiquity. It is a part of the so-called Jurassic Way, which runs along the junction of the upper lias and the lower oolite like a corridor, eventually linking the Bristol Avon with the Humber.* The course of this important trackway across sheet 145 is perfectly clear. It makes its appearance on the bold ridge by the Rollright Stones, where it forms the boundary between Warwickshire and Oxfordshire for part of its course. Keeping along the watershed between the Warwickshire Avon and the Cherwell, it runs past Oatley Hill Farm to Wigginton Heath. Thence it drops down to cross the Cherwell at Banbury. East of Banbury, where it has attracted the name of Banbury Lane for some twenty miles, it follows a winding course along the watershed between the Cherwell and the Great Ouse. For a considerable distance it is now followed by a main road (A422 and B4525), but near Culworth it becomes a narrow lane, running through almost deserted country, past Adstone Lodge and Foxley to Cold Higham. Here we are in the uttermost depths of the Midlands. After Cold Higham it crosses Watling Street, runs past the important Iron Age hill-fort of Hunsbury, and reaches the crossing of the Nene at Northampton. There is no need to trace it farther. Mr O. G. S. Crawford believes the Jurassic Way to be of Iron Age date in view of its strong associations with hill-forts and finds of this period, though he does not dismiss the possibility of its being older. Whether it goes back to the Iron Age or the Bronze Age, however, it has lost its original character as a wide trackway across open country. To see what it was once like we have to turn to the chalk downlands, notably the Ridgeway that follows the crest of the Berkshire Downs or the Icknield Way near Royston in Hertfordshire.

In its present form the Banbury Lane represents a great narrowing down of what was originally not a single track but a more or less open corridor (so that one cannot be too precise about its prehistoric course), bounded on either side by dense forest, in places several miles wide. The narrowing down of this primitive trade-route took place, perhaps

PLATE 96. *An unusual feature on an English road, this tunnel on the A3066 at Beaminster, Dorset, dates from 1831-2. It was built in order to improve the ancient road over the steep-sided Horn Hill into Somerset, and largely paid for by Giles Russell, a major local landowner, as a piece of genuine public beneficence. It was designed and constructed by one of the new generation of civil engineers, M. Lang, in a form that presages early Victorian railway architecture, which at that time had not yet appeared.*

* See the essay by W. F. Grimes in *Aspects of Archaeology in Britain and Beyond* (H.W. Edwards, 1951), pp. 144-71, and some pages in O.G.S. Crawford, *Archaeology in the Field* (Phoenix House, 1953), pp. 81-5.

in stages, in Saxon and early medieval times as more and more land was taken in for arable cultivation. On the chalk downlands, which have been under sheep pasture ever since the Iron Age, something like the original appearance of a similar trackway has been preserved, but in the arable Midlands it must have disappeared fairly early. We know that in the eleventh century the Jurassic Way in Oxfordshire was the main road to Northampton, probably joining it with the important town of Gloucester, and throughout the Middle Ages it was a market-road, linking one market town with the next in a long series. Its present course can almost certainly be dated from late Saxon times. Northampton began life as a fortified position in the early tenth century – it is first recorded as a name in the year 917 – and soon became the shire town. From this time we can probably date the development of Banbury Lane as a road rather than a wide corridor.

Deviations from ancient routes appeared at an early date. It is clear from the map (and other evidence) that the original trackway near Great Rollright ran due north, across the Stour and straight up Traitor's Ford Lane (this must be a medieval name), along the broken lip of the escarpment to Edge Hill. Thence it described a great arc through Fenny Compton and Byfield to rejoin the other road at Cold Higham (Crawford). Crawford considers that the Saxon road to Northampton was a later shortening of this ancient trackway; even so, parts of the Banbury 'cut-off' are themselves prehistoric in date.

The other deviation, that from near Culworth to Watling Street, is of recent date. The old lane was in use down to comparatively recent times as a through road from Northampton to Banbury. On the first edition of the 1-inch map (1834) it is shown as boldly as the lanes linking the villages of Canons Ashby and Moreton Pinkney, and similarly on the map of 1887. The Lane must have fallen out of use in this stretch within living memory.

There is at least one other prehistoric ridgeway on sheet 145. This has continued in use to the present day and carries a vast traffic between Oxford and Coventry and Birmingham. It is now A423, which began as a prehistoric ridgeway along the watershed between the Cherwell and the Evenlode. It ran from a crossing of the Thames at or near Oxford (perhaps ultimately from the Berkshire Ridgeway) northwards to join the Jurassic Way near Banbury. There are remains of long barrows and of megalithic tombs at various points along its course. Later it was taken over and paved by the Romans from a point north of Oxford to Sturdy's Castle, where it met the east-west road of Akeman Street. Medieval

PLATE 97. *One of at least three lines of the so-called Ridgeway, near Aldworth, Berkshire. How old is it? It was certainly used in medieval times but it is doubtful if it is prehistoric, even though traces of Bronze Age and Iron Age fields lie on either side of it. In fact a little further to the north-west this track is cut by a Bronze Age ditch.*

196

charters along its course refer to it as 'the ridgeway'. It apparently remained in continuous use throughout medieval times; it figures as the main road from Oxford to Banbury in Ogilby's road-book (1675); it was turnpiked in the eighteenth century and it still follows its original course after some three thousand years. Because it has remained in use all this time, and has been continually adapted to heavier traffic, it has lost its original character except in two respects. It still commands extensive and airy views over the valleys to the east and west, and in places its broad grass verges betray something of its original width before the road was metalled.

Of the Roman roads of the district, one need say little. Akeman Street will serve as an example. A good deal of it to the east of the Cherwell remains in use as a main road (A41 and A4095), the only important break in the line being caused by the growth of the Saxon town of Bicester, a mile to the north, in place of the now-vanished Romano-British town of Alchester. Just short of the Cherwell, however, the line of the road disappears from the 1-inch map, and to the west of the river for many miles it can be followed only as a continuous hedge-line, a field-path, and a bit of lane here and there. Its entire course can, however, be traced without much hesitation.

Among other features of the road it is interesting to see how it still forms the northern boundary of Kirtlington Park, to the east of the Cherwell, and the southern boundary of Tackley Park, on the other side of the river. The immense continuity of English boundaries is fascinating. Akeman Street was the boundary between what is now Tackley Park and Whitehill Farm as early as the year 1004 when King Ethelred gave the small estate of Whitehill to St Frideswide's monastery at Oxford, and it is still a boundary though the Roman road has vanished from sight. Not many miles away, two estates meet, between Wootton and Steeple Barton, precisely where they met in a charter dated 958, and possibly for some considerable time before that.

The colonisation of new land, and its demarcation into private estates, created thousands of miles of *boundaries* for the first time. Often these new boundaries followed a stream or a trackway that already existed, but very often they created their own boundary lanes or *meres* (from the Old English word '*(ge) maere*', 'boundary'). This is the origin of a great number of 'green lanes' on the map which run for a few miles, separating parishes on either side but eventually petering out. They are to be distinguished, therefore, from the green lanes that run for more considerable distances, which are portions of through-roads dating from prehistoric times. Sometimes these ancient estate-boundaries took the form of deep V-shaped ditches, much more impressive than the ordinary ditch for drainage, and therefore puzzling until one realises their special origin.

These green lanes are sometimes ten to fifteen yards wide, still entirely grassed over, and used only by tractors and cattle. An example of this kind is Dornford Lane, which runs parallel with the Banbury to Oxford road for some miles north of Woodstock. The age and original purpose of this road, like that of many similar green lanes, are puzzling. At its northern end it has no obvious beginning, but it assumes a recognisable course at Barton Lodge in Steeple Barton parish. Thence it runs directly southwards for four and a half miles to Woodstock. For centuries the lane served no doubt as a cattle-road, but why did it come into existence at all, and when? It runs so near the ancient Banbury-Oxford road (within a quarter of a mile in places) that it cannot have served as another through road. One might suspect then that it originated as a boundary – a green *mere* between two ancient estates – but there is no sign of a boundary along it today. The parochial and manorial boundaries (both very ancient) follow either the Banbury-Oxford road or else take a winding course between the main road and the lane. At no point on its way to Woodstock is it followed by a boundary that is known to be ancient.

The break in the line of Akeman Street was not 'caused' by the growth of Saxon Bicester which actually lies to the north of the road. The road through the Roman town was abandoned and re-routed just outside it, presumably in the fifth or sixth centuries. Bicester seems to have been a medieval planted town, probably laid out around 1239 along the then main road through the area, the Aylesbury to Banbury road (A41). The adjacent roads were then diverted into the new town.

Dornford Lane is much more likely to have been the former main road into Woodstock from Banbury, which developed after 1154-74, when Woodstock was founded as a royal town by Henry II. The decline of Woodstock relative to Oxford merely led to the increasing importance of the present main road. Dornford Lane itself has an extension which actually by-passes Woodstock to the east and joins the main road to Oxford (A34) further south at Begbroke. It may therefore have had an earlier importance as an alternative main road to Oxford in late Saxon times before the arrival of Woodstock.

PLATE 98. *Packhorse bridge, Wasdale, Cumbria. Bridges of this primitive style and construction are undateable.*

It was not a through-road for Saxon or medieval traffic; it did not come into existence as a boundary; it was not originally a drove-road, for cattle-drovers took over existing tracks and lanes and did not create their own except in special circumstances. We are left with one possibility – that it originated as a road from one of the royal demesne farms to the royal hunting lodge of Woodstock. The Anglo-Saxon kings are known to have used Woodstock (now Blenheim) Park as a hunting-ground. It is first heard of about the year 1000, and a charter of 1005 speaks of the '*haga*' or enclosure which existed here. At the other end of the lane lay the manor of 'Bertone': no amount of ingenuity can carry the lane any farther north than this.

Barton means literally 'barley farm' or 'corn farm', but later came to have the special meaning of 'demesne farm'. Although by 1086 the Barton estate had been split up into a number of manors, of which only one was still in the hands of the king himself, there can be little doubt that before the Conquest the Anglo-Saxon kings had had here an estate of some seven thousand acres which they kept in hand for their own supplies. Nor can there be much doubt that when they were in residence at Woodstock these supplies were called upon, and were carried in carts along the wide green track now called Dornford Lane. The lane came into existence for this special purpose not later than the tenth century: in no other way can we explain its peculiar and limited course. The fact that the lane runs so wide and straight also tells us that when it came into existence the open arable fields of Barton and Wootton did not yet extend so far. It clearly ran through uncultivated land originally.

I have dwelt upon this small piece of local topography in order to show how here and there, and possibly oftener than we think, roads came into existence to serve a special and limited purpose. Most of these curious little by-roads and lanes developed in Saxon times. In the same piece of country, for example, we read of 'the wood way' in Saxon charters: these are the lanes that grew up between certain villages and the distant woods in which they had rights or pickings. Many of these tiny lanes survive, some incorporated into motor roads.

It is likely that a considerable number of Romano-British by-roads came into existence in the same way for limited purposes and yet remain to be discovered on the map or on the ground. Mr Margary's book on *Roman Ways in the Weald* was a revelation of how much can be unearthed by a patient and detailed examination of one region. There can be no doubt that on Sheet 145 of the Ordnance Survey, with which we are immediately concerned, there are by-roads which will prove eventually to be Romano-British in origin. We have been bemused too long by the great military roads of the Romans and have not given enough thought and research to the local 'economic' roads that developed during the two or three centuries that followed the Conquest and the brief phase of military occupation.

It is certainly true that many of the by-roads in an area such as this may well have been used in Roman times though it is difficult to prove. The example of King's Sutton quoted in the Introduction is significant. Its importance as a late Saxon estate centre was probably the result of it being an equally important Roman and even Iron Age estate. A large Roman settlement existed just north of the village and the great Iron Age hill-fort of Rainsborough lies a little to the south-east. Many of the roads, tracks and footpaths which link the village to its neighbours and to the fort were probably used by prehistoric and Roman people.

In many parts of England, roads marked as 'Salt Way' may be found. On Sheet 145 there is a short stretch of lane so described immediately south of Banbury. Salt was one of the very few necessaries of life that could not be produced anywhere and had to be transported from the centres of production on the sea coasts, on tidal rivers, and from certain inland centres. At Ingoldmells, to the north of Skegness, heaps of debris have been found to be the result of salt-workings in the late Bronze Age. In 1086 there were 278 salt-pools in Lincolnshire, in Sussex 285, and many other coastal counties had a considerable salt industry at this period.

At an early date, the inland brine springs of Droitwich and Cheshire were discovered and used for the manufacture of salt. The earliest reference to Droitwich salt occurs in 716, when King Ethelbald granted a salt pit there to Evesham Abbey. By 1086, Droitwich salt was being widely distributed over the Midlands; King William himself had eighty-five salt pans here. According to Domesday Book, no fewer than sixty-eight manors and estates had

the right to receive salt from Droitwich, including Princes Risborough, some seventy miles away in Buckinghamshire.* Mr F. T. S. Houghton has worked out many of the salt ways of the West Midlands, and considers that the short stretch of Salt Way near Banbury was part of the route taken between Droitwich and Princes Risborough, by way of Stratford-upon-Avon and Aynho. It is therefore of Saxon date, and is an example of a track used for a special purpose. It is doubtful, however, how far the salt trade created its own lanes and tracks. For the most part it made use of trackways already established and ancient, though it is possible that new pieces of track were trampled out where the direct line required it. Certainly the crossing of the Avon at Stratford is extremely ancient.

Salt ways present no special features that distinguish them from other roads and lanes on the map or on the ground. Nor have the medieval market-roads that developed all over England, particularly in the twelfth and thirteenth centuries, any special characteristics. Most of these, too, developed along existing paths, the paths that ran from village to village in Saxon times, though here and there they may have called for a new piece to complete the chain of paths. Many medieval market towns were originally villages of little note, and have sunk back again into obscurity, but their former importance is betrayed by the spider's net of roads that still converge upon them. Deddington, in north Oxfordshire, is an example of such a village, and there are several similar examples in every English county.

Few new roads were created between Saxon times and the turnpike and 'enclosure' roads of the eighteenth century. Like the salt traffic, the cattle trade that developed so strongly from the sixteenth century onwards moved along existing green lanes and trackways. Since most of England south of the Trent was now in a state of cultivation, there was little opportunity for drovers to strike across country and create new lines of movement, though on the moorlands north of the Trent they may have done so. The drovers' roads of the Midlands were particularly important, for it was along these that the great traffic in cattle from Wales to London and the Midland markets found its leisurely way. The Welsh Road, which appears here and there on the map of the Midlands, refers to this cross-country traffic. This road can be picked up just outside Kenilworth, whence it runs in a south-easterly direction through Offchurch across country to Southam, and thence through an almost uninhabited landscape towards the Northamptonshire uplands. Near Marston Doles the route turned south, past Priors Hardwick, Upper and Lower Boddington to Aston-le-Walls, near which it crosses the Banbury-Daventry road. It goes on to Culworth, where it meets Banbury Lane, and may have proceeded along this Lane to the great markets of Northampton, where the cattle were sold in large numbers for fattening on the rich Midland pastures. In the other direction, one can trace the route vaguely from the Welsh border into the Midlands. The Anchor Inn, on the border of Wales and England, high up on the far western side of Clun Forest, was the great point of assembly for drovers coming out of Wales. Thence one recognised route led on to Ludlow, and so due east through Bewdley and Bromsgrove, through the country south of Birmingham, to the point near Kenilworth where we previously picked it up on the map.

The drove-roads of England have yet to be identified and pieced together. They have been written about in Scotland and Wales, and a fascinating piece of field work and historical research awaits someone in this country who is not afraid to use his feet as well as his head. For many miles along the Leicestershire-Lincolnshire border there runs a green lane known as Sewstern Lane or The Drift. This road has a continuous history from the Bronze Age onwards. After it had been superseded in the seventeenth century by the Great North Road, which runs to the east of it through more inhabited country, Sewstern Lane became

* F. T. S. Houghton, 'Salt Ways', *Transactions of the Birmingham Archaeological Society*, 54, 1932.

a recognised route by which cattle from Scotland and the North of England reached the Midland pastures and London: hence its later name of The Drift. Parts of it have been taken over for a secondary motor road, but much of it remains remote and quiet, rarely disturbed by a human voice.

The old drove-roads made their own contribution to the landscape in the wayside inns that grew up to cater specially for drovers in lonely stretches of country, and in the 'stances' beside them where the cattle were shut up and rested for the night. After the middle of the nineteenth century animals were moved by train (and now by lorry) and the drovers' lanes were deserted for good. Now they make some of the quietest walking in England away from the high moors. For they always avoided towns and traffic; they avoided also the larger roads which became turnpikes in the eighteenth century and were subject to tolls, and they were short-turfed for the cattle and sheep, grazing as they went.

The turnpikes, though important in the history of roads, contributed little to the landscape that did not exist before. For the most part they took over existing routes, though in the hillier parts of the country they were responsible for the making of entirely new stretches of road where the older roads tackled gradients suitable only for foot-passengers and pack-horses. These new roads may often be recognised by the fact that they run for miles without passing through a village, or indeed habitation at all apart from their own toll-houses (their most notable addition to the scene) and an inn or two attracted to the roadside by the prospect of traffic. In the industrial counties such as Lancashire the new towns called for entirely new turnpike roads

Sewstern Lane is a fine example of part of a multiple road system. It does run parallel to the Great North Road (A1) away to its east. But to say it was superseded by the latter in the seventeenth century is not entirely true. In medieval times it was merely an alternative to the already existing Great North Road. The latter was probably always more important, for medieval towns such as Stamford and Grantham lay on its line. When traffic increased from the late seventeenth century onwards, usually only one of the various alternatives was improved. The others were largely abandoned as major routes. They then became very useful as cattleways, unencumbered by wheeled vehicles. Further south in Cambridgeshire there are two or three alternative routes, parallel to and east of the present A1 which had the same origin. The same picture is visible on the London to Norwich road between Newmarket and Thetford across the Breckland.

PLATE 99. *This toll house at Kintbury, on the Bath Road, west of Newbury, Berkshire, is perhaps more exotic than most. It is probably late eighteenth-century and known as Halfway House as it lies roughly halfway between London and Bath.*

between them, and the old road pattern was more drastically altered.

Certain important roads, too, were altered out of all recognition. The Roman Watling Street, which had become the London to Holyhead road, was vastly improved and largely remade by Telford between 1820 and 1828. Cuttings were made to ease the original gradients, causeways laid down in difficult places, and the roadway widened. Much of this engineering work was wasted at the time, for it was done on the eve of the railway age and never put to good use – not until the twentieth century. An incidental effect of the turnpike movement was the construction of fine bridges to carry heavy coach-traffic. There is a notable series over the Thames from Lechlade down to Staines, and there are innumerable others up and down the country. Near Exeter, the old Exeter to Crediton road had been doubled in width (from nine and a half to twenty feet) and so made necessary a new bridge over the Creedy. This bridge (Cowley Bridge), built by James Green, the county surveyor, in 1813-14, is so fine in design that it has already been scheduled and protected as an ancient monument.

Milestones make their appearance along the roads during the reign of Charles II. They were known to the Romans, but no one afterwards used them until the Dover Road was given mile-marks in 1663. Stones were also set up along the Great North Road in 1708, but the first true milestone to be set up in Britain since Roman times was that at Trumpington, just outside Cambridge, in 1727, where it is still to be seen. The earliest milestones were the result of private enterprise. Official milestones were authorised on the London to Chester road in 1744, but they did not become compulsory until 1773. An act of that year ordered all turnpike trusts to provide guide-posts and milestones on their roads.

Guide-posts of a sort are much older than milestones. Rough granite crosses, for example, marked the track across Dartmoor in the thirteenth century; and a German traveller in 1598 found a pre-Reformation wayside cross acting as a guide-post in Kent. A few new guide-posts appeared here and there in the late seventeenth century, and an act of 1698 ordered justices to erect standing-posts at cross-roads; but the act seems to have been ineffective. Guide-posts did not become compulsory until the act of 1773. One of the earliest private guide-posts stands on Broadway Hill, in the Cotswolds, set up by Nathan Izod in 1669. A post dated 1705 stands at Hopton in Derbyshire; and at Bicton, in East Devon, is a fine brick pillar dated 1743, with directions and scriptural texts on its four sides. Yorkshire has many early guide-posts. The older guide-posts stood several feet high for the benefit of travellers in coaches and on horseback, but in recent years those on the main roads have been considerably reduced in height for the convenience of motorists.

In recent years, too, other changes have been made in English roads. Great by-pass roads, like the East Lancashire by-pass, now plunge straight across the country, regardless of contours, using cuttings and embankments to keep as even a gradient as possible. They are entirely without beauty. Is there anything uglier in the whole landscape than an arterial by-pass road, except an airfield? Old roads have been straightened, and have lost all their character, historic and otherwise. Sheet 145 of the Ordnance Survey, with which we began, furnishes an excellent example to finish with. The main road from Oxford to Bicester (A43) runs dead straight for several miles and might well be taken for a fine piece of Roman road. But the first edition of the one-inch map, dated 1833, shows a very different sort of road, a narrow Saxon road winding and zig-zagging every few yards. Only in recent years has it been straightened.

PLATE 100. *The Grand Union Canal, Braunston Junction, Northamptonshire. The Oxford Canal was cut here in 1774 and the Grand Junction was opened in 1796. Today it is hard to realise that the canal was the late eighteenth-century equivalent to the M1, which lies five miles away to the east.*

Canals

The canals of England are mainly the creation of the last forty years of the eighteenth century and the first quarter of the nineteenth, and they introduced a number of distinctive changes into the landscape. Not only did they bring stretches of water into country often lacking in them, as in many parts of the Midlands, with consequent changes in bird and plant life, but they also brought – mostly for the first time – aqueducts, cuttings and embankments, tunnels, locks, lifts and inclined planes, and many attractive bridges, and they greatly influenced the growth and appearance of many towns. One town, indeed, was entirely the creation of canals (Stourport in Worcestershire) and is worth seeing solely on that account.

It is true that the Romans had constructed two or three artificial waterways in this country large enough to be regarded as canals: Car Dike that winds from Peterborough up to Lincoln, the Foss Dike joining the Witham and the Trent, and perhaps the Itchen Dike from Winchester to the Itchen. But these were hardly distinguishable from drainage channels, having none of the features that we associate with canals. The first true canal, with locks and a towpath, was that constructed by the municipal authorities of Exeter between 1564 and 1567 to allow barges to pass around the weirs on the river and to reach the city. On this canal pound-locks were used for the first time in England, i.e., an upper and a lower gate fitted with sluices and enclosing a chamber into which boats passed to be raised or lowered to the next level. The Exeter canal had three locks of this type. It was a small undertaking, only sixteen feet wide, three feet deep, and about three miles long, but it was a remarkable work for its time, all the more so because it was a municipal enterprise. Since then it has been

As already noted, the Car Dike, north of Peterborough, is now known not to have been a canal but a Roman catch-water drain.

204

three times enlarged, in width, length and depth. It became a favourite walk in the eighteenth century for the citizens of Exeter, and remained so until recent years. Perhaps it still is, for it still winds peacefully between the elm-shaded meadow. of the Exe valley past congenial inns.

The Exeter canal remained the only one of its kind for almost two hundred years, until James Brindley made his first canal for the Duke of Bridgewater in 1760. In the meantime more than a thousand miles of rivers had been made navigable, but these made no noticeable change in the landscape. But Brindley's canal from the coal-mines at Worsley to Manchester had several features hitherto unknown. His principle was to keep his canal as level as possible. To achieve this he carried it over roads and streams by means of aqueducts, of which the most notable was that at Barton (two hundred yards long and nearly forty feet above the Irwell), crossed valleys by embankments, cut through hills where they were unavoidable, and followed the contours where possible. At times the Worsley canal followed a most circuitous route in order to maintain a level course, and this excessive winding remained a feature of the early canals. On reaching Worsley the canal tunnelled into the sandstone cliff to reach the coal workings some three-quarters of a mile inside the hill, where it divided into channels that eventually reached a length of several miles. The village of Worsley was transformed by this undertaking, the first of many to be so affected by canals. When Josiah Wedgwood visited it in 1773 it had 'the appearance of a considerable Seaport town. His Grace has built some hundreds of houses, and is every year adding considerably to their number.'

Later canals became more daring in their engineering as experience was gained. The Grand Trunk Canal (1766-77) not only made use of aqueducts, cuttings and embankments, but was carried through the hill country between the Mersey and Trent basins by means of five tunnels, of which the Harecastle Tunnel near Kidsgrove was 2,880 yards long and more than two hundred feet beneath the surface at its deepest point. One can still see this triumph of Brindley's engineering skill, though it is now disused, having been superseded by a second tunnel, parallel with the first, which was constructed by Telford in 1827. Altogether the Grand Trunk Canal had five tunnels and seventy-six locks on its ninety-three mile course from the Mersey to Shardlow, near which it entered the Trent. Shardlow was transformed from a quiet farming village into an inland port like Worsley, but with even wider connexions. Wharves were constructed to handle the coal and timber traffic, and tall red-brick warehouses arose after 1777 for iron, for cheese, for corn and salt. By the early nineteenth century three 'large carrying establishments' had made their headquarters here, of which Sutton & Co. carried on a great trade with Hull and Gainsborough, Liverpool and Manchester, the Cheshire salt works and the Potteries, and with Birmingham, Dudley and the Black Country. For many years Shardlow was 'an improving place', but the Derbyshire directory for 1857 observes that business had declined greatly after the opening of the Midland and other railways. But one can still go to Shardlow, which has sunk back into obscurity, and see the tall warehouses, the wharves, and the later Georgian Shardlow Hall where the prosperous James Sutton lived, and all the other evidences of a place that was virtually created by the canal age.

More striking, however, than Shardlow is Stourport, at the confluence of the Stour with the Severn. Before 1772 only a little ale-house stood here, on a sandy waste. With the completion of the Staffordshire and Worcestershire Canal in that year, and the refusal of the town of Bewdley to have anything to do with it, a new town shot up at the point where the canal joined the Severn. Soon there were extensive wharves and basins, tall warehouses, boat-building yards, and 'a considerable iron foundry belonging to Messrs Baldwin'. Just as Shardlow was a great inland distributing centre for the east Midlands, where mining, industry and agriculture mingled their products, so Stourport became the emporium for the west Midlands, connected by river and canal with most parts of the kingdom.

Some notable canal engineering was carried out by men like Rennie and Telford. Rennie built the beautiful aqueduct carrying the Lancaster Canal over the Lune; but even more striking was the Pontcysyllte aqueduct, constructed by Telford between 1795 and 1805, carrying the Ellesmere Canal over the Dee. This, perhaps the greatest monument in stone of English canal engineering, is over a thousand feet long and 121 feet above the river. On the same canal may be seen the Chirk aqueduct and tunnel. Telford's canals took a much more direct course than Brindley's, and so involved much more dramatic engineering, of which a splendid example is the bridge over the deep cutting near Tyrley, on the Shropshire Union Canal.

Tunnels, too, became bolder in conception. The Sapperton tunnel (1789) at the summit of the Thames and Severn Canal bores through the Cotswolds for more than two miles. The Pennines presented the most formidable obstacles of all to the canals, but even they were successfully overcome. The Standedge tunnel, at the highest point (637 feet) of the Huddersfield Canal, was 5,415 yards long. On the little canal linking Tavistock with the navigable Tamar in Devon, the Morwell Down tunnel (1804-17) was a mile and a half long and emerged at its western end nearly 240 feet above the river meadows. This drop was overcome by means of an inclined plane, up and down which the loaded barges were carried on trolleys. For many years the quay at Morwellham was

a scene of busy industry, with its unloading barges, and shouting sailors, and hammering workmen, and train of waggons ascending or descending the inclined plane. A quantity of ore is here shipped off to distant smelting-houses. It is curious to enter the well-swept yard, and observe the different wooden shafts down which distinct ores from various mines are poured. Then it is to be collected, and placed on board the vessels bound for distant quarters. These ships in return bring coals, and lime-stone, and many other commodities. *

By the end of the nineteenth century the quay was deserted; and now it is a grass-grown waste covered in part with the ruins of houses and other buildings. The canal was derelict for many years, but now flows again to produce electricity for the neighbourhood; and it still makes a pleasant summer evening walk from Tavistock to the tunnel mouth.

By the 1820s some three thousand miles of canals had been made, the industrial districts in particular being a network of grimy waterways. But all over the pastoral Midlands and the south of England too, the canals flowed clear and sparkling in the sunshine, something new in the landscape with their towpaths, lock-keepers' cottages, stables for canal horses, their Navigation or Canal Inns where they met a main road, and their long and narrow gaily painted boats. The early canals were contour canals, winding about for miles in order to circumvent a hill; but the later ones were made as straight as possible by means of cuttings and embankments. Sometimes an older canal was straightened by later engineers. The Oxford Canal, for example, was shortened by thirteen and a half miles between 1829 and 1834. The old course and the new can be seen

This description of Pontcysyllte aqueduct is misleading. It certainly contains some substantial stonework but the outstanding feature is the cast-iron water trough which carries the canal across the masonry piers.

Morwellham is no longer a grass-grown waste. It has been completely restored and its former importance can be readily appreciated, even if it has now lost its earlier charm.

* Quoted by Finberg, *Devonshire Studies*, p. 170.

particularly between Hawkesbury Lock, where it joins the Coventry canal, and Hillmorton near Rugby. In 1868 the Fenny Compton tunnel, on the same canal, was removed and replaced by a cutting.

By vastly cheapening the carriage of heavy materials over long distances, the canals also brought about indirect changes in the landscape. Thomas Pennant observed in 1782 that the Grand Junction Canal, between Trent and Mersey, had brought in new building materials: 'the cottage, instead of being half covered with miserable thatch, is now covered with a substantial covering of tiles or slates, brought from the distant hills of Wales or Cumberland. The fields, which before were barren, are now drained, and by the assistance of manure, conveyed on the canal toll-free, are clothed with a beautiful verdure.' But it was left mainly to the railways to break down finally the various regional traditions of building in England, and to put an end to the use of age-old local building materials in favour of standardised brick and slate.

One very special place to appreciate this and many other aspects of the English landscape is in the meadows south-west of Braunston, Northamptonshire. There, on either side of the River Leam, lie the wonderfully preserved sites of the deserted villages of Braunstonbury and Wolfhamcote, both apparently finally abandoned in the sixteenth century, together with the latter's tiny church. They are hemmed in on the east by the Grand Junction Canal which still flourishes, on the north by the straight alignment of the shortened Oxford Canal, on the west by the former Great Central Railway line constructed in 1896 and on the south by the embankment of the old Daventry to Leamington railway. All these lines of communication cut through the ridge-and-furrow of the open fields of the villages, as does the wandering line of the original Oxford Canal to the south-east and west.

Railways

Two generations of canal-building brought about great alterations in the landscape of England, now matured by centuries of slow growth, but these changes were highly localised. They were confined for the most part to the close proximity of the waterways and some parts of the country hardly knew them at all. The railways made a more massive impact. Not only were they greater in mileage, penetrating to remote places unknown to

PLATE 102. *Box Tunnel on the Great Western Railway near Bath. Railway builders gave a special dignity and significance to the treatment of tunnel entrances. This western portal to Box Tunnel is nearly twice the height required for modern traffic. Even the short tunnels on this part of the line are treated on a grand scale.*

the canals and sometimes even to the roads, but they began – from an engineering point of view – where the canals left off. Striking though the tunnels and cuttings and aqueducts of the canal engineers had been, they were soon surpassed in size and grandeur by those of the railways. The canals had indeed created two classes of people without whom the railways could not have been built – the civil engineers at one end of the scale, and the navvies (the 'inland navigators' of the canal era) at the other. Almost from the start therefore the railways manipulated the landscape on a grand scale. Nothing like their earthworks had been seen since the earlier Iron Age of pre-Roman times. We take the railways so much for granted. Indeed, we see little of their grandeur from the line itself as we cross the Wharncliffe Viaduct on the Great Western Railway, or the beautiful bridge over the Thames at Maidenhead, and plunge into the Classical-Renaissance portal of Box Tunnel; or as we traverse the great Tring cutting on the old London and North Western. We must walk to see all this, and it is more difficult to walk along the railways than along the canals with their sequestered towpaths. The early lithographs of J. C. Bourne, John Britton, A. F. Tait and others show us best the magnitude of the physical changes that the railways brought about in both town and country.

In *Dombey and Son*, too, Dickens – an incomparable reporter of the contemporary scene – makes us feel what a convulsion the making of a railway was. Here is Camden Town in the year 1836 when the London and Birmingham Railway was under construction in the locality which Dickens calls Staggs's Garden:

The first shock of a great earthquake had, just at that period, rent the whole neighbourhood to its centre. Traces of its course were visible on every side. Houses were knocked down; streets broken through and stopped; deep pits and trenches dug in the ground; enormous heaps of earth and clay thrown up; buildings that were undermined and shaking, propped by great beams of wood. Here, a chaos of carts, overthrown and jumbled together, lay topsy-turvy at the bottom of a steep unnatural hill; there, confused treasures of iron soaked and rusted in something that had accidentally become a pond. Everywhere were bridges that led nowhere; thoroughfares that were wholly impassable; Babel towers of chimneys, wanting half their height; temporary wooden houses and enclosures, in the most unlikely situations; carcasses of ragged tenements, and fragments of unfinished walls and arches, and piles of scaffolding, and wildernesses of bricks, and giant forms of cranes, and tripods straddling above nothing. There were a hundred thousand shapes and substances of incompleteness, wildly mingled out of their places, upside down, burrowing in the earth, aspiring in the air, mouldering in the water, and unintelligible as any dream. Hot springs and fiery eruptions, the usual attendants upon earthquakes, lent their contributions of confusion to the scene. Boiling water hissed and heaved within dilapidated walls; whence, also, the glare and roar of flames came issuing forth; and mounds of ashes blocked up rights of way, and wholly changed the law and custom of the neighbourhood.

In short, the yet unfinished and unopened Railroad was in progress; and, from the very core of all this dire disorder, trailed smoothly away, upon its mighty course of civilization and improvement.

But as yet, the neighbourhood was too shy to own the Railroad. One or two bold speculators had projected streets; and one had built a little, but had stopped among the mud and ashes to consider farther of it. A brand-new Tavern, redolent of fresh mortar and size, and fronting nothing at all, had taken for its sign The Railway Arms; but that might be rash enterprise – and then it hoped to sell drink to the workmen. So, the Excavator's house of Call had sprung up from a beer-shop; and the old-established Ham and Beef Shop had become the Railway Eating House, with a roast leg of pork daily, through interested motives of a similar immediate and popular description. Lodging-house keepers were favourable in like manner; and for the like reasons were not to be trusted. The general belief was very slow. There were frowsy fields, and cow-houses, and dunghills, and dustheaps, and ditches, and gardens, and summerhouses, and carpet-beating grounds, at the very door of the Railway. Little tumuli of oyster shells in the oyster season, and of lobster shells in the lobster season, and of broken crockery and faded cabbage leaves in all seasons, encroached upon its high places. Posts, and rails, and old cautions to trespassers, and backs of mean houses, and patches of wretched vegetation, stared it out of countenance. Nothing was the better for it, or thought of being so. If the miserable waste ground lying near it could have laughed, it would have laughed it to scorn, like many of the miserable neighbours.

Bourne's lithograph (Plate 95) of the excavation at Park Village near Camden Town, showing the works in progress in September 1836, must be the identical scene to that described by Dickens.

The railway pushed on to Birmingham, the army of navvies departed, the convulsion subsided, and within a very few years

there was no such place as Staggs's Gardens. It had vanished from the earth. Where the old rotten summerhouses once had stood, palaces now reared their heads, and granite columns of gigantic girth opened a vista to the railway world beyond. The miserable waste ground, where the refuse-matter had been heaped of yore, was swallowed up and gone; and in its frowsy stead were tiers of warehouses, crammed with rich goods and costly merchandise. The old by-streets now swarmed with passengers and vehicles of every kind; the new streets that had stopped disheartened in the mud and wagon-ruts, formed towns within themselves, originating wholesome comforts and conveniences belonging to themselves, and never tried nor thought of until they sprung into existence. Bridges that had led to nothing, led to villas, gardens, churches, healthy public walks. The carcasses of houses, and beginnings of new throughfares, had started off upon the line at steam's own speed, and shot away into the country in a monster train.

As to the neighbourhood which had hesitated to acknowledge the railroad in its straggling days, that had grown wise and penitent, as any Christian might in such a case, and now boasted of its powerful and prosperous relation. There were railway patterns in its drapers' shops, and railway journals in the windows of its newsmen. There were railway hotels, office-houses, lodging-houses, boarding-houses; railway plans, maps, views, wrappers, bottles, sandwich-boxes, and time-tables; railway hackney-coach and cabstands; railway omnibuses, railway streets and buildings, railway hangers-on and parasites, and flatterers out of all calculation. There was even railway time observed in clocks, as if the sun itself had given in. Among the vanquished was the master chimney-sweeper, whilom incredulous at Stagg's Gardens, who now lived in a stuccoed house three storeys high, and gave himself out, with golden flourishes upon a varnished board, as contractor for the cleansing of railway chimneys by machinery.

To and from the heart of this great change, all day and night, throbbing currents rushed and returned incessantly like its life's blood. Crowds of people and mountains of goods, departing and arriving scores upon scores of times in every four-and-twenty hours, produced a fermentation in the place that was always in action. The very houses seemed disposed to pack up and take trips. Wonderful Members of Parliament, who, little more than twenty years before, had made themselves merry with the wild railroad theories of engineers, and given them the liveliest rubs in cross-examination, went down into the north with their watches in their hands, and sent on messages before by the electric telegraph, to say that they were coming. Night and day the conquering engines rumbled at their distant work, or advancing smoothly to their journey's end, and gliding like tame dragons into the allotted corners grooved out to the inch for their reception, stood bubbling and trembling there, making the walls quake, as if they were dilating with the secret knowledge of great powers yet unsuspected in them, and strong purposes not yet achieved.

But Staggs's Gardens had been cut up root and branch.

Dr Johnson had deplored the effect that canals would have upon the privacy of the landed class. The railways aroused an even greater opposition for this as well as for numerous other reasons, and not only among those who quietly enjoyed the amenities of a large estate. At Helpston in Northamptonshire, Clare recorded in his diary for 4 June 1825:

Saw three fellows at the end of Royce Wood, who I found were laying out the plan for an iron railway from Manchester to London. It is to cross over Round Oak spring by Royce Wood corner for Woodcroft Castle. I little thought that fresh intrusions would interrupt and spoil my solitudes. After the enclosure they will despoil a boggy place that is famous for orchises at Royce Wood end.

Nothing came of this particular project, not at least for many years, and Clare continued to enjoy the orchises of Royce Wood undisturbed. But the battle to preserve beloved solitudes flared up repeatedly in patches all over the country, precisely as it does today with the threat of new airfields and military training areas. The price of solitude in the modern world is eternal vigilance. In 1844 Wordsworth was aroused by the proposal to construct a railway from Kendal to the shores of Lake Windermere:

> *Is then no nook of English ground secure*
> *From rash assault?*

His two long letters to the *Morning Post* marshal every conservative argument against the proposal, and conclude:

> *We have too much hurrying about in these islands; much for idle pleasure, and more from over activity in the pursuit of wealth, without regard to the good or happiness of others.*

> *Proud were ye, Mountains, when, in times of old,*
> *Your patriot sons, to stem invasive war,*
> *Intrenched your brows; ye gloried in each scar:*
> *Now, for your shame, a Power, the Thirst of Gold,*
> *That rules o'er Britain like a baneful star,*
> *Wills that your peace, your beauty, shall be sold,*
> *And clear way made for her triumphal car*
> *Through the beloved retreats your arms enfold!*

> *Heard YE that Whistle? As her long-linked Train*
> *Swept onwards, did the vision cross your view?*
> *Yes, ye were startled; – and, in balance true,*
> *Weighing the mischief with the promised gain,*
> *Mountains, and Vales, and Floods, I call on you*
> *To share the passion of a just disdain.*

PLATE 103. *West Cranmore Station, Somerset, typical of the rural branch lines of the country. This one was built by the East Somerset Railway Company between 1858-62. It was one of three separate lines, each belonging to a different company, laid to the small cathedral city of Wells between 1859-70. Wells then only had 7,500 people. The East Somerset line, later taken over by the Great Western Railway, could never have made a profit. It was only a single track and had a gradient of 1 in 50 or worse for several miles. Yet it, together with the other numerous Somerset railways, knitted town and country together in a way that had never been achieved before. All lines were closed to passengers in the 1960s.*

But the conservatives, however right they were – and we have lost nearly all our privacy and silence since they wrote – lost all along the line. The new railways 'slashed like a knife through the delicate tissues of a settled rural civilization. They left their scars on park and copse; they raised high walls of earth across the meadows – "your railroad mounds, vaster than the walls of Babylon," Ruskin called them; they brutally amputated every hill on their way.'*

The magnitude of the early railway works was enhanced by the severe limitation the engineers placed upon themselves as regards gradients. Brunel would have nothing steeper than 1 in 660 for the first eighty-five miles out of Paddington; Robert Stephenson planned the London and Birmingham Railway with no gradient steeper than 1 in 330 (except the first rise from Euston to Camden); and Locke nothing steeper than 1 in 250 on the difficult London and Southampton line. So we get on the London and Birmingham route the vast cuttings at Tring (two and a half miles long and at times nearly sixty feet deep) and Roade (one and a half miles long and nearly seventy feet deep), and the embankments at Boxmoor and Wolverton. On the London and Southampton line sixteen million cubic feet of earth were moved in making the cuttings and embankments, mostly between Basingstoke and Winchester: some of the most extensive cuttings in the world are on this stretch of line. On the Great Western route we have such major engineering achievements as the Wharncliffe Viaduct over the Brent valley at Hanwell, the Sonning cutting, the embankment west of Chippenham (and the fine viaduct over the town itself), the Box tunnel, and the series of tunnels, cuttings and embankments between Bath and Bristol.

At times the railway altered almost the whole aspect of a town, or at least of distant views of it. The Great Western Railway's embankments and viaducts changed the prospect of

PLATE 104. *Viaduct, Ribblehead, Yorkshire, on the Settle-Carlisle line. Scenically perhaps the most attractive line in England. It was built by the Midland Railway in 1870-5 as a third route to the North. It was not actually needed and was probably hardly worth constructing. Yet it was a triumph of Victorian engineering and now adds more to the English landscape than most railway lines do.*

* C. Barman, *Early British Railways* (Penguin Books, 1950), p.25.

PLATE 105. *Crewe Station in 1848.*
The early railway stations were
often a pleasure to contemplate –
imposing sometimes, and
sometimes faintly romantic, like
the first Crewe Station. Few stations
of the first generation survived the
vast increase of railway traffic, but
some did and they are well worth
seeing. Railways added a vast
amount of detail to the English
landscape, besides manipulating it
at times on a large scale.

The speed of change which Professor Hoskins deplored is
well brought out here by his remarks about a stopping
train through Rutland. Not only does Rutland no longer
exist, swallowed up by a greater Leicestershire, but the
trains which cross the old county now only stop at Oak-
ham, its last surviving station. The rest have been
demolished, vandalised or turned into country cot-
tages. Even so the slow trains from Peterborough to Leic-
ester, via Stamford, Oakham and Melton Mowbray, give
us, visually, one of the great railway journeys for those
who can appreciate the English landscape. The barley
still shakes, the meadows still have their cattle and the
superb spires still stand proud above their villages.

Bath; the viaduct over the Mersey at Stockport brought a fine geometrical composition into the urban landscape. Indeed the railways created as much beauty as they inadvertently destroyed, but of a totally different kind. The great gashes they inflicted on the landscape in their cuttings and embankments healed over, and wild flowers grew abundantly once more. Going down to the south-west in spring, the cuttings through Somerset and Devon sparkle with primroses. Even in Clare's own country, the railway has been absorbed into the landscape, and one can enjoy the consequent pleasure of trundling through Rutland in a stopping-train on a fine summer morning: the barley fields shaking in the wind, the slow sedgy streams with their willows shading meditative cattle, the elegant limestone spires across the meadows, the early Victorian stations built of the sheep-grey Ketton stone and still unaltered, the warm brown roofs of the villages half buried in the trees, and the summer light flashing everywhere. True that the railway did not invent much of this beauty, but it gave us new vistas of it.

Or there is the grander scenery, and the more spectacular engineering, of the railway from Settle up to Carlisle, some of the finest railway landscape in Britain; and the route over Shap with its visions of the Lakeland mountains; and there are the superb night scenes from the railway viaducts that span the industrial towns of Lancashire and Yorkshire. There are the elaborate tunnel entrances like Box and Bramhope and others, the great viaducts like Monsal Dale and Dutton, the bridges like Saltash and Severn; and the charming survivors among early railway stations that one comes across unexpectedly almost anywhere in England. All the convulsions and brutal gashings of the rural landscape by the railway engineers have long been smoothed over and forgotten; and we take the railway earthworks and monuments as much for granted as we do the hedges and fields of the enclosure commissioners or the churches of our medieval forefathers.

The railways not only made a direct physical impact on the landscape: their indirect effects were equally powerful and far-reaching. The diary of a Middlesex parson, the Rev B. J. Armstrong, shows us what a devastating effect they were having as early as the 1830s.*

* R. M. Robbins, 'A Middlesex Diary', *Transactions of the London and Middlesex Archaeological Society*, XI, 1954, pp. 105-14.

His father had decided in the year 1830 to move out of London and to take a small house in the country.

It was thought advisable to take some small place in the country for the benefit of our health . . . He took a very pretty and rather commodious cottage-residence at Southall Green, Middlesex, about a mile out of the high road to Uxbridge, and exactly 10 miles from Tyburn Gate. Our intention was to reside half the year at Southall, and the remainder in London, and I remember we moved there on the 26th June, 1830 . . . My delight at everything I saw was beyond bounds – gardens were allotted my sister and self – there was the canal to fish in – a pony to ride – besides animals of different kinds . . . Having been long pent up in town, Annie and myself viewed Southall as a second Paradise, and I remember I nearly hung myself on my pin-before the very first morning after our arrival, in attempting to scale the yard gates to see the country beyond them.

Eight years later the main line from Paddington to the west was opened through Middlesex. West Drayton (for Uxbridge) was the first station; and in the following year stations were built at Ealing, Hanwell and Southall. The effect on Southall is duly recorded in Armstrong's diary:

A remarkable change for the worse took place about this time in the hitherto retired neighbourhood of Southall Green. The railway spread dissatisfaction and immorality among the poor, the place being inundated with worthless and overpaid navigators ['navvies']; the very appearance of the country was altered, some families left, and the rusticity of the village gave place to a London-out-of-town character. Moss-grown cottages retired before new ones with bright red tiles, picturesque hedgerows were succeeded by prim iron railings, and the village inn, once a pretty cottage with a swinging sign, is transmogrified to the 'Railway Tavern' with an intimation gaudily set forth that 'London porter' and other luxuries hitherto unknown to the aborigines were to be procured within.

These immediate effects were observable only near the stations, but as the railways extended rapidly to all parts of the country their effects on local building and building materials grew correspondingly wide. In Middlesex the impact came soonest, and was most violent. The older houses had been built of a homely and native brown stock brick, and the farm buildings largely of wood. Between 1800 and 1850, however, a hard soapy-looking yellow brick was pouring up the Thames from Suffolk, and most of the new Middlesex churches were built of it. 'From 1850 onwards' – with the triumph of the railways – 'every kind of material was poured on to the unprotesting soil: harsh red bricks, sometimes glazed; in the north, yellow-green brick from Three Counties, near Hitchin; slates, pantiles, green tiles; stucco, artificial stone, and concrete.'* What happened in Middlesex eventually happened all over England, and as Midland bricks and Welsh slates – and later more unspeakable materials like asbestos and corrugated iron – flooded into every corner of provincial England, the ancient local materials that fitted their own regions so well, for they came out of their very soil, disappeared one by one. In Oxfordshire the Stonesfield slate-pits and mines shut down one by one during the second half of the nineteenth century;† in Leicestershire the Swithland slate-quarries, which had been worked since Henry III's time, shut down altogether in 1887; and so it was in nearly every county in England. All regional styles and all local materials were exterminated except where the well-to-do could afford to build deliberately in the old manner, with the aid of an architect. What had been the living style of a whole region, modified to suit all classes of people, became a piece of pleasant antiquarianism for a rich man.

The nineteenth-century expansion of London in general and west London in particular was complex and not by any means always related to the arrival of the railways. In many areas the coming of the horse trams and later the electric trams, of which almost all traces have gone, were a far greater influence. Often the policies of individual railway companies determined what happened. As Professor Simmonds has pointed out the Great Western was mainly concerned with long distance traffic in its early years. Though stations were built on the main line west of Paddington after its opening in 1838 the initial suburban service was poor and the passenger receipts small. Only at Ealing was there large-scale housing development at this time. It was not until the Metropolitan Railway was linked to this line at Paddington, thus enabling through trains to run to the City, that traffic developed and new housing estates appeared elsewhere. Even then the existing double track limited services. Only when the track was quadrupled in 1879 did residential development begin in earnest in this part of London. Though Ealing itself doubled in size between 1861 and 1871 and grew by over half in each of the two following decades, the first of these increases can hardly have been the result of the railway services although the later ones may have been.

* R. M. Robbins, *Middlesex* (Collins, 1953), p. 165.
† The Duke of Marlborough managed to keep a pit open until 1909 (W. J. Arkell, *Oxford Stone*, Faber, 1947, p. 140).

Chapter 9
THE LANDSCAPE OF TOWNS

Introduction

Writing in the 1950s, Professor Hoskins rightly criticised the lack of detailed topographical studies of towns at that time. Since then the situation has improved greatly. There have been numerous large-scale excavations on historic towns, many individual historical studies and a variety of general works on urban origins and development. As a result we now know much more about the beginnings of towns in England as well as about their growth at all periods.

Professor Hoskins divided towns into those he called planned, those described as open-field towns and those which were market towns. While there is still much validity in that classification, it is perhaps more interesting to analyse towns, at least to begin with, in terms of their origin.

The most important and certainly the commonest form of town is the planned town, using the work 'planned' in its widest sense. It is now clear that there are very few towns which just grew because they were at suitable locations. Certainly geography helped and prevailing economic conditions played an important part, but most towns seem to have come into existence as a result of conscious decisions. Thus the term planning encompasses not only those places whose form shows clearly that an overall scheme lay behind the layout of streets, but also towns which, whatever form they acquired, were pushed into existence and developed by the active support of individuals or institutions.

Excluding Roman towns, the earliest planned towns of England can be identified in late Saxon times. These appear to be of two types. The first are those which developed from what have been called 'proto-urban' settlements. That is they are places which, well before 800 AD, had characteristics which were already marked as different in function from the normal agricultural settlements of the period. The most important of these characteristics were that they were the administrative centres of royal estates, or more rarely great ecclesiastical estates. They were already the centres of civil administration, often derived from earlier minor kingdoms or tribal units, they usually possessed an early minster church and so were centres of ecclesiastical administration and they had already acquired some marketing functions more important than those of their neighbours. Most of these places also are physically very close to known important earlier settlements such as Roman towns, large Roman villas or a semi-urban Roman settlement, or even an Iron Age hill-fort, the latter often re-used temporarily in early Saxon times.

The implication of all this is that such places had perhaps been important as estates or administrative centres as well as having marketing functions long before late Saxon times and thus could be developed into true towns fairly easily. They also had a pattern of routeways radiating from them, originating from centuries before. These later towns might then have been either assisted in their development by their royal or ecclesiastical lords or owners, or actually given a regular street pattern and/or a market place to encourage them to grow and expand. Towns of this category include Canterbury, Rochester and Faversham in Kent, Abingdon in Berkshire, Bradford on Avon in Wilt-

PLATE 106. *This simple building in the Lea Valley at Walthamstow in London was, at the end of its life, a pumping station belonging to the Metropolitan Water Board. Together with the great reservoirs that lie around it typifies the enormous impact of Victorian and later public works on the English landscape. Yet its full history is much more complicated. It stands on the site of a watermill recorded in Domesday Book as belonging to the Manor of Walthamstow. The mill was used for grinding corn until the seventeenth century. Then it was variously used to produce gunpowder, flour and paper. The existing building dates from the 1740s when it became an oil mill for linseed. In 1808 it was bought by the British Copper Company and was used for producing copper sheets. In 1860 it was purchased by the East London Water Company and rebuilt as a pumping station. The tower was added in 1864 and it passed to the Metropolitan Water Board in 1904.*

PLATE 107. *The urban motorway of Newcastle-upon-Tyne is perhaps the ultimate in the drive to destroy totally the historic landscape of towns for the sake of short-term convenience and gain.*

shire, Dorchester in Dorset, Lincoln, York and Carlisle. Some of these have rectangular layouts of streets which seem to date from late Saxon times, as at Winchester and Guildford.

By far the largest and most important of this type of town, curiously ignored by Professor Hoskins here, and elsewhere, was London. As recent work indicated, it too was redeveloped within its older Roman walls on a huge scale in late Saxon times. The surviving street plan of the City, with the exception of the late nineteenth-century alterations, is in fact arranged in a regular grid which dates from the end of the Saxon period.

The second type of late Saxon town, which overlaps in some cases with the first, is the fortified burghs. These were founded either by the late Saxon kings from Alfred onwards to protect their kingdom from the Scandinavian invaders or by the Scandinavians themselves, partly for defence, and partly for the encouragement of trade. The Alfredian burghs of southern England include Shaftesbury and Wareham in Dorset, and Wilton and Cricklade in Wiltshire. Worcester, Hereford and Towcester, Warwick and Stafford are among the later English burghs, while the Scandinavian burghs include Derby, Manchester and Leicester.

Some towns had more than one burgh. Stamford, one of Hoskins' 'open-field' towns, is actually made up of a Danish burgh, founded in 877 on the north side of the River Welland and consisting of a roughly rectangular block bisected by the east-west High Street, and an English burgh to the south of the river founded by King Edward in 918, and consisting of a neat rectangular area bisected by the north-south St Martins High Street.

Cambridge is even more complex. North of the River Cam, re-using the older Roman town, was the late eighth-century Mercian burgh which had another fortified town south of the river crossing added to it in the late ninth century by the Danish soldiers and traders. The latter had the present Bridge Street as its main road with the significantly dedicated St Clements Church halfway along it. A few years later in 917 King Edward added a vast planned town to the south, laid out on a slightly skewed grid and with a massive open market place on its east. This work in Cambridge was also accompanied by the diversion of the river from its original channel to one alongside the new town. Most of this grid, incidentally, was later destroyed by the growth of the University and Colleges, though fragments of it still exist.

The next type of planned town includes those which are reasonably well dated to the tenth to thirteenth centuries and which were clearly new planned urban centres added on to existing villages by their owners as attempts to encourage trade. Many of the towns on the Banbury map which Professor Hoskins referred to in the previous chapter fall into this category. Bicester (1239), Banbury (1123-38), Woodstock (1154-74), Chipping Norton (about 1150) and Deddington (before 1190) are examples. Elsewhere in England there are many more. Daventry and Oundle in Northamptonshire, Ely and Wisbech in Cambridgeshire, St Albans and Peterborough are more examples. Some of these were strictly castle towns, that is, they were planted against the gates of a newly built castle of the late eleventh century, such as Ludlow, Alnwick, Pontefract and Launceston. All these, if examined carefully, show in their arrangements of streets or patterns of roads the impact imposed on them by their 'planning lords'.

The best of all the planned towns are those such as New Winchelsea (1288) and Salisbury (1290) which were apparently laid out *de novo* on previously empty sites from the late eleventh century to the four-

PLATE 108. *Bolton Town Hall, Lancashire, by William Hill, 1866-73. A Victorian public building on a grand scale, even if the French top of the tower sits rather oddly on the rest of the classical design.*

teenth century, again as deliberate acts of commercial exploitation. Such towns often show their unencumbered planned origins by the grid-pattern of streets, or generally rectangular layout, and they include not only the obvious planned towns such as those noted by Professor Hoskins at Kingston-upon-Hull (1293) and Stratford-upon-Avon (1196) but also Newmarket, Suffolk (1217-23), Market Harborough (1167-77), Liverpool (1207), Leeds (1207) and North Shields (1225). All these still have clues in their plans to show their origins. At Leeds, for example, the grid of streets between the present railway station and the significantly named The Headrow, though now much mutilated by modern development, is still that laid out by Maurice de Paynel in the early thirteenth century.

New towns continued to be founded right through the medieval period though after the early thirteenth century the changing economic conditions were no longer ideal for their development and the process tailed off. Queenborough, Kent (1368) is said to be the latest medieval planned town, though Bewdley, Worcestershire (soon after 1477), is probably the last one.

During the High Middle Ages, many of these towns were successful and soon expanded. Many merely developed by ribbon expansion along existing streets, but others had additional planned elements added, as had happened earlier at Cambridge and Stamford. Banbury had a completely new suburb significantly called Newland added to the older town between 1250 and 1285, only a little over a hundred years after it had been first founded, a mark of its success, while Eynsham, also in Oxfordshire, has a neat rectangular block of properties, bisected by Newland Street which dates from 1215 when a charter was acquired for an extension. The original town had been founded with a new market place in 1135-9 by the Benedictine abbey there.

After the sixteenth century few new towns were established. Whitehaven in Cumbria was begun in 1660 by the local Lowther family and given a spacious grid of streets and a new harbour. It soon became a successful coal port and ship-building centre. The growth of the British Empire and in particular the requirements of the Royal Navy produced Chatham in 1622 and Devonport in the late seventeenth century. At the old medieval naval base of Portsmouth the planned suburb of Portsea was added in the early eighteenth century to house the workers in the new and expanded dockyard.

More important in producing new forms of urban life was the general prosperity of the late seventeenth and eighteenth centuries, coupled with new ideas of social life and architecture brought in from abroad. Up to then there had been little social division in towns and houses were crowded in on themselves in a formless way. Expansion of population was often solved by sub-division of plots and infilling of open spaces, particularly markets. But from the 1630s the idea of high class residential areas was introduced from Italy. The first expression of this was the Earl of Bedford's estate of Covent Garden in London which included the idea of an Italian piazza or open space surrounded by terraces of uniform houses. The concept was taken up elsewhere in London and the beginnings of the great pattern of squares (Bloomsbury Square in 1661, St James's Square in 1665 and Soho Square in 1690) with their associated terraced streets began to emerge. This concept of squares, and more particularly terraced houses, was to dominate urban planning for the next two hundred years. It first produced the glories of Bath, and later still Buxton and a whole series of resort towns such as Tunbridge Wells, Cheltenham and Leamington Spa.

The development of industry, and the coming of the railways, produced towns that were essentially planned, at least in outline, even if the detailed building work was done piecemeal. Middlesbrough is especially mentioned by Professor Hoskins, as is Stourport as a canal town. Goole, in Humberside, was a planned canal port founded by the Aire and Calder Navigation Company in 1819 while the railway towns of Crewe, Wolverton and Eastleigh have been discussed earlier. Other resort towns came in the nineteenth century. The earliest is Scarborough, begun in the seventeenth century; the most famous, with its magnificent squares and ubiquitous terraces, is Brighton, begun soon after 1750. Melcombe Regis acquired the first of its grand planned terraces in the 1780s. Grid planning was immensely popular and extensions of old medieval towns as well as the new industrial towns went on apace in this fashion. In Birmingham the Colmore family laid out a new suburb on a neat grid in the 1740s on their land north-west of the existing town centre. Its traces are still just visible amongst the wreckage of the modern urban motorway system. Ashton-under-Lyne was

217

Bedford Square, London. Up until the middle of the seventeenth century this part of London (Holborn) was still open fields. Houses and some streets appeared after 1660, but it was not until 1775 when Bedford Square was laid out that the growth of Bloomsbury began. Within fifty years the area was entirely built over with a population of nearly 70,000. Bedford Square is not only the oldest of the Bloomsbury development, it is also the only one that remains complete.

given a rigid grid of wide streets by the Earls of Stamford after 1758 when it was becoming an important cotton town.

Planning of this type covered large areas of most English towns by the late nineteenth century. The process has continued ever since. New towns have continued to appear, though by the late nineteenth century novel concepts of housing produced very different layouts and appearance, best seen at, for example, Letchworth, the first garden city in 1903, and later at Welwyn Garden City in 1920. More recently, a whole new series of planned towns, including Crawley, Bracknell, Stevenage, Harlow and most notable of all, Milton Keynes, have appeared.

Much of the foregoing has concentrated on the origins and physical plans of towns. But much exists in their architecture to tell us of the social conditions, wealth, success or decline of towns. Not all periods of a town's history are visible in its buildings. In many cases the more successful a town the less likely is the chance of seeing its early development. The late medieval story of a small place such as Thaxted, with its mass of late medieval timber buildings, survives because it failed to develop after its early period of prosperity as a wool town. The joys of Stourport result from the failure of the canals and their replacement by railways. Birmingham is less attractive because it has remained the commercial centre of the Midlands. All towns, if one wishes to understand landscapes rather than to gain inner pleasure from beauty, have much to offer, despite Professor Hoskins' strictures. The modern centre of Coventry is as much a reflection of mid-twentieth-century ideals, demands and greed, as the centre of Saffron Walden is of those of the sixteenth and seventeenth centuries. The gentility of Harrogate shows what upper-class people thought suitable

in the early nineteenth century, as Basingstoke, with its urban carriageways and new industries, shows our demands today. Milton Keynes can tell us a great deal about late twentieth-century hopes and aims in a democratic car-owning society, quite apart from having the best range of modern domestic architecture in England.

Detailed work in recent years has given us new insights into how nineteenth-century towns developed. Professor Dyos' study of Camberwell was the first in a series of examinations which have enabled us to see how the ubiquitous terraced streets of our great cities were laid out and slowly built up in a highly complex way, for a whole series of social and economic reasons. Today we often ignore large areas of terraced housing and merely regard it as 'late nineteenth-century development', forgetting perhaps that most of the population was then housed in them and indeed still is today. We ought to be more concerned as to exactly how they came into being. Even the great spread of inter-war surburban houses, such as those which line the Kingston by-pass in Surrey, have a fascinating story to tell of the growth of such areas if we are prepared to look at them properly.

Not all towns were a success and the English landscape is littered with total failures. Lydford, in Devon, still has the abandoned streets of a late Saxon burgh which never succeeded. Newport in the Isle of Wight with its grid of lanes and isolated Guildhall is a failed planned town of 1177-84, as are the villages of Hindon, Wiltshire (1219-20), Holme in Cambridgeshire (before 1107) and Newborough in Staffordshire (1100-39). Dunwich in Suffolk was swept away by the sea, while at a later date Tenbury Wells, founded as a spa in 1839, never took off. Even in this century there have been failures. Mundesley in Norfolk was intended to be a new resort town in 1900 but never succeeded.

THE LANDSCAPE OF TOWNS

There are many different ways of looking at a town for the first time. One of them – a little old-fashioned perhaps, for I do not see many people doing it nowadays – is to walk around it guide-book in hand, best of all with one of those old Murray's *Handbooks for Travellers*, the most catholic, the most informative, the most solid guide-books ever written in this country; still well worth buying though the last one came out nearly fifty years ago and one must hunt for them with increasing difficulty in the second-hand bookshops.

We may study with our guide-books all the historic, individual features of a town and get to know them. But then – if we are taking our time and stay to look at the town as a whole, walk around it in the cool and quiet of the evening when the shops are shut, and the traffic has gone home, and we can really see its contours and its bone-structure – other questions begin to arise in the mind, which even the best of guide-books does not answer. Why is the town just like this, this shape, this plan, this size? Why do its streets run in this particular way and not in some other way that seems more logical to us? Why are there sometimes two market places, why are the ancient churches just where they are? – and so on. In short, what gives the town this particular landscape?

Here even the best of guide-books fails us. Indeed, there are no books at all to answer our question. The historians also fail us – in this country, at least – for they have not studied the topography of towns as they have in Germany and France. We have nothing like Louis Halphen's great topographical study of the growth of Paris; or the work of Keussen and Koebner on the physical development of Cologne, or of Des Marez on the city of Ghent. This lack is astonishing when one thinks of the innumerable ancient towns of England that richly deserve such a study. There are, of course, many scholarly books on boroughs in their institutional aspects, their political history and their administration. But one looks in vain for any discussion of their physical growth, where their original core lay, of the directions in which they grew, and when and why, and of what accounts for their street plan and their shape today. The nearest we have to this in England is one chapter by the American scholar Carl Stephenson in his book *Borough and Town*.* Written over twenty years ago, it is admittedly a tentative sketch put on in the hope that some English historians and archaeologists would set to work in a more expert way and on a bigger scale. But still very little has been done: only medieval Lincoln and modern Brighton have had some attention recently.

What is the point of studying towns in this way? For me, at least – and I think for most people who travel around this country for pleasure, that is, to see things – it is simply that one gets a greater depth of pleasure out of knowing the anatomy of a town and why it takes that particular form and not just its superficial features, however attractive they may be individually. It may well be that when the archaeologists and historians have studied a sufficient number of towns intensively in this country, as they have done abroad, we shall add something appreciable to our knowledge of English history, knowledge which we could get in no other way. But this is looking a long way ahead. In the meantime one studies them as landscapes, so to speak, simply to heighten one's pleasure in sight-seeing, to get behind the superficial appearances, to uncover the layers of the palimpsest and to see, for example, a piece of the tenth century in the way a street makes an abrupt turn or does something else unexpected.

* Cambridge, Massachusetts: Medieval Academy of America, 1933.

The Planned Town

Street-plans raise a multitude of questions. Why are certain English towns, for example, laid out on a gridiron pattern with straight streets crossing each other at right angles, sometimes at fixed distances apart, like a mid-western American city? Towns, moreover, so utterly dissimilar in other ways – Salisbury and Middlesbrough, Barrow-in-Furness and Winchelsea? From a topographical point of view, these planned towns are the simplest towns to understand: but even here we are confronted with a number of questions at the outset. Why are there so few planned towns in this country? Why were most English towns left to grow up in more or less haphazard fashion? What determined that a particular town should be planned with this regular layout of streets and building-plots? Why, again, are the planned towns scattered about the country in so haphazard a way, and so different in age and social type – Salisbury's plan belongs to the thirteenth century (Fig. 9, p. 93), Middlesbrough's to the nineteenth. And why are certain parts of a great city like Birmingham planned on the gridiron pattern, and the rest of it just a jumbled, inchoate mess?

We look into the records and another question emerges. While some, indeed most, planned towns established themselves successfully, others proved completely abortive, never came to life at all despite all the activity of the planners, including the king himself. For the viability of towns depends in the last resort on a solid economic foundation. Planned towns were deliberate attempts to exploit the economic possibilities of a site; and like any other investment could go wrong. On the southern shore of Poole Bay in Dorset, directly opposite the ancient port of Poole, is the site of a completely still-born royal town – Nova Villa. King Edward I, that great town-planner, gave it a charter in 1286, conferring upon it all the liberties and privileges of the City of London. A site was chosen; two town-planners appointed (one of them a parson), the town marked out on the ground: but all in vain. Nothing happened. In Elizabethan days, three hundred years later, the solitary farm of Newton, standing upon the heath that petered out in the muddy flats of the bay, alone marked the site of Edward I's 'new town'.

Leaving aside the Romans, whose tradition of town-planning had been completely forgotten after their departure, the earliest piece of town-planning that we know of in England is that carried out by Abbot Baldwin at Bury St Edmunds, between 1066 and 1086. This plan is still very easily picked out today as one walks about the streets of Bury. The little border town of Ludlow may well be a twelfth-century example of planning on a smaller and more rudimentary scale, but the most notable examples come from the thirteenth century – Salisbury, New Winchelsea, the five bastide towns laid out by Edward I in North Wales, and part of Kingston-upon-Hull, laid out by Edward from 1293 onwards. Hull was already an important seaport in the twelfth century. Edward did not create it from nothing, but he founded a new town – King's Town – on the old site, which he manipulated especially on the western side. At Stratford-upon-Avon, the Bishop of Worcester (who owned the entire manor) obtained the grant of a market in 1196 and proceeded to lay out a new town forthwith. He set aside an area of one hundred and nine acres to the east of the original Saxon village (called Old Town to this day) and on it laid out a regular plan of streets – three running parallel with the river and three others crossing them at right angles. This elementary plan survives unchanged as the core of the modern town.

The impulse to produce planned towns, such as it was, had died out by 1300. Then we get no more until the planned development of more or less large estates in the late eighteenth-century towns – notably, of course, the spas, but also in such unlikely places as Birmingham and (early in the nineteenth century) Ashton-under-Lyne. Finally, in the middle decades of the nineteenth century, we get once again whole new towns created on the gridiron pattern, of which the outstanding

As already discussed, Bury St Edmunds is not the earliest planned town. There are numerous towns which had already been founded in late Saxon times either as commercial centres or as fortified burghs.

Again, as discussed in the Introduction, medieval towns continued to be founded until the fifteenth century.

examples are the iron and steel towns of Middlesbrough and Barrow-in-Furness. It is curious, by the way, that the gridiron plan should have gone on so long. It is the simplest and most obvious layout, but there are, of course, other patterns – such as the radial pattern of so many modern housing estates – and it is odd that these others should not have been tried out until within our own time.

When we study the planned towns of England, we arrive at the first, and obvious, conclusion that to make a planned town required the absolute ownership of the site by one man or corporation. This immediately limited the number of towns that could be planned, for most English towns have developed from villages, and their sites had been partly built on for centuries before they developed into towns. More important than that (for medieval village buildings could have been swept away as easily as the Romans had swept away the native British buildings for their planned towns) – a variety of ownerships and rights had grown up that precluded a unified plan even as early as the twelfth or thirteenth century. True, these property rights could have been dealt with by a determined planner, but the fact remains that they were not. At Bury, for instance, the abbey owned the whole site and could lay it out as it pleased. At Salisbury, in the 1220s, the Bishop of Sarum was able to plan a complete new city on his own meadows by the Avon (Fig. 9). At New Winchelsea and in North Wales, the king was dealing with his own land, as he was also on the abortive site of New Town beside Poole Bay. In Birmingham the planned area – all that part to the west of Snow Hill station today – was formerly the New Hall estate of the Colmore family. Their park was given over as a whole for building development, and laid out on the gridiron pattern in the middle decades of the eighteenth century. At Barrow-in-Furness the site of the new town was owned by the dukes of Devonshire, one of whom was responsible for its planning in the middle decades of the nineteenth century. At Middlesbrough in 1829 a syndicate of six Quakers bought a site of five hundred acres beside the Tees, and created their planned town upon the empty farmland, drawing their straight lines and making their rectangles without hindrance from any legal or physical obstacle.

Very few English towns can really be said to have 'developed' from villages. Almost all had some form of conscious planning or deliberate encouragement from their lords to give them urban status. It is possible that a few minor markets did grow slowly from an earlier village but they are very difficult to discover. Chatteris in the Cambridgeshire fens might be a rare example.

Much of the original Middlesbrough no longer exists. Most of the slums which developed from the complex succession of nineteenth-century grid blocks have now been swept away in modern re-development.

But to say that the planned town required a single ownership of the site does not go to the root of the matter. Most English towns have grown from Anglo-Saxon villages, but, particularly in the twelfth and thirteenth centuries, landowners were founding new towns all over England – and indeed all over Europe. In the one county of Devon, for example, sixty or so boroughs were created by optimistic landowners, of which one half failed to come to anything. Population was increasing, trade and industry growing; it was an expanding economy with wonderful new opportunities for making money if one could only strike the right spot.

So landowners, from the king down to relatively small provincial lords, founded boroughs right and left, especially where they saw merchants and traders already congregating at some convenient spot – near the protection of a castle or an abbey, which were considerable markets also, at some important river-crossing, and so on. Why, then, were only half-a-dozen of these new towns properly laid out on a predetermined plan, and the vast majority left to grow haphazard with narrow, irregular, winding streets, odd little lanes everywhere, and all the other attributes of the picturesque today? There were two principal reasons for this: one was that medieval men had no *a priori* love of symmetry. The planned town is an aberration, not the norm. Secondly, the planning of a new town – laying out the lines of streets, lanes, markets, churches and house-plots over a considerable area – required, after all, the investment of a large amount of capital, and a greater degree of economic optimism than most landowners could contemplate. The planned town is the product of the big capitalists – kings, bishops, abbots, in medieval times; town corporations, dukes and Quaker syndicates in modern times. And today, only the state can

PLATE 110. *West Pier, Brighton, Sussex. Brighton is usually seen as a genteel late eighteenth-century resort favoured by the Prince of Wales. So it was, though its real period of early development was in the 1820s, still as a select upper-class watering place. Then in 1841 the railway arrived, and the 'people's Brighton' began. It expanded from 47,000 people in 1841 to 102,000 in 1901 and in 1860 nearly 150,000 people came to the town by excursion train in two successive days. Now millions of visitors come every year for day trips and holidays. The West Pier, built in 1863-6 and lengthened in 1893, represents the later Brighton as the famous Pavilion does its beginning.*

222

PLATE 111. *Scarborough. The first settlement can be precisely dated. It was in 966 or 967 that the Norsman Thorgills Skarthi (Hare Lip) founded it below the great fortified headland that was thereafter called Skarthi's Burh or stronghold. The earliest village probably lay along the waterfront of the inner harbour. In the mid-twelfth century a castle was built on the headland and a new town laid out below it. Within a hundred years the town had grown westwards and in 1256 Henry III granted land outside the walls for a new planned extension to the borough. This extension is today marked by the street called Newborough. Scarborough remained a prosperous if small town until the seventeenth century when, after the discovery of medicinal springs, it became a fashionable spa. Sea bathing developed in the mid-eighteenth century but it still remained somewhat select until the railway arrived. The mighty Grand Hotel of 1863 and the rows of Victorian terraces tell of a different type of resort when it became Yorkshire's equivalent to Lancashire's Blackpool.*

afford to lay out a complete new town.

Most landlords, even bishops and abbots, made no attempt to lay out their new towns. They gave them charters, sometimes supplied building materials, offered low rents and other inducements, but they were content to let the town grow – if it was to grow – as it liked within the prescribed area. And when that area was satisfactorily filled, they were prepared to extend the boundaries of the borough by granting more land for building, as happened at Scarborough in 1256 (Plate 111) or at Newcastle-on-Tyne in 1298. To plan a whole town at once was a highly risky investment. We know, for example, that at Kingston-upon-Hull fewer than half the building plots in the royal town had been taken up by 1320, a generation after the original planning. At New Winchelsea many of the thirty-nine squares or chequers into which the town-site had been divided in the 1280s were never built upon, but remained under grass and can be seen to this day.

These were all royal foundations. Few other landowners could afford to wait a generation for the return of their money, if it was to come back at all. It was far safer to start a town off with a charter, a market and a fair, and a few other practical inducements to settlers, and then to sit back and hope for the best. Let it grow automatically as new groups of traders and merchants directed their steps there and decided eventually to settle and build there. No landowner – not even the king – could create a new town if people did not want it. It remained empty or half-empty despite all the inducements.

We do not know why New Town, on Poole Bay, failed so completely to come off. It is one of those nice little problems of local history. In a general way, I suppose it was still-born because the town of Poole lay only four miles across the bay, founded about forty years before by William Longsword, Earl of Salisbury, and the new town of Edward's, for all its royal backing and privileges of the City of London, could not compete with it. The earl had got in first on this wonderful anchorage, and the advantage remained with his town.

Down in Cornwall, it was difficult to attract the natives into the new towns at all. Like all Celtic people they preferred to live in the country. So, though medieval landowners founded nearly forty boroughs in the county, few of them ever got going as towns. Most were futile experiments. In fact they became the rotten

It is likely that Newtown in Poole Harbour failed, as Professor Hoskins suggests, because of the proximity of Poole. This was not an uncommon feature. The Bishops of Winchester laid out a new town at their manor of Downton in Wiltshire, in 1208-9. It failed because in 1219 the Bishop of Salisbury founded New Salisbury, eight miles to the north on a better site. Now only a great rectangular green, known as the Borough, exists at Downton to mark this abortive town.

boroughs of later centuries. Even those that succeeded in coming alive were populated in their early days mostly by foreigners, that is, by non-Cornishmen, or they too would have failed.

There were in fact great risks in starting a new town, or at least in investing money in it. One needed considerable capital and a long-term view to risk a completely planned town, and preferably also the certainty that the demand was there and could not fail – as in New Sarum in the thirteenth century or Middlesbrough and Barrow in the nineteenth. And so, for these and other reasons, the planned town has always been the exception in England, and derives most of its special interest from that fact.

As suggested above, planned towns are probably the norm rather than the exception in England.

The Open-Field Town

The planned towns are the easiest kind of urban landscape to understand, and perhaps for that reason the least interesting to the curious traveller – however attractive they may be to look at. They satisfy our curiosity too soon. Now let us explore what lies behind the contemporary appearance of quite another group of towns: towns which reveal nothing at first sight of their secret, physical history, and which indeed seem to have little or nothing in common as one looks at them and around their streets. As we explore the ramifications of their anatomy we shall encounter a good deal of the stupidity, the greed and self-interest, the plain conservatism – just human resistance to change of any kind – as well as the pure evil of human nature, working itself out in bricks and stone and mortar.

Let us look at those towns that grew up in the midst of their own open fields, that entered the nineteenth century with their population rising at a phenomenal rate, but were wholly unable to expand their building area to meet this rise in numbers. They were still held within the vice of their own fields, with all the complicated property rights which made it impossible to secure land for building development. Most effective of all in stopping any new building were the Lammas pasture rights – that is, the right of burgesses, or some of them, to graze their cattle and sheep over the open fields after the harvest had been taken in. The town fields might well be private property and held by only half-a-dozen farmers. The burgess might have no land at all in the fields; but he had this right to graze his cattle after Lammas over any man's lands, freely and wherever he liked. It sounds a trivial thing – this common pasture right for six months of the year – but it had the most devastating effect on town development, in the Midlands above all. The consequences are almost unbelievable until one follows them out.

There are, in the east Midlands, three towns lying fairly close together that illustrate well the physical consequences of this situation – Nottingham, Leicester and Stamford. Until about two hundred years ago, they had developed along pretty much the same lines. They differ very markedly from each other today. For in each instance the problem of expansion was solved or evaded in a different way, and produced as a result towns with very different characteristics. Nottingham failed to solve the problem until too late and created as a consequence some of the worst slums in any town in England. Leicester solved it just in time and produced a town that spilled widely across the surrounding fields and gave its working class bigger and better houses, and wider streets, than almost anywhere else in industrial England. Stamford failed entirely to solve the problem of its open fields; but whereas Nottingham created its slums, Stamford fossilised into the beautiful seventeenth- and eighteenth-century town we see today, a museum piece from a pre-industrial England.

Some two to three hundred years ago, Nottingham was one of the most beautiful towns in England. All travellers were agreed about this. Thomas Baskerville, who saw it in the 1680s, called it 'Paradise Restored, for here you find large streets, fair built houses, fine

PLATE 112. *This now historic photograph of Leeds shows how the nineteenth-century terraced houses were fitted into the pre-existing pattern of fields. The agricultural past thus shows through into the urban present.*

women, and many coaches rattling about, and their shops full of merchantable goods'. For Celia Fiennes, a few years later, it was a favourite town by which she judged all others – and generally found them wanting. It was, she said, the neatest town she had ever seen. And Dr Charles Deering, who settled there after a wandering career, said that 'were a naturalist in Quest of an exquisite Spot to build a Town or a City, could he meet with one that would better answer his Wishes?'

Three generations later, Nottingham had become a squalid mess. 'I believe,' said the commissioner who reported on it to the Health of Towns Commission in 1845,

that nowhere else shall we find so large a mass of inhabitants crowded into courts, alleys, and lanes as in Nottingham, and those, too, of the worst possible construction. Here they are so clustered upon each other; court within court, yard within yard, and lane within lane, in a manner to defy description . . . Some parts of Nottingham [are] so very bad as hardly to be surpassed in misery by anything to be found within the entire range of our manufacturing cities.

In an England that contained the slums of Manchester and Liverpool, Leeds and east London, this was strong language indeed.

What had happened to destroy so utterly the Paradise Restored of Thomas Baskerville, the neat town of Celia Fiennes, the exquisite spot of Charles Deering, to destroy it in the short space of three generations? To the north and south of the town, gripping it along three quarters of its circuit, lay nearly eleven hundred acres of open fields, far more than enough land for housing the new industrial population. But until these fields were enclosed, until their multitudinous strips were reallotted in large compact blocks of land,

and until the rights of common pasture over them were extinguished, it was impossible to get a single acre for building. The burgesses with pasture rights steadfastly refused to allow the enclosure of the fields. Borough elections were fought on this issue. Candidates who wanted enclosure were burned in effigy, their supporters wheeled about in muck-carts in the robust eighteenth-century fashion. Even the freeholders in the fields – who were willing to have enclosure so that they could farm more efficiently or sell land for building – were helpless in the face of the burgesses who might have no land but who hoped to get a piece in time, or who already held these rights to graze their cattle and sheep.

This 'Cowocracy', as they were called, were not entirely blind to the evils of slums and overcrowding. But they had a lively fear that enclosure might rob them of their valuable rights – rights which made a real difference to their standard and their mode of living – in the interests of the large freeholders and a corporation known to be corrupt. Then, too, there were those who opposed enclosure because there was no guarantee that any open spaces would be reserved for the public benefit; and, as things stood, the slum-dweller in Nottingham could at least walk in the adjacent fields and get some fresh air. Enclosure might result in every acre being grabbed by private owners, who would sell for speculative building.

Most of the opponents of enclosure at Nottingham were not, therefore, mere villains. They had some good reason on their side. But their refusal to enclose had the effect of creating another class of opponents of a blacker hue – the owners of slum property. The town could not grow outwards. So every garden, every orchard, every foot of open space within the old confines, was doled out piecemeal at exorbitant prices for building. Even streets were too extravagant of space: courts and alleys enabled more houses to be packed into a given area: and where, in Deering's day, the apple or the cherry orchard had blown in springtime, courts of back-to-back houses now faced each other across an open drain (Fig. 13). In some parts there were eight hundred persons living – if that is the word – on one acre of ground: one person to every six square yards.

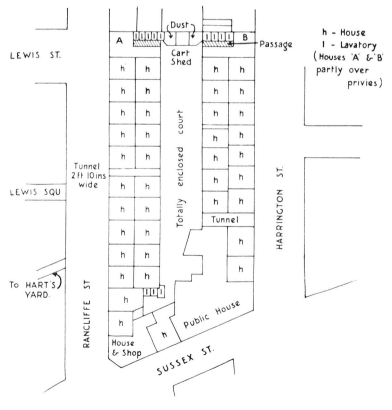

FIG. 13.
Plan of a typical court in Nottingham (taken from the Report of the Royal Commission on the State of the Large Towns, 1845) *showing the intense pressure on building land as a result of the failure to enclose the surrounding open fields. Notice the back-to-back houses, the tunnel entrances to the completely enclosed court, and the primitive sanitation.*

Even the schools were built in the corners of crowded burial grounds, or over public sewers into which they slowly sank. Rents for these appalling houses – eight thousand back-to-backs, rising three storeys with single rooms piled one on top of the other – took a high proportion of a working-class income. Nottingham's own historian, Dr Chambers, reckons that altogether the slum property of the town produced an annual return of forty thousand pounds, some of which went to building-clubs financed by small artisans. Not all the slum-owners were big men.

So an unholy alliance of cow-keepers and slum-owners repeatedly elected the kind of corporation that would fight to the death 'the unsightly monster' of enclosure – as the mayor called it in 1825. When, at last, the reformed corporation carried through the enclosure in 1845, and the town could burst outwards, the damage had been done (Fig. 14). Three times as many people had been packed into the old confines as could prudently be housed there, even by the low standards of a hundred years ago, and the slums of Nottingham have remained a byword down to our own day. Not until the 1920s and 1930s could a real clearance be made of this formidable mess, and a newer Nottingham begin to appear out of it.

FIG. 14. HOUSING DEVELOPMENT IN NOTTINGHAMHIRE AFTER THE ENCLOSURE OF THE OPEN FIELDS
The map shows the development of part of Clay Field after the enclosure. The heavy black lines represent the boundaries of the separate allotments made to private owners by the enclosure commissioners. There were about four hundred of these allotments, most of which were immediately 'developed' by their owners without the slightest reference to neighbouring allotments and owners. The pattern of the roads and streets was largely determined by the medieval footpaths and furlongs of the open fields. Thus Victorian Nottingham is largely built upon lines determined many centuries ago (see J.D. Chambers, A Century of Nottingham History, 1851-1951, *University of Nottingham, 1952). Reproduced by permission of Dr J.D. Chambers and of the Ordnance Survey.*

At Leicester, twenty miles away, with much the same kind of industrial and population history, things happened quite differently. Here the three open fields which practically surrounded the ancient town had all been enclosed before the need for more building land had become desperate. One great field, lying to the east and north-east of the town, had been enclosed in 1764 – in good time for the population increase – and the town proceeded to grow comfortably in that direction. There was almost unlimited space for Leicester to expand; and in 1845 the commissioners were able to report that the town 'was spread over an unusual extent of ground in proportion to its population'. Many large gardens were still to be seen, even in the centre of the town. The newer streets were wider than the average of manufacturing towns. The wind could blow through them and the sun shine upon them, unlike the courts of Nottingham. The working-class homes seldom rose above two storeys. Moreover, these houses had four rooms, and each room was bigger than its Nottingham counterpart; and there was rarely more than one family per house. They generally had ample yards, often little gardens, and were better built than those of most industrial towns. Leicester was no Paradise Restored: its flat site led to difficult drainage problems and mortality was high even by the standards of the time, but there was nothing remotely resembling the horrors of Nottingham.

Stamford presented quite another case again. The open fields hemmed in the town along its entire northern side, while on the southern side Burghley Park and the farmlands of the Cecils offered not an acre for expansion. Here the open fields survived until 1872. Until that late date, the Cecils successfully opposed any move to enclose the fields, for reasons which were never fully disclosed at the time. But the main reason is clear enough. The borough of Stamford returned two members to Parliament, the franchise being restricted to householders. Since the end of the seventeenth century the Cecils, at Burghley House just outside the town, had controlled the election of both members by a combination of methods that seemed to leave no loophole for a mistake. There was, indeed, one possible loophole. Squatters on the waste of the manor, at the fringe of the open fields, erected hovels and tried to stake a claim. But the Marquess of Exeter (as the Cecils had become in 1801) pulled down these hovels instantly, and prosecuted the squatters. Why? Because every house that went up and stayed up represented a certain vote against his political nominees. With all his elaborate political machinery – his control of all the tradesmen in the town and of all the town's six advowsons, his ownership of some two hundred houses each carrying a vote, his absolute control of the Mayor, the corporation and all the corporation offices – the Marquess of Exeter could not be absolutely certain that the remaining voters would not one day oust his candidates. There were too many houses he did not own; and he could not afford to see any more built. In a town that chafed under this tyranny, every new house that went up was a vote against the Cecil interest.

For the same reason, therefore, he could not allow the open fields to be enclosed. That would have meant some twelve hundred acres freed for building, a catastrophic thought. True, he owned a good deal of this land and could stop any building on his own acres. But there was much he did not own. As lord of the manor, his consent was necessary to the procuring of any act of parliament for the enclosure of the town fields: and that consent was never forthcoming. If Stamford had been a vigorous industrial town like Nottingham or Leicester, the results of this feudal control would have been disastrous for the health and housing of the population. But Lord Exeter also saw to it that Stamford should never attract any industry. In 1846 there was a good chance that the new main line of railway from London to York would pass through Stamford instead of Peterborough, then a place of no consequence. The people of Stamford were passionately anxious that the railway should come their way, for it was plain enough that the great coaching trade, by which they lived, was doomed. For reasons we need not go into, Lord Exeter successfully prevented the main line from entering the town: it was taken through Peterborough instead. Stamford was killed: in the 1850s its population, which until then had been rising steadily, actually began to fall. There was no housing problem here. The open fields remained open for another generation – until the secret ballot came in 1872, but by then grass was growing in the streets of the town.

Other towns in the Midlands, towns such as Coventry for example, faced the same problem of how to get building land for their physical expansion. Some towns, like Leicester, solved the problem with no difficulty. Others, like Nottingham and Stamford, failed – though the failure was due to entirely different political circumstances. At Nottingham it was the shortsighted conservatism of the townspeople themselves, fighting a minority who wanted change and improvement; at Stamford it was an aristocratic landlord fighting for his archaic political privileges against the townspeople. And there at Stamford, the beautiful town that Celia Fiennes and Defoe had admired so much remained almost exactly as they had seen it: but fossilised, moribund. Peterborough became the great railway and engineering centre that Stamford might well have become. But now that the human misery of the transition is over and forgotten, and now that we see modern Peterborough, we may perhaps be grateful to the Cecils for the feudal obstinacy which kept their town from growing, and preserved it for our pleasure today. There are too many Peterboroughs, and not enough Stamfords, in modern England.

The Market Town

The majority of old towns have grown up as market towns, and they all present their own special problems. This makes them more varied to look at, and in general perhaps more picturesque, but it is not easy to make them intelligible to someone who has not seen them. The market place was the growing point of most towns, and they have taken their shape around it. Standing in the market place, we are – not always but very often – at the origin of things. As we study its shape, its size, its layout in relation to the parish church, and the details of its topography, we are confronted by a whole series of questions. If we could answer these, I feel we should know a lot more than we do about the earliest history of the place and the way it has grown. What accounts for the differences from town to town, or the similarities between them?

In the Midlands, even in the large industrial towns, we find markets still being carried on with stalls pitched in a large open space, covering perhaps a couple of acres, exactly in the medieval fashion. The covered stalls with their piles of goods of every description, the traders shouting their wares from every stall under the open sky, all this is purely medieval; and around these open markets stand the lordly twentieth-century shops, the nearest to the London shops that the town can show. It is a curious survival: the Middle Ages incapsulated in the twentieth-century industrial town. Such great open-air markets can be seen at Northampton, Newark and Leicester, for example, and most notable of all was that at Nottingham, where the vast triangular market place covers five-and-a-half acres and was once even larger. Only in recent years has it been taken over as the civic centre, and the Goose Fair relegated to the outer suburbs; but for something like a thousand years it was the market place. At Leicester the market place occupied the whole of the south-eastern quarter of the walled town. It has shrunk a little since it first started there, perhaps in the tenth century, but it is still one of the largest open-air markets in the country.

Yet at Stamford, thirty miles away, not an industrial town but indeed always a market

PLATE 114. *Boston, Lincolnshire. The great tower or Stump of St Botolph's church dominates both the town and the river which gave it its prosperity. The Witham is edged by warehouses, mainly of the eighteenth century. These reflect a relatively late period of modest success for the town. Of its earlier medieval greatness little more than the church and the town plan survives.*

town for a very rich countryside, the market place has shrunk to a fraction of its original size. Red Lion Square, covering about half an acre at the most, and mostly taken up by the Great North Road, represents just the shrunken remains of a market place that once covered about five times that area.

Not all market places were vast squares or rectangles or triangles, set aside for the purpose. At Marlborough and Thame, both ancient Saxon towns, the present-day main street – of immense width and length – once served as the open-air market. Stalls were set up to a considerable depth on either side of the main road, which swelled out like a sausage-shaped balloon for half a mile or so and then closed in again. All this must have taken shape before there were any houses on the scene. Not until much later were these immense spaces lined with buildings, and even then the houses and shops were kept well back so as not to interfere with the immemorial rights of the stall-holders. In such towns as Marlborough and Thame – and many others – the market places were never built upon, but remain wide and open to this day. Probably they owe their exceptional size to the fact that Marlborough was a great sheep market from the earliest times, and Thame possibly a great cattle-market. Both needed all the space they could get. In scores of other towns, on the other hand, the market places have been partly built over, so that one gets a broad main street, a block of buildings down one side and behind that again a narrow street running parallel to the main street.

Thame is certainly a planned town, founded by the Bishops of Lincoln in 1219-21, and Marlborough is likely to have the same origin. Balloon- or cigar-shaped market places in new towns are relatively common, as it was one of the easiest ways to create an open space along an existing main road.

There seem to be no discoverable rules about the shape of market places, why some take the form of a large open square – often set rather apart from the main flow of traffic – and some a swelling, a sort of aneurism, in the main artery of trade. The triangular shape is also common: starting with a broad base, narrowing steadily as one goes away from it for a quarter to half a mile, until one reaches the outlet in a main road of the normal width. St Albans is a good example of this type, if we think away the large block of building that lies between the present market place and the street called Chequer Street that lies behind. One would like to know what these various shapes mean. Perhaps they reflect nothing at all except the accidents of conception: but I suspect that there is often, in fact, a buried clue here, and that if we could unearth it we should know something about the early growth of many market towns that no documents will ever tell us.

The centre of Royston, Hertfordshire, founded by the adjacent priory of Austin Canons in about 1189, has this characteristic. The original cigar-shaped market place was entirely built over, presumably at an early date, for then a second, triangular, market place was added to the east. This too has partly been encroached upon.

St Albans is thus a planned town of late Saxon date.

Very occasionally there is a document that gives us a clue. Thus the chronicler of St Albans monastery tells us that about the year 950 Abbot Wulsin laid out the rudimentary town outside the north gate of the abbey. It took the form of an open space tapering from a broad base outside the abbey walls, northwards to a point at which he built St Peter's church. Facing this triangular space, created for the benefit of traders, the abbot divided up the land on either side into a series of narrow plots on which traders and others were encouraged to settle permanently, building their houses with timber and other materials provided by him. The triangular plan of the market place, which determined the shape of the town here, is now seen to be a perfectly rational shape for its purpose. Traders would naturally regard stall-sites close to the abbey wall as the best for business. As many as possible would cluster at that end, and the stalls would thin out quickly as one went northwards away from the abbey towards the open country, with all its dangers for the peaceful trader. The triangular shape gave the maximum protection of the greatest number of traders; but whether it represents a fairly general type of early plan – say pre-Conquest – I do not know.

Such a market place was covered with booths and stalls for different types of traders. The next stage developed when the stalls were covered over and became permanent. The last stage was reached when the permanent stalls became houses or shops. At this point it might well happen that blocks of shops and houses would be built down one side of the market place, taking the place of a number of stalls, and so creating the plan, described

above, where the original open space is reduced to a broad main street, with a detached block of buildings down one side, behind which is a narrow back street, as at St Albans, or Kimbolton in Huntingdonshire, to speak of only two examples. This happened at Stamford, also, though the buildings put up in the market place there formed irregular blocks. And the records at St Albans and Stamford show that these permanent buildings had made their appearance by the early fourteenth century. We should be safe in saying that this building-over of ancient market places was the result of the great expansion of trade and population in the boom of the thirteenth century. But why did they choose to build on their own valuable market places instead of expanding outwards into suburbs? After all, suburbs have a very respectable antiquity. They were well developed outside the walls of many English towns by the thirteenth century, even a little earlier in some places.

The relationship of market place and church raises yet other questions. That the two are almost invariably found together is a commonplace: but why, at Market Harborough, does the church of St Dionysius spring grandly up from the market place without any green space around it, without a vestige of a church-yard? The answer to this question takes us back to the very origins of the town in the middle years of the twelfth century. Before that it was simply a part of the open fields of Great Bowden, a village a mile or two away. With the expansion of trade and industry in the twelfth century – perhaps the most prolific of all centuries for new towns until we come to the nineteenth – a few traders assembled periodically near a crossing place over the river Welland. An informal and unofficial

Kimbolton, now in Cambridgeshire, is not an example of encroachment. The broad rectangular market place, laid out at the gates of the former castle there, still exists as it was originally planned. The back lane marks the line of the old through road of the area which was then diverted around four right-angle bends to enable it to enter the new market place.

PLATE 115. *Thame, Oxfordshire, belonged to the Bishops of Lincoln who were great town planners. It was probably set up around 1150 and given this huge market place along an existing road running north to south. But the main through road from Oxford to Aylesbury ran from east to west a little to the north of the new town. So, in 1219 this road had to be turned into Thame town centre, a diversion of almost a mile. By 1221 the town was so successful that encroachments on the market place began. Their successors still stand in the middle distance.*

233

market began to develop. In such a casual way many an English town was conceived. This is no guesswork; we know from the records that it often happened like this.

By the year 1203 the casual assembly at Harborough was sufficiently well established and viable to attract the notice of the Crown – ever on the look-out for revenue – and the infant township was called upon to pay three marks into the Exchequer for the right to hold a regular weekly market. Some forty years later, the town had grown big enough to call for a church of its own, instead of attending the mother church of Great Bowden. But the new town church, large and imposing though it was, was allowed only to be a dependent chapel of the mother-church, without the right of burial of the dead. This right, which was a source of income to the medieval rectors, was carefully reserved to the mother-church. When the men of Market Harborough died they were carried back to Great Bowden for burial, back to the country village on whose fields their town had sprung up. Their own church of St Dionysius was allowed no churchyard. Wherever we see an ancient town church without a churchyard, we may well suspect that the town is the daughter of some mother village near by – now completely overshadowed by its offspring – and that it came into existence at a comparatively late date, since the Norman Conquest anyway, and most probably in the twelfth or thirteenth century.

At King's Lynn one's curiosity is immediately aroused by two great market places with a splendid church beside each: the Saturday market shadowed by St Margaret's church, the Tuesday market by St Nicholas. Here again, we are taken back to the very beginning of the town, to the years just after the Norman Conquest – for King's Lynn is not really old by English standards. It was a town created on the marshland by the first Bishop of Norwich (Herbert Losinga, 1091-1119), to whom the site belonged and who saw its wonderful possibilities. It was he who created the Saturday market and built the church of St Margaret beside it, just before the end of the eleventh century. And it was his successor, William de Turbe (1146-74) who, two generations later, had to extend the limits of the successful town over the marshland to the north, where he established another market place and built the church of St Nicholas beside it. Hence the two: the Saturday market in the original town, the Tuesday market in its twelfth-century extension. Each symbolises a distinct phase in the physical history of Lynn.

This is much too bald an account of what lies behind the landscape of this fascinating town: and across the grey waters of the Wash lies another town of the same type and date and manner of origin – Boston. Lynn was created by a Norman bishop, Boston by a great Breton lord almost simultaneously. But they did not get in each other's way: more than twenty miles of water lay between them and they drew their vigour and their sustenance from different parts of England.

What I have tried to do in this chapter is to suggest a way of looking at towns as though they were a special kind of landscape – as indeed they are – to get behind the guide-books and the individual buildings to the secret history of these places: to draw attention to what I think are some of the significant bits of urban landscape that point the way into this secret history. But there is – for all our reflection – so much we do not know about even the simplest town scene.

There are so many towns to be seen, and each must be – or ought to be – approached for

Professor Hoskins' description of the growth of Market Harborough is splendid and was based on his own detailed research (Trans. Leics. Arch. Soc. XXV (1949), 56-68). However it is now clear that Market Harborough is indeed a true 'New Town'. Here again the old north to south and east to west through-roads were diverted to pass through the new market place, so producing the dangerous corners which still exist in the town today.

Again therefore, King's Lynn is a double new town. Boston (1086-1113) too is a planted town, its plan related to the curving banks of the River Witham along which came the trade which made it the second most prosperous town after London by 1206.

PLATE 116. *Kimbolton, Huntingdonshire (Cambridgeshire). Not an example of the infilling of a market place, but a perfect instance of a small planned town. The original through road is still in existence at the top and the bottom of the picture. It now leads, via sharp bends, into the town, whose broad market place was laid out at the gate of Kimbolton Castle probably around 1200. The medieval castle has long since gone, its site occupied by the great house, built by Sir John Vanbrugh for the fourth Earl of Manchester between 1707-14. The back lane, roughly on the line of the original through road, is exactly that.*

PLATE 117. *Wool Merchant's House, Lavenham, Suffolk. A glorious fifteenth-century structure with a central open hall and elaborate cross-wing. It was in the height of fashion when it was built. Yet it has only survived because Lavenham, as a town, failed. In a more successful town the house would have undoubtedly been destroyed long ago.*

the first time on foot: certainly all the smaller towns. For only on foot does one detect the subtle rise and fall of ground to which the earliest settlers were so sensitive, or alignments in the town scene that may throw light on some fundamental change of plan: or the names of streets and lanes that set the mind working at once. No one could see Old Town Street, at Plymouth, without beginning at once to speculate about the significance of a name like this: and in fact the name takes us back to the very beginnings, to the poverty-stricken little Saxon village of farmers and fishermen, well down behind the Hoe, out of which this great naval city has grown. And then there are all the seaside towns and the dockyard towns, about which I have said nothing. The landscape of towns, indeed, requires a whole book to itself.

One needs the published histories of the towns and behind them the town records themselves. And slowly one pieces together from the records, from the archaeological finds in the local museum, and from the evidence of one's own eyes, what has happened. It would be an interminable occupation were it not for the fact that what one learns about the landscape of one town often throws a flash of light upon a topographical puzzle in another. A pattern begins to form. It is still too early to generalise much about this subject – if indeed one will ever be able to. But in the meantime how pleasant it is to find oneself arriving in the evening for the first time in some lively little English market town, where one can forget for a while the noisy onward march of science, and settle down to meditate upon the civilised past.

Chapter 10
THE LANDSCAPE TODAY

Introduction

There is little that can be added to this chapter, containing as it does Professor Hoskins' evocative explanation of the piece of the English landscape visible from the window of his study in Oxfordshire.

One might add that despite his strictures on modern landscapes, there is much to see from any window in England if only the viewer is prepared to try and understand it. Not all the views may be as pleasurable as that of North Oxfordshire but the history of at least part of the English landscape can be seen from all of them whether it be the story of the development of a north London suburb, seen by a student from a garret window in Stoke Newington, the growth of a medieval town viewed by a young man from the upper windows of an eighteenth-century house in the centre of Lichfield, Staffordshire, or the development of a Cambridgeshire village in front of an ageing civil servant from a study in a 1960s neo-Georgian estate house.

Professor Hoskins saw little in the modern development of the English landscape that filled him with pleasure and one has great sympathy for his feelings. Yet two points come to mind. One is that if aesthetic pleasure is separated from objective study then the most dreadful landscapes can come alive after close research and bring with them their own form of satisfaction. The other is that the English landscape has never been static but has always been changing, for better or worse. Today we are passing through a period which can perhaps be regarded as a disaster. Yet it is not the faceless planners, mindless civil servants, wild military men or politicians who are always to blame. Ultimately they merely carry out what we as a democratic society demand. It is we who want broad motorways, cheap coal, instant electricity, subsidised food, and protection from alleged enemies without care for the past or indeed thought for the future. Perhaps we have achieved in our landscape what we deserve.

THE LANDSCAPE TODAY

The industrial revolution and the creation of parks around the country houses have taken us down to the later years of the nineteenth century. Since that time, and especially since the year 1914, every single change in the English landscape has either uglified it or destroyed its meaning, or both. Of all the changes in the last two generations, only the great reservoirs of water for the industrial cities of the North and Midlands have added anything to the scene that one can contemplate without pain. It is a distasteful subject but it must be faced for a few moments.

The country houses decay and fall: hardly a week passes when one does not see the auctioneer's notice of the impending sale and dissolution of some big estate. The house is seized by the demolition contractors, its park invaded and churned up by the tractors and trailers of the timber merchant. Down comes the house; down come the tall trees, naked and gashed lies the once beautiful park. Or if it stands near a town, the political planners swarm into the house, turn it into a rabbit-warren of black-hatted officers of This and That, and the park becomes a site for some 'overspill' – a word as beastly as the thing it describes. We may indeed find the great house still standing tidily in a timbered park: but it is occupied by what the villagers describe detachedly as 'the atom men', something remote from the rest of us, though not remote in the sense they themselves like to think. And if the planners are really fortunate, they fill the house with their paper and their black hats, and open-cast mining of coal or iron ore simultaneously finishes off the park. They can sit at their big desks and contemplate with an exquisite joy how everything is now being put to a good use. Demos and Science are the joint Emperors.

Beyond the park, in some parts of England such as East Anglia, the bulldozer rams at the old hedges, blots them out to make fields big and vacant enough for the machines of the new ranch-farming and the business-men farmers of five to ten thousand acres. Fortunately, the tractor and the bulldozer cannot easily destroy the great hedge-banks and stone walls of the anciently enclosed parts of England; nor is it worth doing, for the good farmer knows the value of these banks and walls as shelter, and of the hedges for timber. Much of the old field pattern therefore remains, with its tangle of deep lanes and thick hedges.

What else has happened in the immemorial landscape of the English countryside? Airfields have flayed it bare wherever there are level, well-drained stretches of land, above all in eastern England. Poor devastated Lincolnshire and Suffolk! And those long gentle lines of the dip-slope of the Cotswolds, those misty uplands of the sheep-grey oolite, how they have lent themselves to the villainous requirements of the new age! Over them drones, day after day, the obscene shape of the atom-bomber, laying a trail like a filthy slug upon Constable's and Gainsborough's sky. England of the Nissen hut, the 'pre-fab', and the electric fence, of the high barbed wire around some unmentionable devilment; England of the arterial by-pass, treeless and stinking of diesel oil, murderous with lorries; England of the bombing-range wherever there was once silence, as on Otmoor or the marshlands of Lincolnshire; England of battle-training areas on the Breckland heaths, and tanks crashing through empty ruined Wiltshire villages; England of high explosive falling upon the prehistoric monuments of Dartmoor. Barbaric England of the scientists, the military men, and the politicians: let us turn away and contemplate the past before all is lost to the vandals.

The view from this room where I write these last pages is small, but it will serve as an epitome of the gentle unravished English landscape. Circumscribed as it is, with tall trees closing it in barely half a mile away, it contains in its detail something of every age from the Saxon to the nineteenth century. A house has stood on this site since the year 1216, when the Bishop of Lincoln ordained a vicarage here, but it has been rebuilt over and over again, and last of all in 1856. Down the garden, sloping to the river, the aged and useless apple

PLATE 118. *Early Warning Radar Station, Fylingdales Moor, North Yorkshire. The landscape we deserve? Even the preparation for Armageddon produces its own strangely attractive vision.*

PLATE 119. *Middle Barton, Oxfordshire today. Compare this photograph with the plan of the village in 1795 (Fig. 5). The old pattern of streets and houses is still just visible but it is being rapidly engulfed by the ubiquitous housing estates and 'infill' as the drive for 'a home in the country' goes on apace.*

trees are the successors of those that grew here in the time of Charles I, when the glebe terrier of 1634 speaks of 'one orchard, one backside, and two little gardens'. Beyond the apple trees and within a few feet of the river is a large raised platform, visible in winter before its annual submergence in weeds, part of a vanished building, and there are clear lines of stone walls adjoining it. Almost certainly this is the site of one of the three water-mills recorded on the estate in Domesday Book. Below it flows the Dorn, known to the Saxons as the Milk, from the cloudiness of its water after rain: and one still sees it as the Saxons saw it a thousand years ago, as I saw it a few minutes ago in the thin rain drifting down from the Cotswolds.

Across the stream, tumbling fast on its way to Glyme and Evenlode, one sees a wide sedgy hollow planted with willow saplings, from which flocks of goldfinches rise with a flash of wings on sunny mornings. This hollow, enclosed by a massive earthen bank, was the fishpond begun by the lord of the manor before his death in 1175, and completed by his son: 'Odo de Berton grants to Roger de St John the land between the garden of Roger and the road to the bridge together with the moor where Thomas de St John began to make his fishpond, rendering yearly a pair of spurs or twopence.'

This was about the year 1200 (the charter is undated), but there is the fishpond today. And there is the lane dropping down to the stone bridge that was rebuilt in 1948, but unquestionably on the site of the stone bridge which is mentioned as a landmark in an even earlier charter. And 'the moor' is the description of the scene before it had been claimed for cultivation. We catch a sight of an earlier world in the bare words of this charter.

Beyond the fishpond, the ground rises to form the other side of the valley, fields with their broken hedges of twisted hawthorns. What age are these hedges? They were not here in 1685, when another glebe terrier shows that the parish still had its open fields. But they were probably made before 1750, by which date the enclosure had apparently been accomplished. One or two hedge-banks are, however, medieval in origin, for the St Johns had a separate enclosed pasture called Grascroft from the early 1200s onwards, and this ancient field comes into the view also.

A little to the right, on the other side of the lane, the eye dwells upon a small park, with a boating-lake catching the light, and some modest landscaping; and through the bare winter trees one sees the chimneys of a seemly Victorian 'big house'. The house and park were made as late as the 1870s. It must be one of the last parks to be made in England, for landowners began to feel the pinch of falling rents soon after that. The house, in fact, is older, for the work of the 1870s, though apparently a complete rebuilding, is merely a stone casing around a house originally built by a successful merchant of the Staple, whose inscription is still over the door: *'Thinke and Thanke Anno 1570'*. Three hundred years later his house was remodelled by another successful bourgeois – this time a wealthy Oxford brewer.

But this was an old, long-cultivated estate when John Dormer the merchant stapler acquired it, with a history stretching back to pre-Conquest days, when it was one of the demesne-farms of the Anglo-Saxon kings. When they hunted in Woodstock Park, five miles away, in the tenth and eleventh centuries, they called upon the produce of this large estate (about seven thousand acres then) to feed their household; and one can walk, after a morning's writing, along the broad green lane that was first made to connect the estate with the hunting-park. It was a royal estate in Saxon times, but how far back into that age? What was it when the Saxons captured Eynsham, not many miles away, in the year 571? We do not yet know, but here in this room one is reaching back, in a view embracing a few hundred acres at the most, through ten centuries of English life, and discerning shadowy depths beyond that again.

By opening the window and leaning out, the parish church comes into view across the lane, a lonely building now, empty and cold and bare except for one hour each week. It was rebuilt about the year 1300, when the village was large and flourishing: this was the high farming period of the Middle Ages. But the font is of the twelfth century, so there was

PLATE 120. *Didcot Power Station,*
Oxfordshire. The modern landscape.

a church here then; and deep in the churchyard to the east of the chancel is a buried wall which is perhaps the east wall of a Saxon church. For though it stands so isolated today from human kind, St Mary's church was a mother-church for a wide area round about, as befitted the spiritual centre of a royal estate; and we do not know how far back a building stood on this site. A Roman coin came from under the tower at the restoration of 1855, but one cannot make too much of that.

And then, finally, out of sight but only fifty or sixty yards from this room in the field next the garden, there lies buried the main street of the old village that was wiped out by the Black Death. One walks between the banks that show where the houses stood, marking how blocks of squared masonry thrust in one place out of the turf (a more important building than most of them), and how the tree-roots twist among the rubble footings of the peasant dwellings; and one picks up pieces of twelfth- and thirteenth-century pottery – mere sherds, bits of rim, of sides, of bases, but all dateable: nothing later than the Black Death, when the great silence descended.

Not every small view in England is so full of detail as this, upon the oolite of north Oxfordshire, for this was a rich and favoured countryside that was beloved of owners of Roman villas, even in places of Bronze Age men. The cultural humus of sixty generations or more lies upon it. But most of England is a thousand years old, and in the walk of a few miles one would touch nearly every century in that long stretch of time.

Know most of the rooms of thy native country before thou goest over the threshold thereof.
Especially seeing England presents thee with so many observables.

SELECT BIBLIOGRAPHY

General Studies

ASTON, M., *Interpreting the Landscape,* Batsford, 1985.
ASTON, M. and ROWLEY, T., *Landscape Archaeology,* David & Charles, 1974.
BERESFORD, M. W., *History on the Ground,* Lutterworth, 1957.
  Time and Place, Hambledon Press, 1985.
DARBY, H. C., *A New Historical Geography of England,* Cambridge University Press, 1973.
GELLING, M., *Signposts to the Past,* J. M. Dent, 1978.
  Place-Names in the Landscape, J. M. Dent, 1984.
MUIR, R., *Reading the Landscape,* Michael Joseph, 1981.
  History from the Air, Michael Joseph, 1983.
ROGERS, A. and ROWLEY, T. (eds), *Landscape and Documents,* Bedford Square Press, 1974.
TAYLOR, C. C., *Fieldwork in Medieval Archaeology,* Batsford, 1974.
  Fields in the English Landscape, J. M. Dent, 1975.

---

1 The Landscape before the English Settlement

BOWEN, H. C., *Ancient Fields,* British Association for the Advancement of Science, 1961.
BRADLEY, R., *The Prehistoric Settlement of Britain,* Routledge and Kegan Paul, 1978.
CLARK, GRAHAME, *Archaeology and Society,* Methuen, 1939. *Prehistoric England,* Batsford, 1940.
COLLINGWOOD, R. C., and MYRES,
  J. N. L., *Roman Britain and the English Settlements,* Oxford: Clarendon Press, revised edn 1937.
CRAWFORD, O. G. S., *Archaeology in the Field,* Phoenix House, 1953, revised edn 1960.
CURWEN, E. C., *Air Photography and the Evolution of the Corn-Field,* Black, 2nd edn 1938.
Field Archaeology, H.M.S.O., revised edn 1963.
FINBERG, H. P. R., *Roman and Saxon Withington,* University of Leicester, Department of English Local History, Occasional Paper no. 8, 1955.
FOSTER, I. L., and ALCOCK, L., *Culture and Environment,* Routledge & Kegan Paul, 1963.
FOWLER, P. J., *Approaches to Archaeology,* A. and C. Black, 1977.
  The Farming of Prehistoric Britain, Cambridge University Press, 1983.
FOX, SIR CYRIL F., *The Archaeology of the Cambridge Region,* Cambridge University Press, 2nd edn 1948.
FRERE, S. S. and ST JOSEPH, J. K., *Roman Britain from the Air,* Cambridge University Press, 1983.
GODWIN, H., *The History of the British Flora,* Cambridge University Press, 1956.
Historian's Guide to Ordnance Survey Maps, H.M.S.O., 1964.
LONGWORTH, I. and CHERRY, J. (eds), *Archaeology in Britain since 1945,* British Museum Publications, 1986.
MARGARY, I. D., *Roman Roads in Britain,* Phoenix House, revised edn 1967.
MEGAW, J. V. S. and SIMPSON, G. (eds), *Introduction to British Prehistory,* Leicester University Press, 1978.
MERCER, R. (ed.), *Farming Practice in British Prehistory,* Edinburgh University Press, 1981.
Ordnance Survey Map of Roman Britain, H.M.S.O., 1956 edn.
Ordnance Survey Map of Southern Britain in the Iron Age, H.M.S.O., 1962.
PHILIPS, C. W. (ed.), *The Fenland in Roman Times,* Royal Geographical Society, 1970.
RILEY, D. N., *Early Landscapes from the Air,* University of Sheffield, 1980.
SIMMONS, I. and TOOLEY, M., *The Environment in British Prehistory,* Duckworth, 1981.
THOMAS, CHARLES (ed.), *Rural Settlement in Roman Britain,* Council of British Archaeology, Research Report 7, 1966.
  Christian Antiquities of Camborne, St Austell: H. E. Warne, 1967.
WILSON, D. R., *Air Photo Interpretation for Archaeologists,* Batsford, 1982.

---

2 The English Settlement

BAKER, A. R. H., 'Howard Levi Gray and English Field Systems: an evaluation', *Agricultural History,* 39, 1963, pp. 86-91.
COLLINGWOOD, R. G., and MYRES, J. N. L., *Roman Britain and the English Settlements,* Oxford: Clarendon Press, revised edn 1937.

CRAWFORD, O. G. S., *Archaeology in the Field,* Phoenix House, 1953, revised edn 1960.

DARBY, H. C., *The Domesday Geography of England,* Cambridge University Press: vol. 1, Eastern England, 1952; vol. 2, Midland England (with I. B. Terrett), 1954; vol. 3, Northern England (with I. S. Maxwell), 1962; vol. 4, South-East England (with E. M. J. Campbell), 1962; vol. 5, South-West England (with R. Welldon Finn), 1967; Domesday Gazetteer, 1975.

Dodgshon, R. A., *The Origins of British Field Systems,* Academic Press, 1980.

EKWALL, E., *The Concise Oxford Dictionary of English Place-Names,* Clarendon Press, 4th edn 1966.

EVERITT, A., *Continuity and Colonization,* Leicester University Press, 1986.

FAULL, M. (ed.), *Studies in Late Saxon Settlement,* Oxford University, Dept. for External Studies, 1984.

FINBERG, H. P. R., *The Early Charters of Devon and Cornwall,* University of Leicester, Department of English Local History, Occasional Paper no. 2, 1953, new edn 1963.
The Early Charters of the West Midlands, Leicester University Press, Studies in Early English History no. 2, 1961.
The Early Charters of Wessex, Studies in Early English History no. 3, 1964.

GRAY, H. L., *English Field Systems,* Cambridge, Massachusetts: Harvard University Press, Harvard Historical Studies vol. 22, 1915.

HART, C. R., *The Early Charters of Essex,* University of Leicester, Department of English Local History, Occasional Papers nos. 10 and 11, 1957.
The Early Charters of Eastern England, Leicester University Press, 1966.

HOOKE, D. (ed.), *Medieval Villages,* Oxford University Committee for Archaeology, 1984.
The Anglo-Saxon Landscape, Manchester University Press, 1985.

HOSKINS, W. G., *Provincial England,* Macmillan, 1963, Chapter 2. *Fieldwork in Local History,* Faber, 1967.

HOSKINS, W. G., and FINBERG, H. P. R., *Devonshire Studies,* Jonathan Cape, 1952.

MEANEY, AUDREY, *A Gazetteer of Early Anglo-Saxon Burial Sites,* Allen & Unwin, 1964.

PAGE, W., 'The Origins and Forms of Hertfordshire Towns and Villages', *Archaeologia,* LXIX, 1917-18.

RACKHAM, O., *Trees and Woodland in the British Landscape,* J. M. Dent, 1976.
Ancient Woodland, Edward Arnold, 1980.

REANEY, P. H., *The Origin of English Place-Names,* Routledge & Kegan Paul, 3rd imp. 1964.

ROWLEY, T., *Villages in the Landscape,* J. M. Dent, 1978.

SAWYER, P. H., *From Roman Britain to Norman England,* Methuen, 1978.
English Medieval Settlement, Edward Arnold, 1979.

SEEBOHM, F., *The English Village Community,* Cambridge University Press, 1926 edn.

TAYLOR, C. C., *Village and Farmstead,* George Philip, 1983.

THORPE, H., 'The Green Villages of County Durham', *Proceedings of the Institute of British Geographers,* 1951.
'Rural Settlement', Chapter 19 in J. WREFORD WATSON and J. B. SISSONS (eds.), *The British Isles: a Systematic Geography,* Edinburgh: Nelson, 1964.

3 The Colonisation of Medieval England

ABERG, F. A. (ed.), *Medieval Moated Sites,* Council for British Archaeology, 1978.

ALLEN BROWN, R., *English Castles,* Batsford, 1976.

BERESFORD, M. W., *New Towns of the Middle Ages,* Lutterworth Press, 1967.

BERESFORD, M. W. and ST JOSEPH, J. K., *Medieval England: an Aerial Survey,* Cambridge University Press, 1979.

CANTOR, L. (ed.), *The Medieval Landscape,* Croom Helm, 1982.

CRAWFORD, O. G. S., *Archaeology in the Field,* Phoenix House, 1953, revised edn 1960, Chapters 18 and 19.

DARBY, H. C., *The Domesday Geography of England,* Cambridge University Press, 1952-67, 5 vols. and gazetteer. (see Bibliography for Chapter 2 above).
The Medieval Fenland, Cambridge University Press, 1940.

EMERY, F. V., 'Moated Settlements in England', *Geography,* XLII, 1962.

FINBERG, H. P. R., *Tavistock Abbey,* Cambridge University Press, 1951, Chapter 2.

GRAY, H. L., *English Field Systems,* Cambridge, Massachusetts: Harvard University Press, Harvard Historical Studies vol. 22, 1915.

HALLAM, H. E., *The New Lands of Elloe,* University of Leicester, Department of English Local History, Occasional Paper no. 6, 1954.

HELM, P. J., 'The Somerset Levels in the Middle Ages', *Journal of the British Archaeological Association,* 1949.

HOSKINS, W.G., and FINBERG, H. P. R., *Devonshire Studies,* Jonathan Cape, 1952, essays on 'The Open Field in Devon', 'The Making of the Agrarian Landscape' and 'Three Studies in Family History'.

HOSKINS, W. G., and STAMP, SIR DUDLEY, *Common Lands of England and Wales,* Collins, 1963.

LAMBERT, J. M. (and others), *The Making of the Broads,* John Murray, 1960.

MILLER, E., *The Abbey and Bishopric of Ely,* Cambridge University Press, 1951.

NEILSON, N., *A Terrier of Fleet, Lincolnshire,* Oxford University Press, 1920.

PAGE, W., 'The Origins and Forms of Hertfordshire Towns and Villages', *Archaeologia,* LXIX, 1917-18

POWER, EILEEN, *The Medieval English Wool Trade,* Oxford University Press, 1941, Chapter 2.

RAISTRICK, A., *The Story of the Pennine Walls,* Clapham, Yorkshire: The Dalesman Publishing Co., 1946, 2nd edn 1952.

RENN, D. F., *Norman Castles in Britain,* John Baker, 1968.

SAVAGE, SIR WILLIAM, *The Making of Our Towns,* Eyre & Spottiswoode, 1952, Chapters 6 and 7.

SMITH, R. A. L., *Canterbury Cathedral Priory,* Cambridge University Press, 1943, Chapter 11.

4 The Black Death and After

ALLISON, K. J. (and others), *The Deserted Villages of Oxfordshire,* University of Leicester, Department of English Local History, Occasional Paper no. 17, 1965.
The Deserted Villages of Northamptonshire, Occasional Paper no., 18, 1966.

ATKINSON, T. D., *Local Style in English Architecture,* Batsford, 1947.

BARLEY, M., *Houses and History,* Faber & Faber, 1986.

BERESFORD, M.W., 'The Deserted Villages of Warwickshire', *Transactions of the Birmingham Archaeological Society,* 66, 1950.
'The Lost Villages of Yorkshire', *Yorkshire Archaeological Journal,* Parts 148, 149, 150, 1951-3.
The Lost Villages of England, Lutterworth Press, 1954.

BERESFORD, M. W. and HURST, J. G., *Deserted Medieval Villages,* Lutterworth Press, 1971.

HENDERSON, C., and COATES, H., *Old Cornish Bridges and Streams,* Simpkin Marshall, 1928.

HENDERSON, C., and JERVOISE, E., *Old Devon Bridges,* Exeter: A. Wheaton, 1938.

HOSKINS, W. G., *Provincial England,* Macmillan, 1963, Chapter 6.
'Seven Deserted Village Sites in Leicestershire'.
'The Deserted Villages of Leicestershire', in *Essays in Leicestershire History,* Liverpool University Press, 1950.
The Heritage of Leicestershire, Leicester: Edgar Backus, 1946, for Ashby de la Zouch and Kirby Muxloe castles.

HOSKINS, W. G., and FINBERG, H. P. R., *Devonshire Studies,* Jonathan Cape, 1952, essay on 'The Wealth of Medieval Devon'.

JERVOISE, E., *The Ancient Bridges of the South of England,* Architectural Press, 1930.
The Ancient Bridges of the North of England, Architectural Press, 1931.
The Ancient Bridges of Mid and Eastern England, Architectural Press, 1932.

Maps and Plans in the Public Record Office, c. 1410-1860, H.M.S.O., 1967.

MESSENT, C. J. W., *The Ruined Churches of Norfolk,* Norwich: Hunt, 1931.

MOORE, J. S., *Laughton: A Study in the Evolution of the Wealden Landscape,* University of Leicester, Department of English Local History, Occasional Paper no. 19, 1965.

MORRIS, R., *Cathedrals and Abbeys of England,* J. R. Dent, 1979.

MUIR, R., *The Lost Villages of Britain,* Michael Joseph, 1982.

PLATT, C., *The Parish Churches of Medieval England,* Secker & Warburg, 1981.

RAVENSDALE, J. R., *Liable to Floods,* Cambridge University Press, 1974.
RODWELL, R., *The Archaeology of the English Church,* Batsford, 1981.
ROWLEY, R. T. and WOOD, J., *Deserted Villages,* Shire Publications, 1982.
THORPE, HARRY, 'The Lord and the Landscape' (Wormleighton, Warwickshire) in *Transactions of the Birmingham Archaeological Society,* 80, 1965, pp. 38-77.
TOY, S., *The Castles of Great Britain,* Heinemann, 1953.
WOOD, M., *The English Medieval House,* Ferndale, 1981.

---

5 Tudor to Georgian England

BARLEY, M. W., *The English Farmhouse and Cottage,* Routledge & Kegan Paul, 2nd imp. 1967.
BROWN, R. J., *Timber-Framed Buildings in England,* Robert Hale, 1980.
BRUNSKILL, R. W., *Traditional Buildings of Britain,* Gollancz, 1983.
CURTLER, W. H. R., *The Enclosure and Redistribution of our Land,* Oxford: Clarendon Press, 1920.
DARLEY, G., *Villages of Vision,* Architectural Press, 1975.
DEFOE, DANIEL, *A Tour through England and Wales,* Everyman edn, 1928.
GIROUARD, M., *Life in the English Country House,* Yale University Press, 1978.
  The Victorian Country House, Yale University Press, 1979.
GONNER, E. C. K., *Common Land and Inclosure,* Macmillan, 1912.
GOTCH, J. A., *The Growth of the English House,* Batsford, revised edn 1928.
HADFIELD, M., *Landscape with Trees,* Country Life, 1967.
HOSKINS, W. G., *Provincial England,* Macmillan, 1963, Chapter 7, 'The Rebuilding of Rural England, 1570-1640'.
HUSSEY, C., *English Gardens and Landscapes, 1700-1750,* Country Life, 1967.
KERRIDGE, E., *The Agricultural Revolution,* Allen & Unwin, 1967.
LELAND, JOHN, *Itinerary* (ed. Smith, L. T.), Centaur Press, 5 vols., 1964.
MACHIN, R., *The Houses of Yetminster,* Bristol University, 1978.
MERCER, E., *The Vernacular Houses,* H.M.S.O., 1975.
MORRIS, CHRISTOPHER (ed.), *The Journeys of Celia Fiennes,* Cresset Press, 1947.
PARKER, L. A., 'The Agrarian Revolution at Cotesbach, 1501-1612', in *Studies in Leicestershire Agrarian History* (ed. Hoskins, W. G.), Leicester Arch. Society, 1949.
Royal Commission on the Historical Monuments of England, *Houses of the North York Moors,* H.M.S.O., 1987.
STAMP, G. and GOULANCOURT, A., *The English House 1860-1914,* Faber & Faber, 1986.
SUMMERSON, JOHN, *Architecture in Britain, 1530-1830,* Penguin Books, 1953.
THIRSK, JOAN (ed.), *The Agrarian History of England, 1500-1640,* Routledge & Kegan Paul, 1967.
WILLIAMSON, T. and BELLAMY, L., *Property and Landscape,* George Philip, 1987.

---

6 Parliamentary Enclosure and the Landscape

CHAMBERS, J. D., and MINGAY, G. E., *The Agricultural Revolution, 1750-1880,* Batsford, 1966.
CLARE, JOHN, various poems.
CUTLER, W. H. R., *The Enclosure and Redistribution of our Land,* Oxford: Clarendon Press, 1920.
DARBY, H. C., *The Changing Fenland,* Cambridge University Press, 1983.
ELLIS, C. D. B., *Leicestershire and the Quorn Hunt,* Leicester: Edgar Backus, 1951.
GONNER, E. C. K., *Common Land and Inclosure,* Macmillan, 1912.
HARRIS, ALAN, *The Rural Landscape of the East Riding of Yorkshire, 1700-1850,* Oxford University Press, 1961.
HARVEY, N., *A History of Farm Buildings,* David & Charles, 1970.
HIGGS, J. W. Y., *The Land (A Visual History of Modern Britain),* Studio Vista, 1964.
HILLS, R. L. *Machines, Mills, and Uncountable Costly Necessities,* Goose & Son, 1967.
MARSHALL, WILLIAM, *Rural Economy of Norfolk,* 1787.
  Rural Economy of Yorkshire, 1788.
  Rural Economy of Gloucestershire, 1789.
  Rural Economy of the Midland Counties, 1790.

MOORE, N. W., HOOPER, M. D., and DAVIS, B. N. K., 'Hedges: Introduction and Reconnaissance Studies' in *Journal of Applied Ecology,* 4, 1967, pp. 201-20.

ROBINSON, J. M., *Georgian Model Farms,* Oxford University Press, 1983.

TURNER, M., *English Parliamentary Enclosure,* Dawson, 1980.

W. E. Tate's valuable Handlists to the enclosure acts and awards in most of the counties affected by the parliamentary enclosure movement have been published (usually) in the Transactions or Proceedings of the appropriate local historical or antiquarian society, and should be consulted for the detail about each country.

7 *The Industrial Revolution and the Landscape*

AIKIN, J., *A Description of the Country from thirty to forty miles round Manchester,* John Stockdale, 1795.

ALBERT, A. W., *The Turnpike Road System in England,* Cambridge University Press, 1972.

ASHTON, T. S., *The Industrial Revolution 1760-1830,* Oxford University Press, 1948.

AUBIN, R. A., *Topographical Poetry in Eighteenth-Century England,* New York: Modern Language Association of America, 1936.

BARMAN, C., *An Introduction to Railway Architecture,* Art & Technics, 1950.

BIDDLE, G. and NOCK, O.S., *The Railway Heritage of Britain,* Michael Joseph, 1983.

BOOKER, FRANK, *Industrial Archaeology of the Tamar Valley,* Dawlish: David & Charles, 1967.

BRACEGIRDLE, B., *The Archaeology of the Industrial Revolution,* Heinemann, 1973.

CHALONER, W. H., and MUSSON, A. E., *Industry and Technology (A Visual History of Modern Britain),* Studio Vista, 1963.

COURT, W. H. B., *The Rise of the Midland Industries, 1600-1838,* Oxford University Press, 1938.

DEFOE, DANIEL, *A Tour through England and Wales,* Everyman edn 1928.

FALCONER, K., *Guide to England's Industrial Heritage,* Batsford, 1980.

HARRIS, R., *Canals and their Architecture,* Hugh Evelyn, 1969.

HINDLE, B. B., *Medieval Roads,* Shire Publications, 1982.

History of Birmingham, Oxford University Press, 1952, vol. 1: 'Manor and Borough to 1865' by C. Gill, vol. 2: 'Borough and City, 1865-1938' by A Briggs.

HUDSON, KENNETH, *Industrial Archaeology,* John Baker, 1963. *Industrial Archaeology of Southern England,* Dawlish: David & Charles, and Macdonald, 1965.

KLINGENDER, F., *Art and the Industrial Revolution,* Noel Carrington, 1947.

MANTOUX, P. J., *The Industrial Revolution in the Eighteenth Century,* Jonathan Cape, 1928.

SMITH, DAVID, *Industrial Archaeology of the East Midlands,* Dawlish: David & Charles, and Macdonald, 1965.

8 *Roads, Canals and Railways*

Architectural Review, Special Canals Number, July 1949.

BARMAN, CHRISTIAN, *Early British Railways,* Penguin Books, 1950.

BOURNE, J. C., *History and Description of the Great Western Railway,* David Bogue, 1846.

BRITTON, JOHN, *Drawings of the London and Birmingham Railway,* 1839.

BUTTERWORTH, EDWIN, *Views on the Manchester and Leeds Railway,* Blacklock, 1845.

CAFFYN, L., *Working Class Housing in West Yorkshire,* H.M.S.O., 1986.

CHAPMAN, S. D., CHAMBERS, J. D. and SHARPE, T. R. *Industrial Britain,* University Tutorial Press, 1970.

COSSINS, N., *The BP Book of Industrial Archaeology in Britain,* David & Charles, 1987.

CRAWFORD, O. G. S., *Archaeology in the Field,* Phoenix House, 1953.

DOUGHTY, M., *Building the Industrial City,* Leicester University Press, 1986.

HADFIELD, E. C. R., *British Canals,* Phoenix House, revised edn 1959.

HOUGHTON, F. T. S., 'Salt Ways', *Transactions of the Birmingham Archaeological Society,* 54, 1932.

HUDSON, K., *Industrial History from the Air,* Cambridge University Press, 1984.

JACKMAN, W. T., *The Development of Transportation in Modern England,* Cass, 2nd edn (with an introduction by W. H. Chaloner), 1961.

JONES, E., *Industrial Architecture in Britain,* Batsford, 1985.

MARGARY, I. D., *Roman Ways in the Weald,* Phoenix House, 1948.
  Roman Roads in Britain, John Baker, 1973.

NOCK, O. S., *The Railways of Britain, Past and Present,* Batsford, 1948.

PORTEOUS, J., *Canal Ports,* Academic Press, 1977.

PRATT, E. A., *History of Inland Transport and Communication in England,* Kegan Paul, 1909.

SIMMONDS, JACK, *The Railways of Britain,* Routledge, 1961.
  Transport (A Visual History of Modern Britain), Studio Vista, 1962.
  The Railway in Town and Country, David & Charles 1986.

TAIT, A. F., *Views on the London and North Western Railway (Northern Division),* 1848.

TAYLOR, C. C., *Roads and Tracks of Britain,* J. M. Dent, 1979.

WILLIAMS, F., *Our Iron Roads: their history, construction, and social influences,* Ingram, Cooke & Co., 1875.

9 The Landscape of Towns

ASTON, M. and BOND, J., *The Landscape of Towns,* J. M. Dent, 1976.

BALLARD, A., *British Borough Charters, 1042-1216,* Cambridge University Press, 1913.

BALLARD, A., and TAIT, J., *British Borough Charters, 1216-1307,* Cambridge University Press, 1923.

BELOE, E. M., 'Freebridge Marshland Hundred and the Making of Lynn', *Norfolk Archaeology,* XII, 1895.

BERESFORD, M. W., *New Towns of the Middle Ages,* Lutterworth Press, 1967.

CHALKIN, C. W., *The Provincial Towns of Georgian England,* Edward Arnold, 1974.

CHAMBERS, J. D., 'Modern Nottingham in the Making', *Nottingham Journal,* 1945.
  A Century of Nottingham History, 1851-1951, University of Nottingham, 1952.

CHAPMAN, S. D., 'Working-Class Housing in Nottingham during the Industrial Revolution', *Transactions of the Thoroton Society,* 1963.

DYOS, H. J., *Victorian Suburb* (Camberwell), Leicester University Press, 1961.

FOX, LEVI, *Stratford-upon-Avon,* Norwich: Jarrold & Sons, 1963.

GILBERT, E. W., *Brighton, Old Ocean's Bauble,* Methuen, 1954.

GREEN, BARBARA, and YOUNG, RACHEL, *Norwich: the growth of a city,* Norwich Corporation, Museums Committee, 1964.

HART, GWEN, *A History of Cheltenham,* Leicester University Press, 1965.

HASLAM, J. (ed.), *Anglo-Saxon Towns in Southern Britain,* Phillimore, 1984.

HILL, J. W. F. (SIR FRANCIS), *Medieval Lincoln,* Cambridge University Press, new edn 1966.
  Tudor and Stuart Lincoln, Cambridge University Press, 1956.
  Georgian Lincoln, Cambridge University Press, 1966.

History of Birmingham, Oxford University Press, 1952, vol. 1: 'Manor and Borough to 1865' by C. Gill, vol. 2: 'Borough and City, 1865-1938' by A. Briggs.

HODGES, R., *The Origins of Towns,* Duckworth, 1982.

HYDE, F. E., and MARKHAM, F. S., *A History of Stony Stratford,* London and Wolverton: McCorquodale, 1948.

JOHNS, EWART, *British Townscapes,* Edwin Arnold, 1965.

MARSHALL, J. D., *Furness and the Industrial Revolution,* Barrow-in-Furness Corporation, Library and Museum Committee, 1958.

MARTIN, GEOFFREY, *The Town (A Visual History of Modern Britain),* Studio Vista, 1961.

MUTHESIUS, S., *The English Terraced House,* Yale University Press, 1982.

NEWTON, ROBERT, *Victorian Exeter,* Leicester University Press, 1968.

OLIVER, P., DAVIS, I. and BENTLEY, I., *Dunromin,* Barrie & Jenkins, 1981.

RUSSELL, PERCY, *A History of Torquay and the Famous Anchorage of Torbay,* Torquay Natural History Society, 1960.

SAVAGE, SIR WILLIAM, *The Making of our Towns,* Eyre & Spottiswoode, 1952.

STEPHENSON, CARL, *Borough and Town,* Cambridge, Massachusetts: Medieval Academy of America, 1933, especially Chapter 7.

INDEX

Main references are in **bold** type. Page-numbers suffixed by *ill* or *marg* denote topics
referred to only in the captions to *illustrations* or in *marginal notes*.
NB Names of counties are those used in the text; i.e. they are in most cases the names in use
before reorganisation.

251

255